ABANDONED ALABAMA

EXPLORING THE HEART OF DIXIE

LELAND KENT

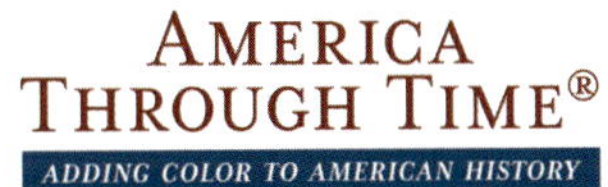

America Through Time is an imprint of Fonthill Media LLC
www.through-time.com
office@through-time.com

Published by Arcadia Publishing by arrangement with Fonthill Media LLC
For all general information, please contact Arcadia Publishing:
Telephone: 843-853-2070
Fax: 843-853-0044
E-mail: sales@arcadiapublishing.com
For customer service and orders:
Toll-Free 1-888-313-2665

www.arcadiapublishing.com

First published 2021

Copyright © Leland Kent 2021

ISBN 978-1-63499-356-2

Typeset in Trade Gothic 10pt on 15pt
Printed and bound in England

CONTENTS

1

CAPITAL CITY LAUNDRY

Founded in 1901, Capital City Laundry was in operation for most of the twentieth century. At its peak, the family-owned-and-operated dry cleaners included a dozen locations across Montgomery, far more than its closest competitor. Shortly after opening, the business was acquired by newcomer Charles Smith, Sr., who further developed and expanded the business. In the 1950s, his son Charles Smith, Jr., an MIT graduate, helped modernize the operation to compete with the new coin-operated laundry phenomenon. The family business amassed into a showcase steam laundry operation. In 1959, Charles Smith III renovated the old laundry building with a new façade.

During the construction of the RSA Energy Plant in 1993, construction crews discovered soil and groundwater contamination with PCE spreading under fifty blocks of downtown Montgomery. The groundwater contamination was first discovered in a city well in 1991 when the city identified tetrachloroethylene (PCE) in public water wells. Two wells were closed, with the city shifting to take its water from the Tallapoosa River upstream or from wells approximately 8 miles south of downtown that were not affected by the plume. City officials say it has no path to escape from its current location, but the groundwater contains contaminants, including carcinogens, that could be harmful if exposed.

The Environmental Protection Agency stepped in after the discovery of the downtown plume. Many of the businesses closed shortly after the EPA began their investigation and have been left abandoned ever since. Some business owners simply shut their doors and disregarded any requests by the EPA. Crews removed the contaminated soil. They also planted trees to absorb any remaining contaminants and installed vapor barriers in some buildings. EPA officials discovered dry-cleaning solvents, cleaning agents, and degreasers in groundwater under the downtown area.

A report by the EPA ties the pollutants to multiple cleaners and gas stations in the area. The EPA lists these businesses as the most likely scenario since the contaminants are present in multiple locations and not traceable to a single source. During the investigation, officials discovered barrels of discarded cleaning chemicals inside one of the dry cleaners. The barrels contained the same chemical that was found in the contaminated groundwater. The EPA first proposed the site, known as the Capital City Plume, be added to the agency's National Priorities List in 2000. A designation on the EPA National Priorities List means a site has known releases or threatens releases of hazardous materials or pollutants.

The city of Montgomery began monitoring groundwater contamination in 2006. In 2011, the U.S. Geological Survey said tree ring analysis pointed to the *Montgomery Advertiser* and the Alabama Department of Education as the most responsible for the plume. The EPA also says the Alabama Attorney General's Office and the Alabama Department of Transportation contributed to the plume.

In 2012, the city, county, state, Montgomery Water Works and Sanitary Sewer Board, the *Montgomery Advertiser*, Standard Roofing of Montgomery, and other businesses formed the Downtown Environmental Alliance to work with the EPA and the Alabama Department of Environmental Management (ADEM) to address remaining needs. The group split costs and paid back the EPA for the costs of investigating the site. The ADEM has overseen the clean-up since 2015. In July 2020, the ADEM recommended that the EPA withdraw its listing of the site, and the site was removed in September 2020. Montgomery's downtown has already undergone an economic resurgence with hotels, museums, new retail shops, and the baseball stadium in recent years. The mayor hopes the decision will allow continued revitalization of the downtown area.

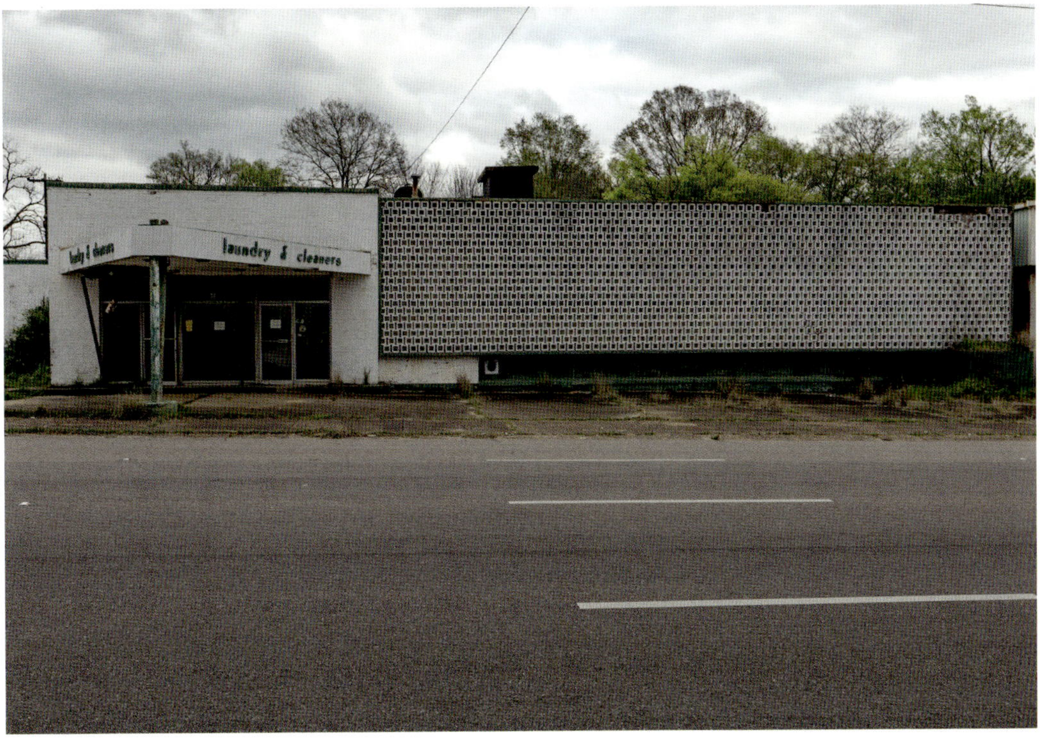

Today, the Capital City Laundry building remains abandoned.

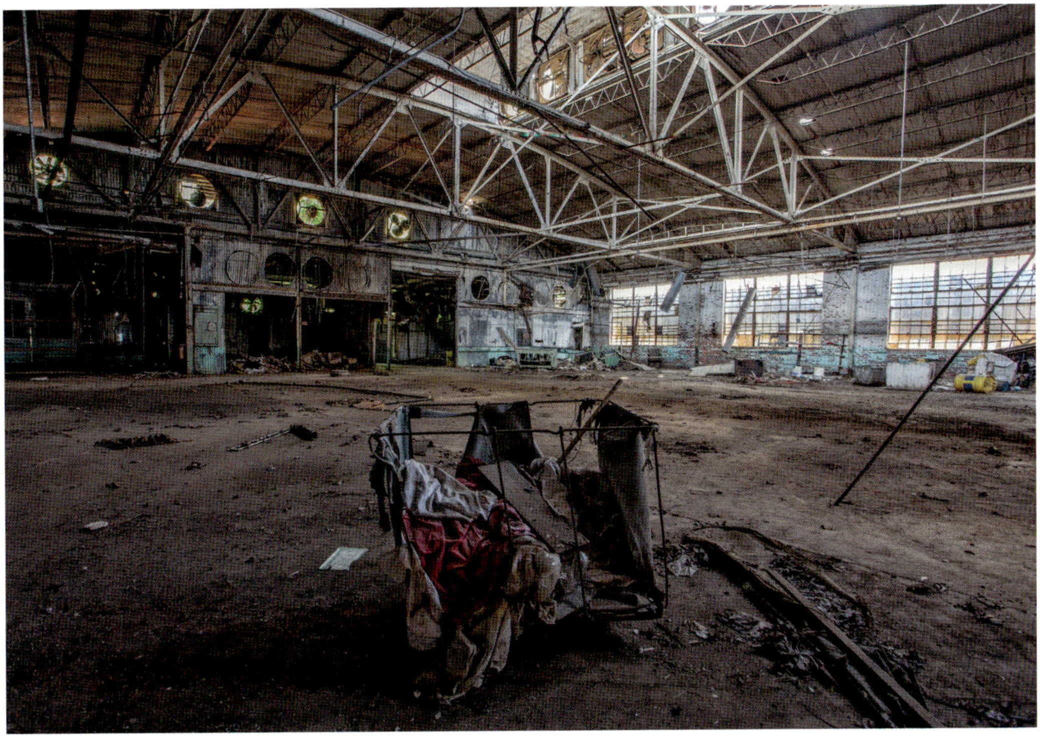

The industrial laundromat headquarters date back to the turn of the twentieth century.

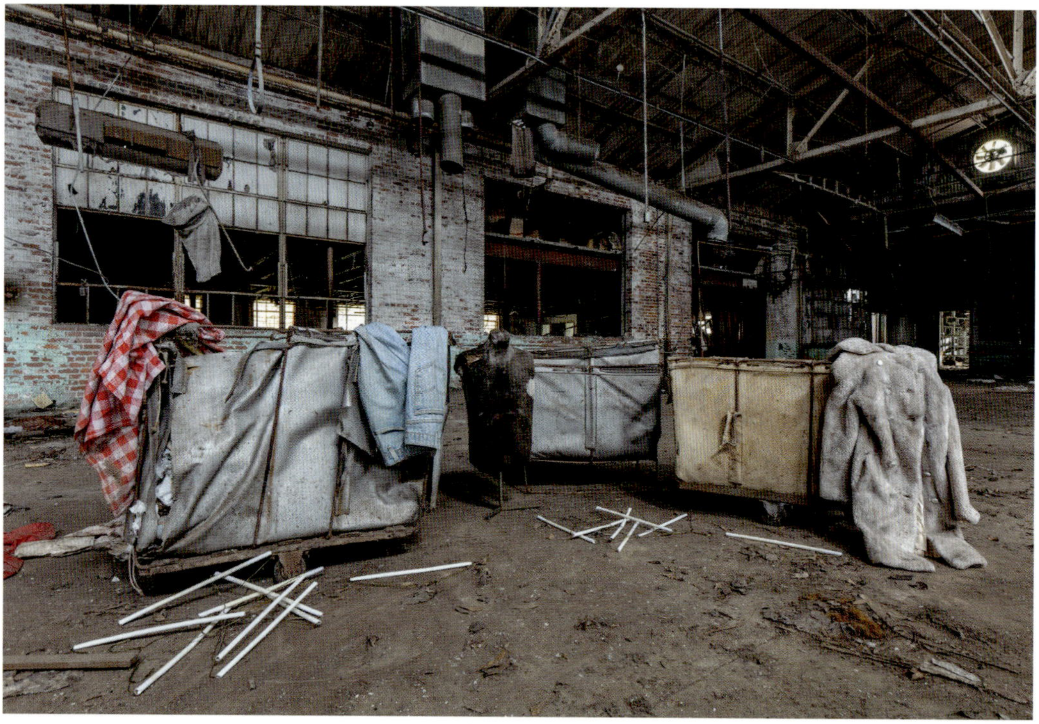

Large linen carts were used to maneuver the clothing around the warehouse.

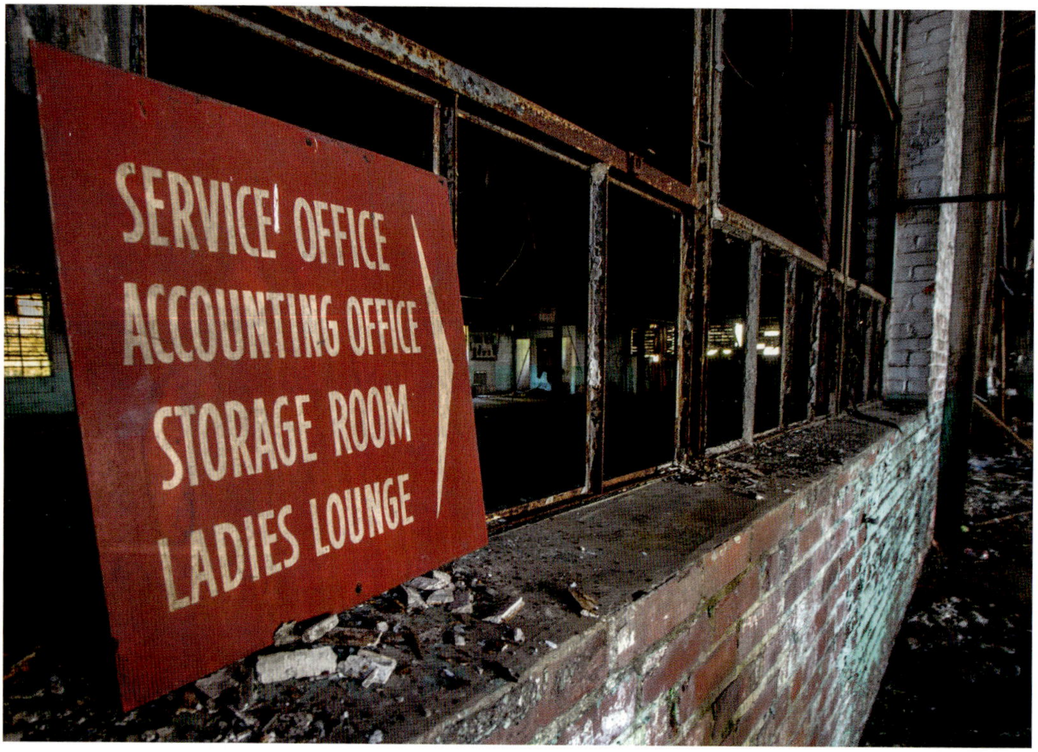

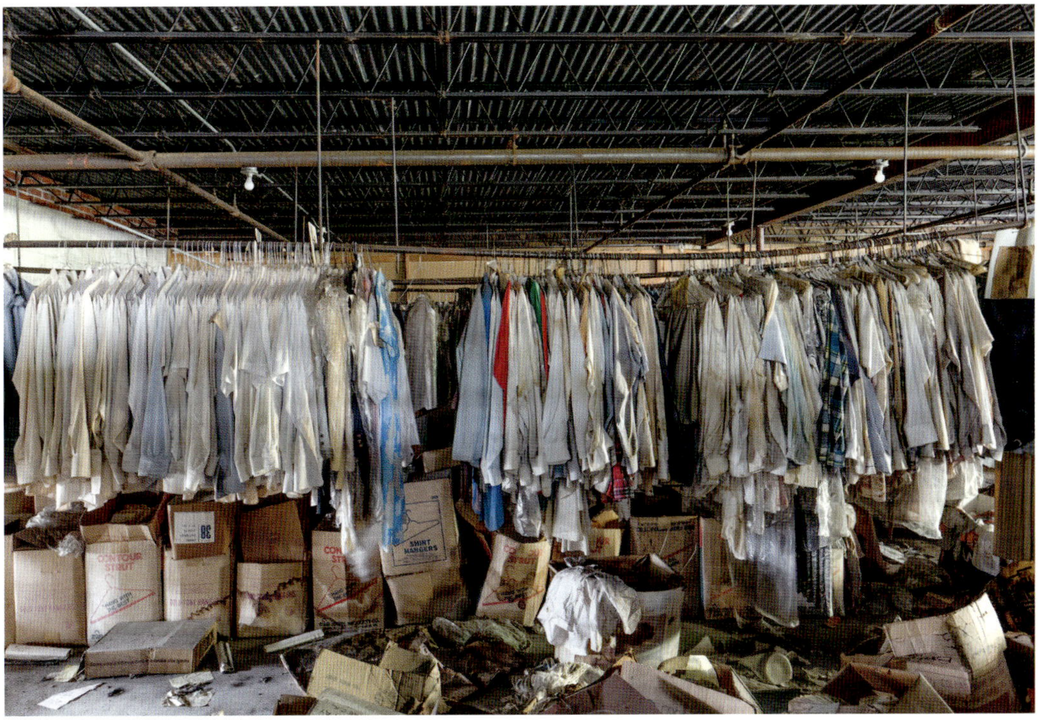

The old dry cleaners' warehouse was packed with forgotten garments.

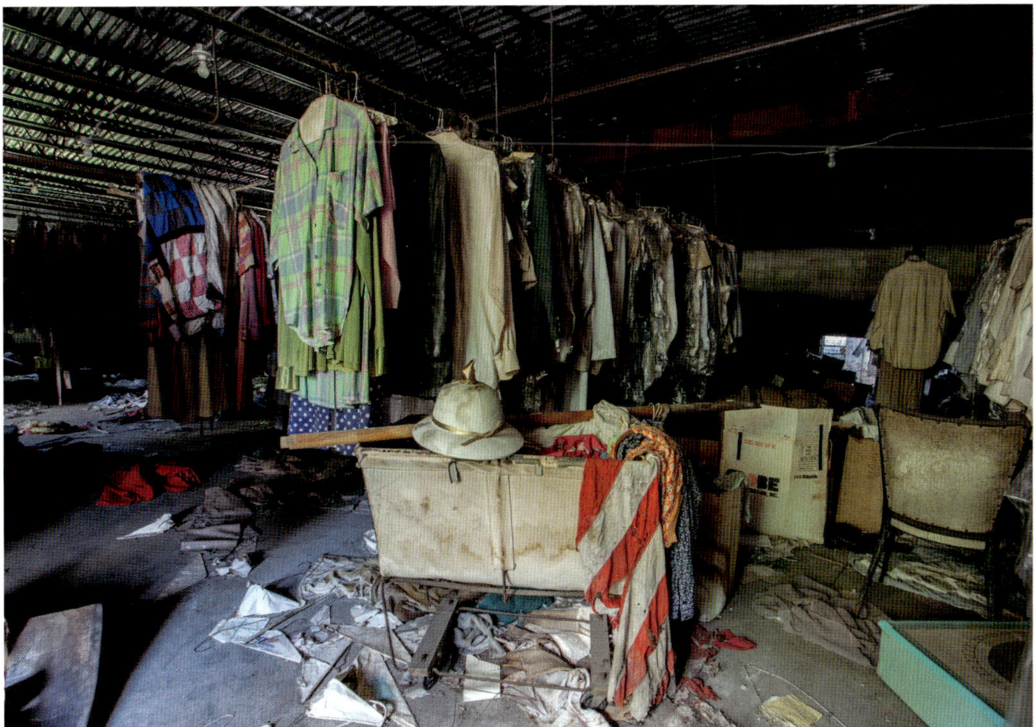

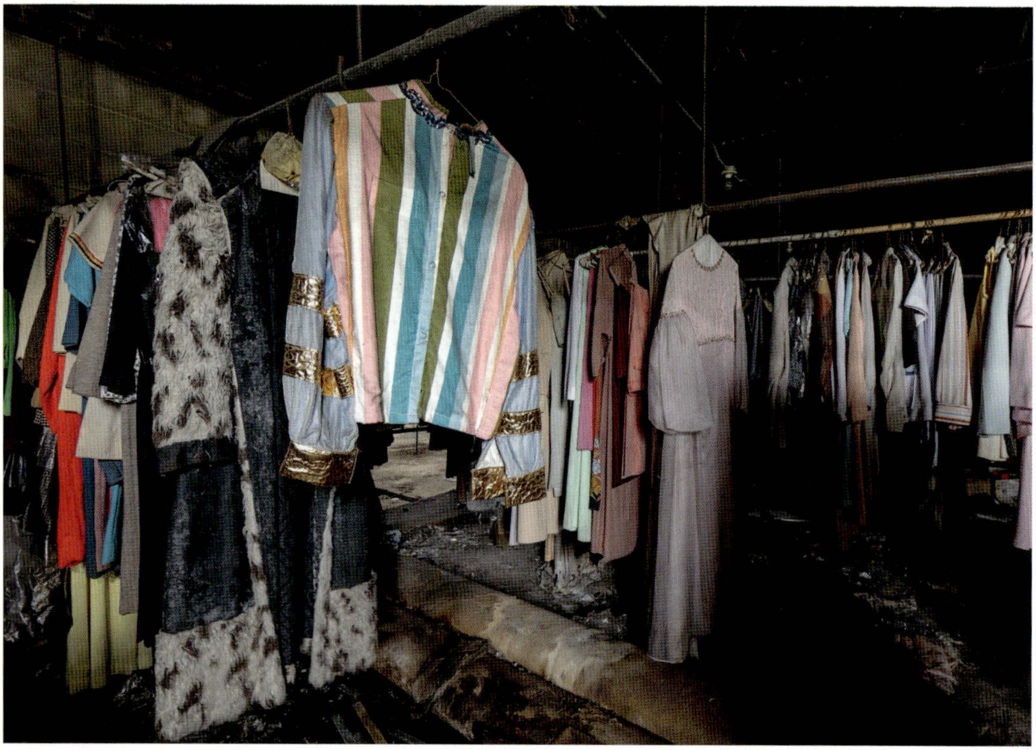

Down every aisle was some sort of unique piece of clothing, all damaged beyond repair.

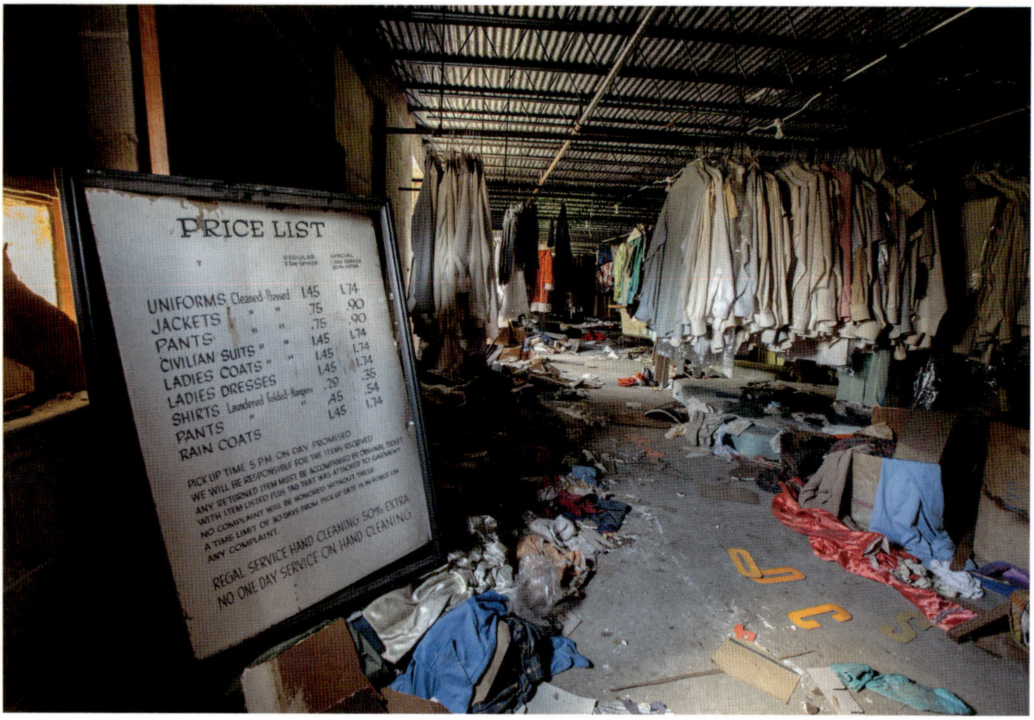

A framed poster-sized price list rests in one corner of the warehouse.

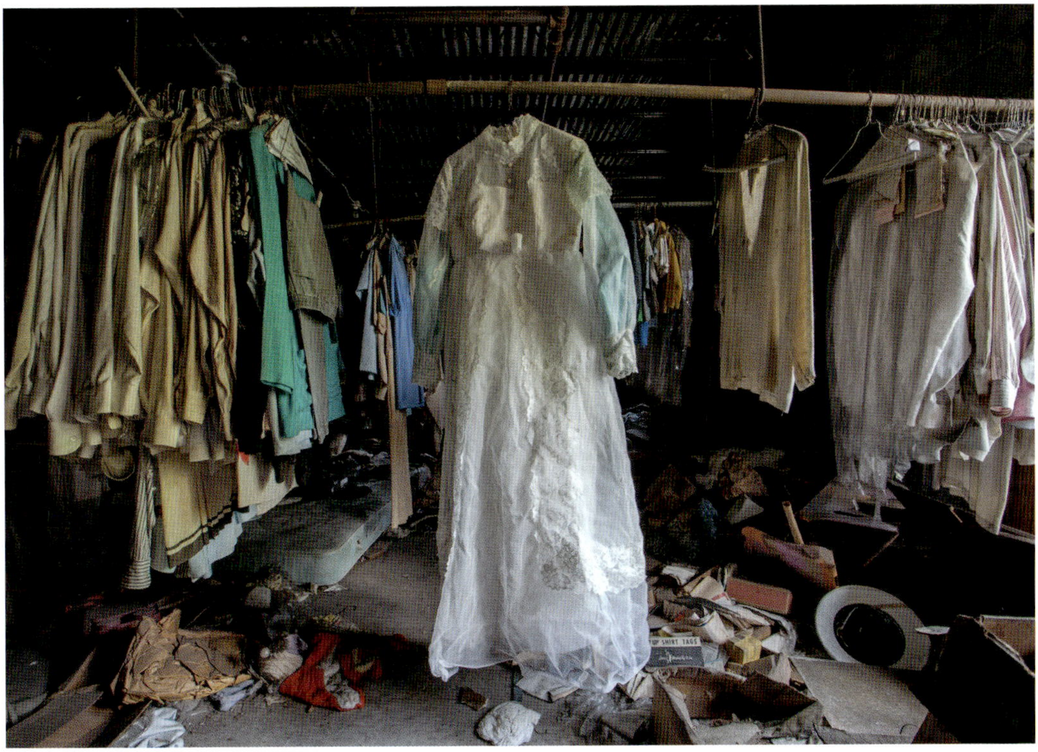

Among the hundreds of items were several amazing vintage wedding dresses like this one.

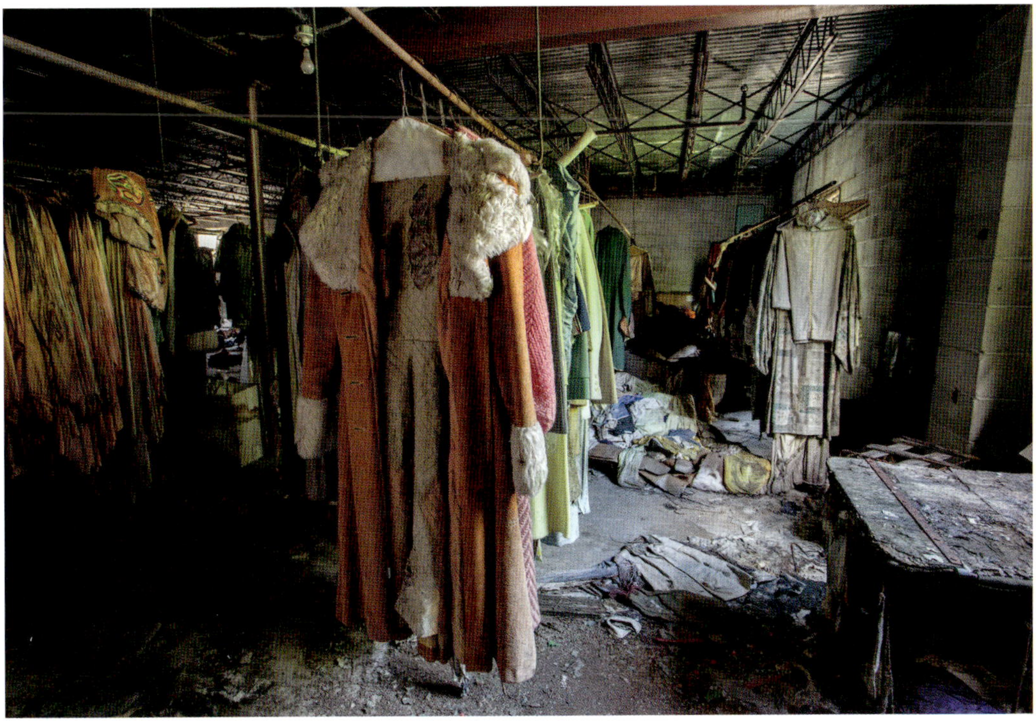

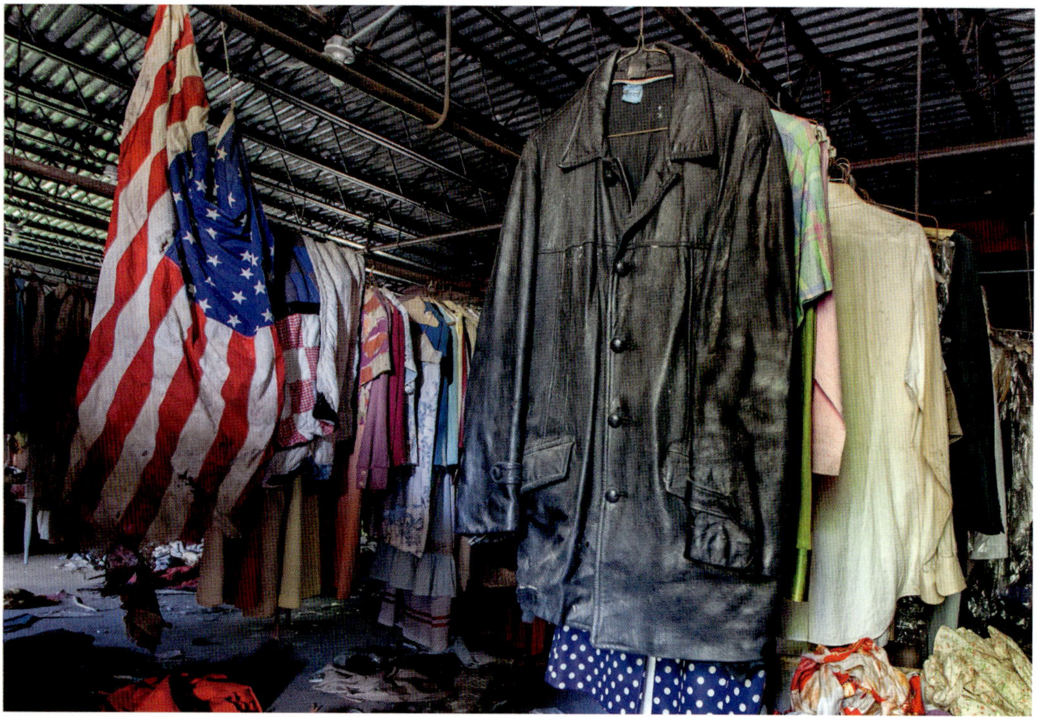

Besides your everyday clothing, the laundromat was filled with costumes, work uniforms, band uniforms, and even American flags.

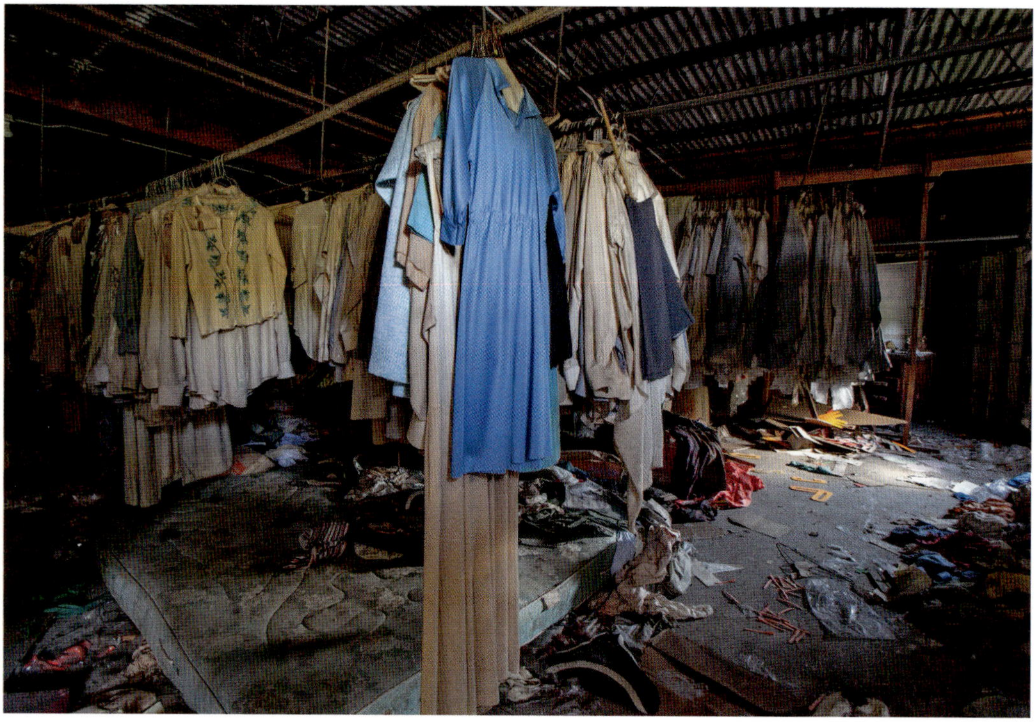

Once upon a time, women brought their Sunday dresses here.

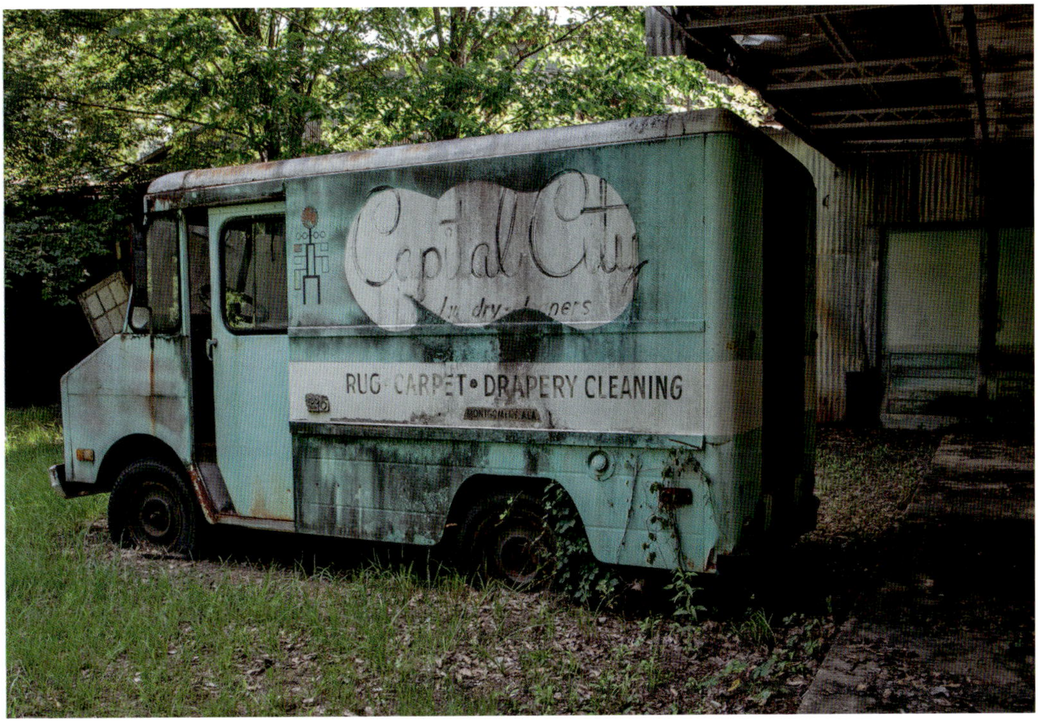

The former Capital City Cleaners' delivery truck sits abandoned behind the building.

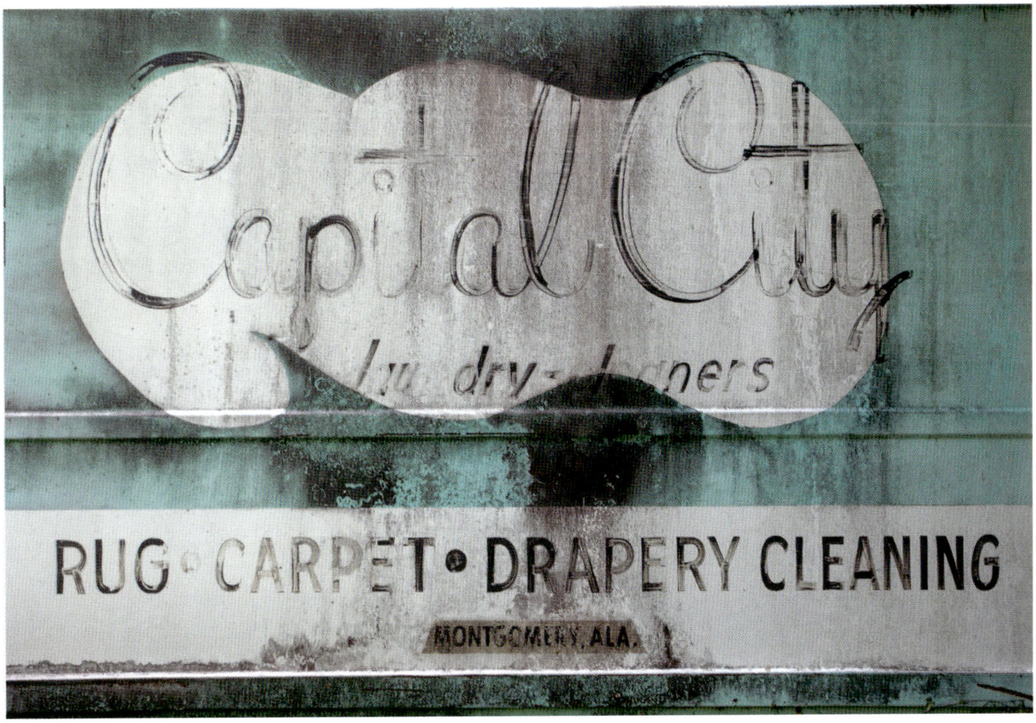

2

COWAN-RAMSER HOUSE

Although the home was last used as White's Funeral Home, this amazing Greek Revival house was originally built as a private residence for William Cowan, one of Eufaula's earliest physicians. Cowan and his wife had eight children, three of whom tragically died young. They also raised his wife's orphaned brother. The couple's daughters married wealthy district attorneys or state senators. One of Cowan's sons served as an officer during the Civil War. In 1859, after Cowan's death, one of his sons inherited the property. A few years later, in 1862, tragedy struck after a member of the Cowan family known for sleepwalking fell from the porch balcony, becoming paralyzed. After the civil war, the property was sold to Jacob Ramser, a Swiss furniture craftsman. While living in Eufaula, he married, became a member of the city council, and held the position of mayor as well as superintendent of education. Ramser and his wife had four children. After his death in 1892, his son inherited the property.

The Lewis family purchased the property in around 1948, and the house was renovated for use as White's Funeral Home. Today, the house is owned by a family member living in Florida. For decades, the Lewis family operated a funeral business downstairs and lived upstairs. When Colonel White passed away, they decided to close the funeral business. His wife continued to live in the house until her death in 2004.

In 2017, a wind storm damaged the roof and broke several windows. The storm damage was exacerbated by Hurricane Michael a year later. The old home suffers from severe water intrusion and deteriorates further with each passing day. The owners have applied for an emergency loan from the Alabama Trust's Endangered Property Trust Fund, but this loan cannot cover the costs. The Eufaula Heritage Association is supporting the restoration of the house. "Places in Peril" listed the house in 2019 to provide statewide awareness of the ongoing issue.

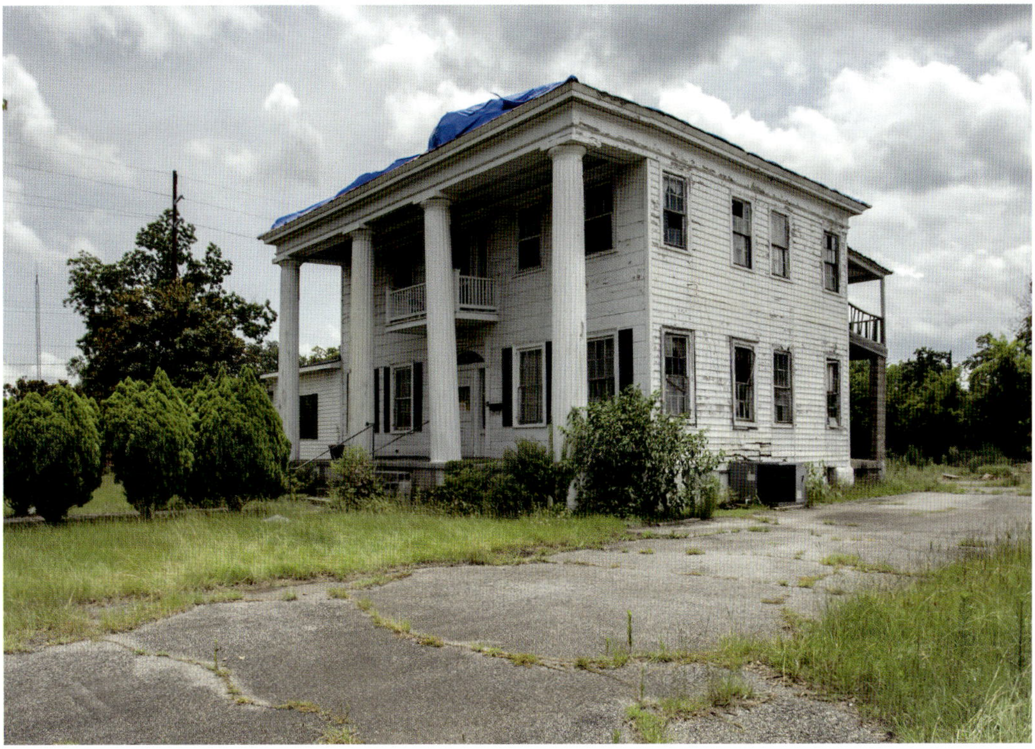

The Cowan-Ramser house is one of the oldest surviving Greek Revival houses in Alabama.

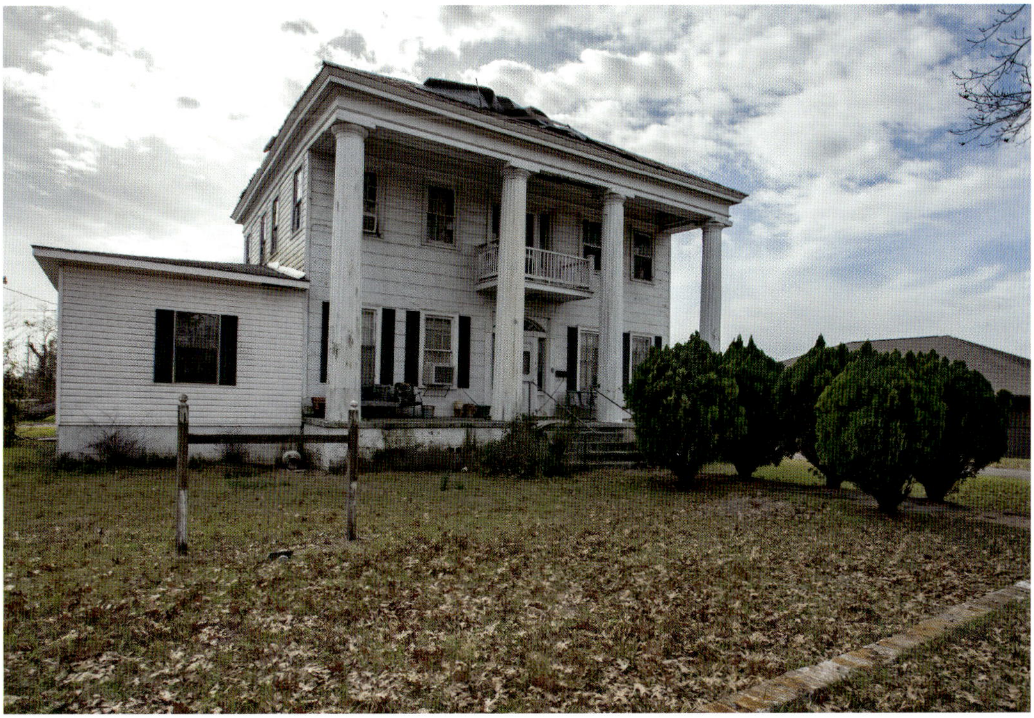

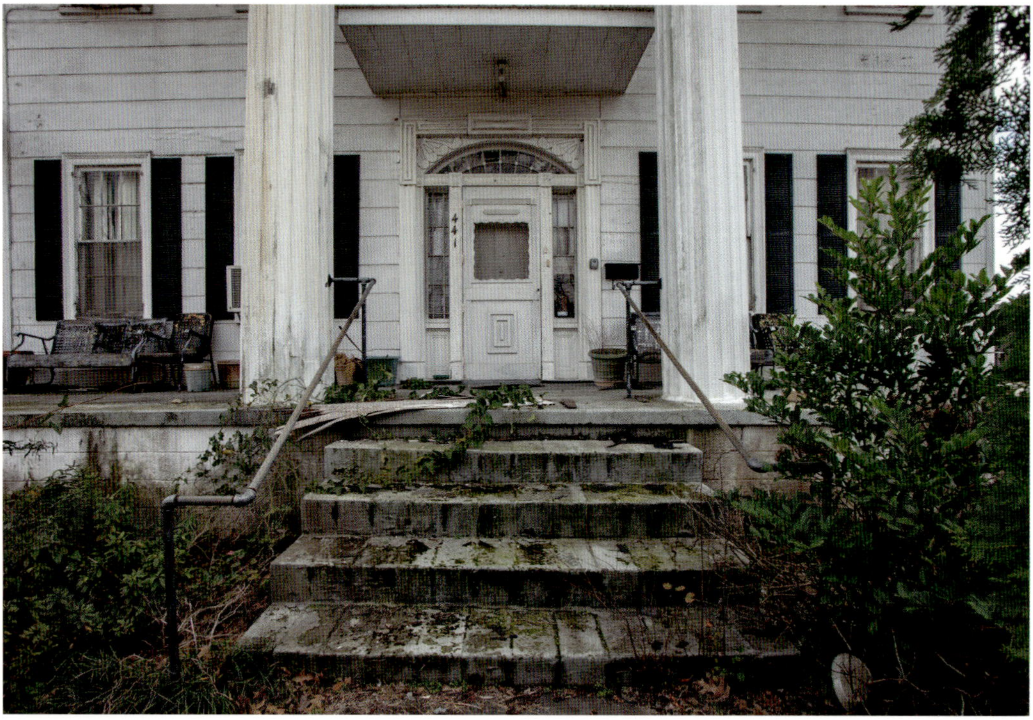

Note the linear pattern carved around the top of the door as a decorative border. This motif is called a Greek key. It is said to represent the twisting path of a labyrinth or maze.

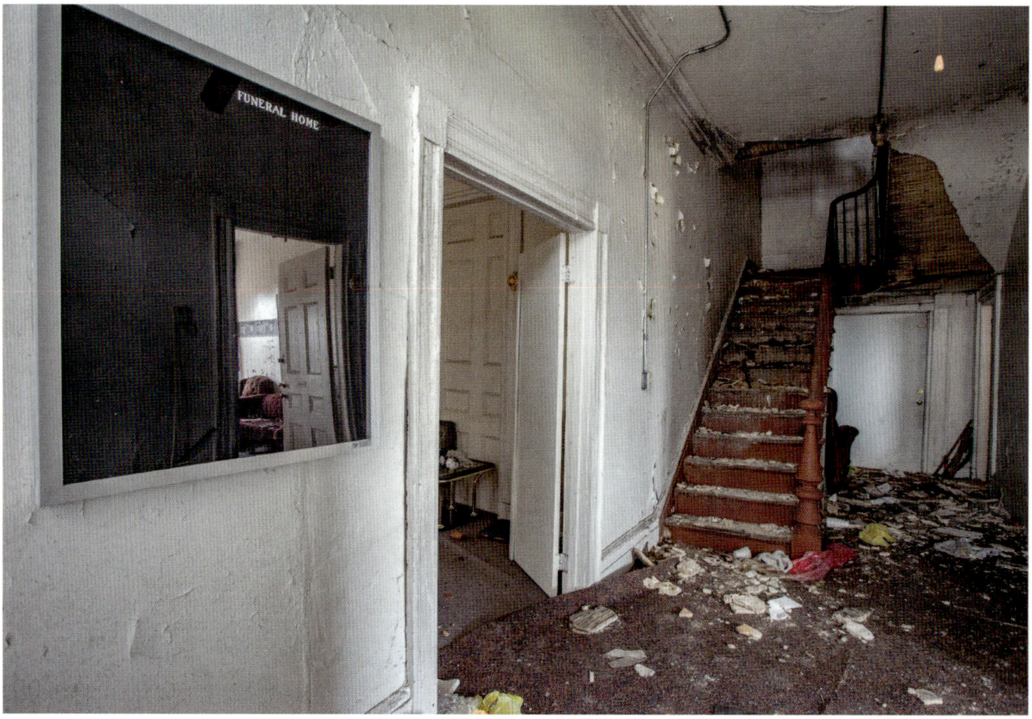

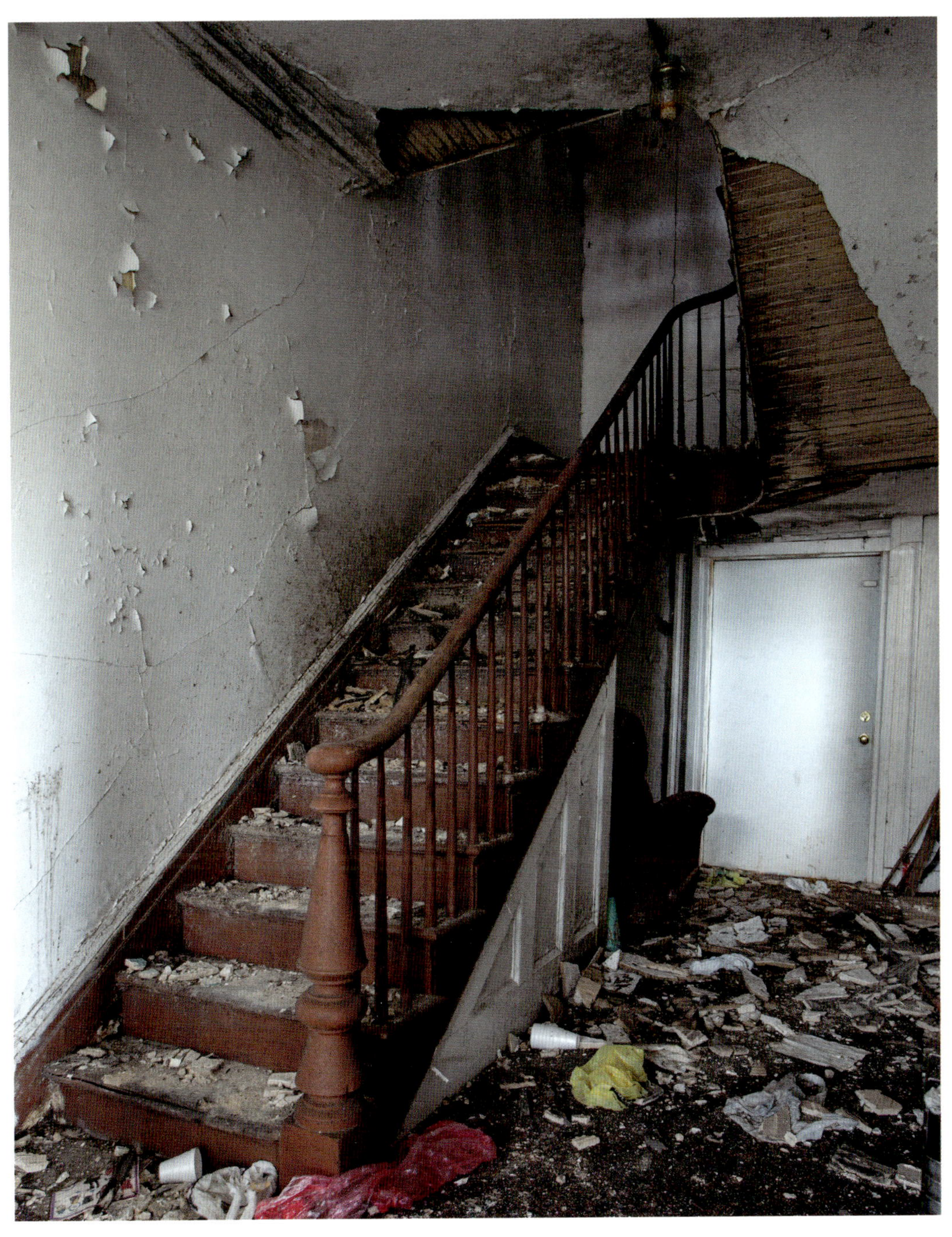

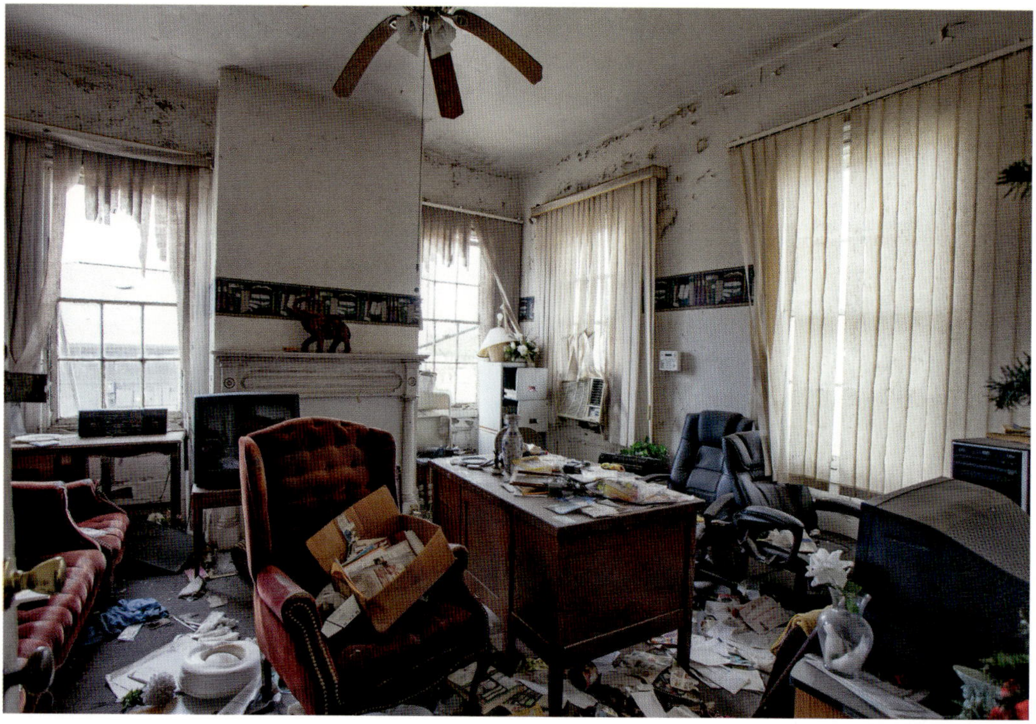

No sense of order remains in the ransacked office.

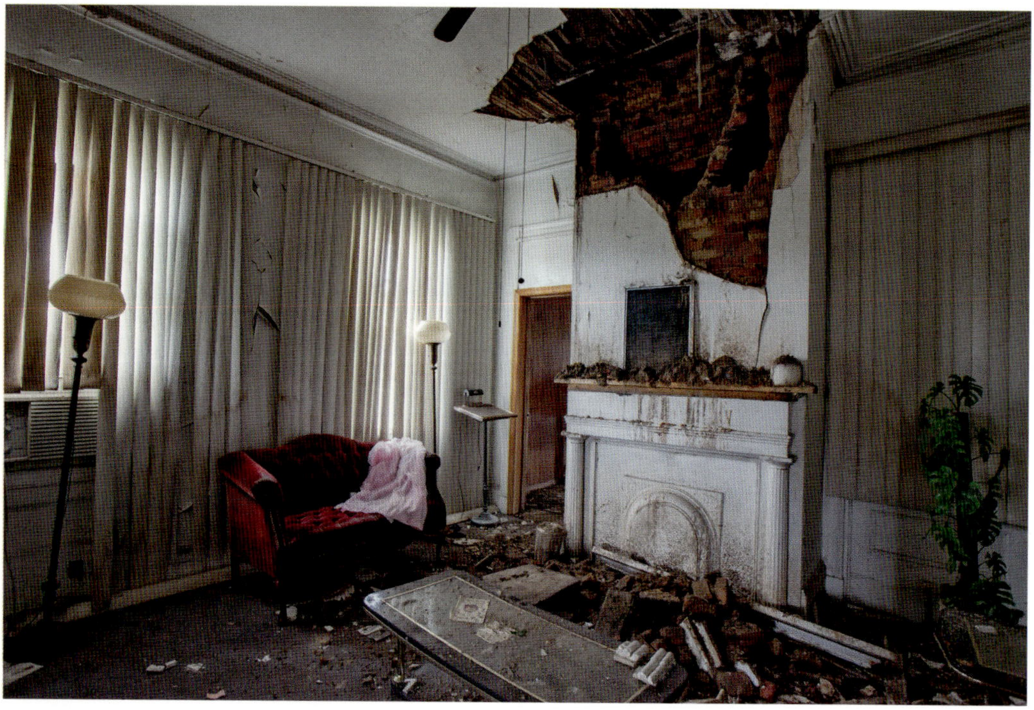

With crumbling brickwork and peeling plaster, this sitting room shows little sign of the home's former glory.
Only the fireplace stands proud, with its miniature Greek columns mirroring the ones on the building's exterior.

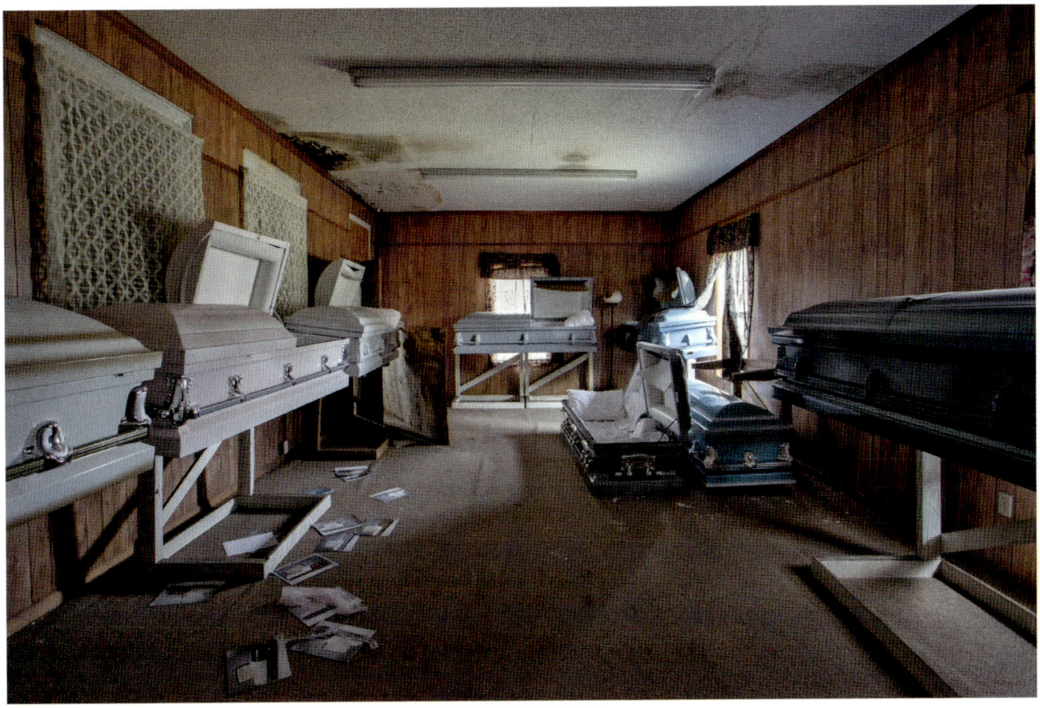

The addition on the side of the house was added when it was converted into White's Funeral Home and housed the casket showroom and embalming room.

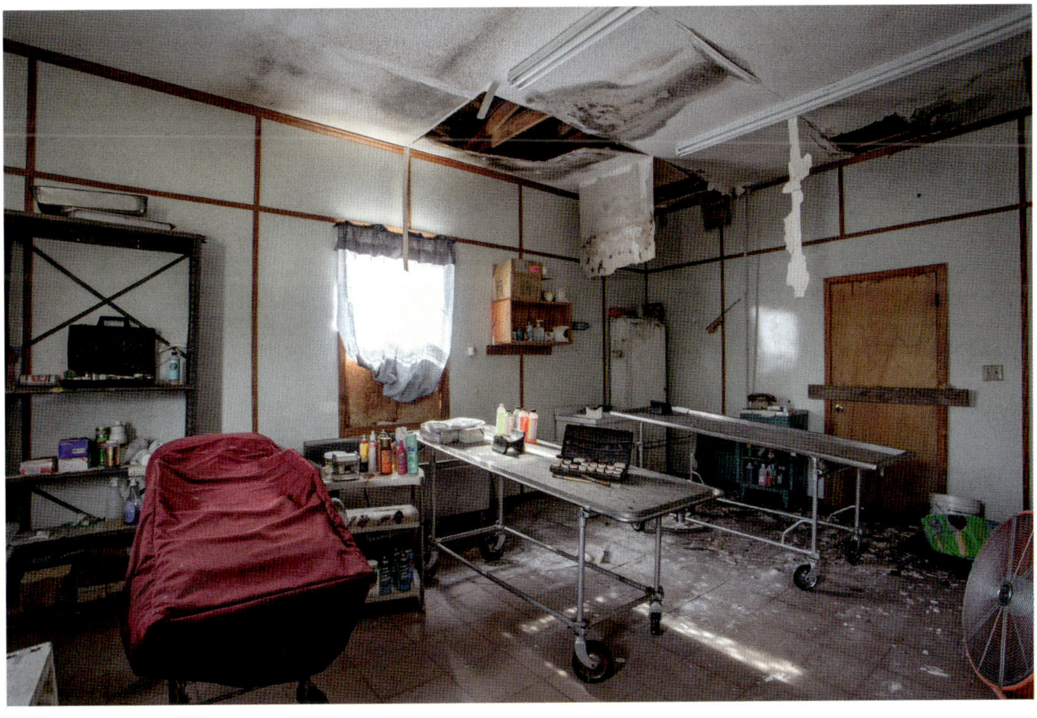

These old metal stretchers were once used to lay out dead bodies. The deceased would then be made to look presentable for grieving loved ones.

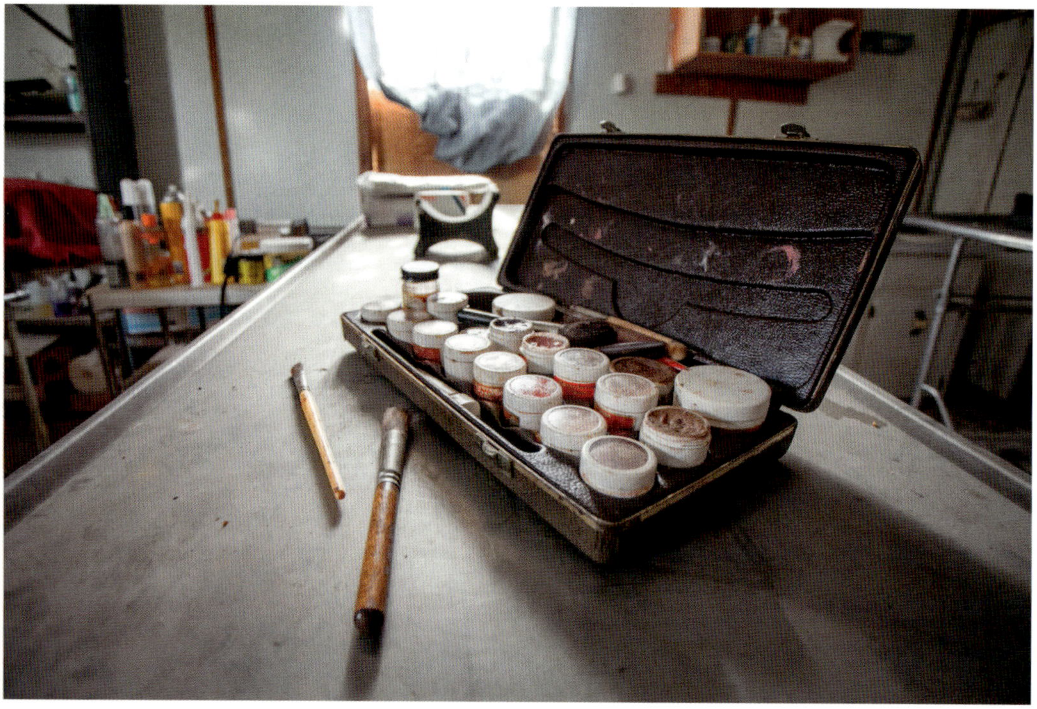

A collection of cosmetic powders and balms—make-up for the dead. All of the tools of the undertaker's trade were squeezed into this small space.

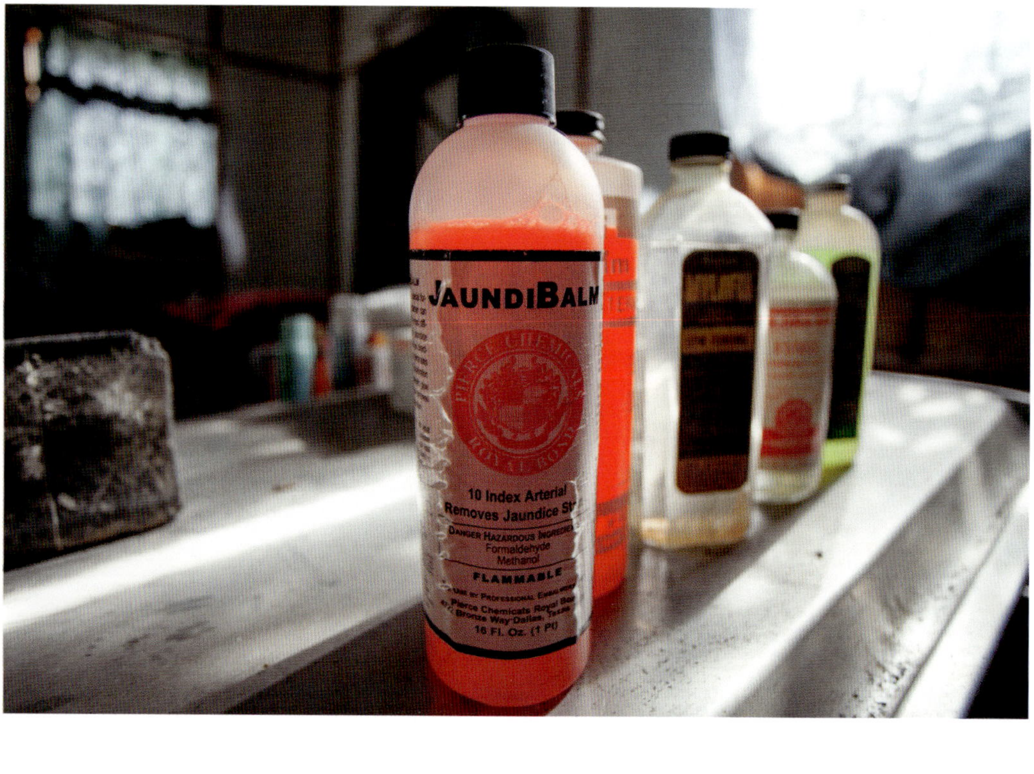

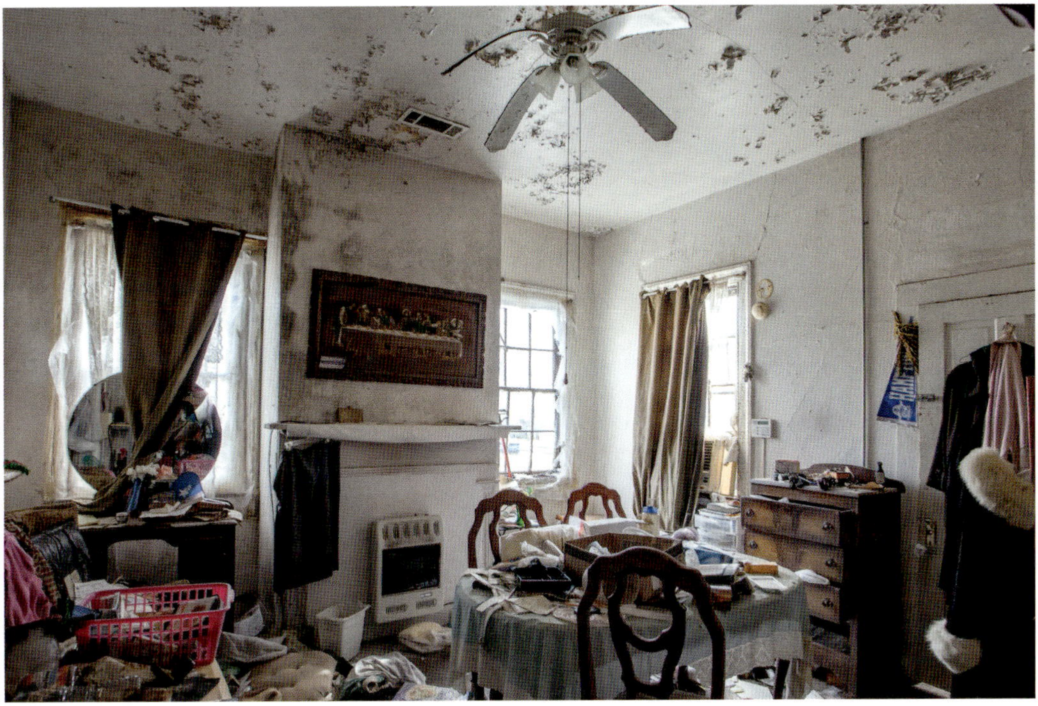

After decades in the death business, the funeral director passed away in 1992 and the business closed.

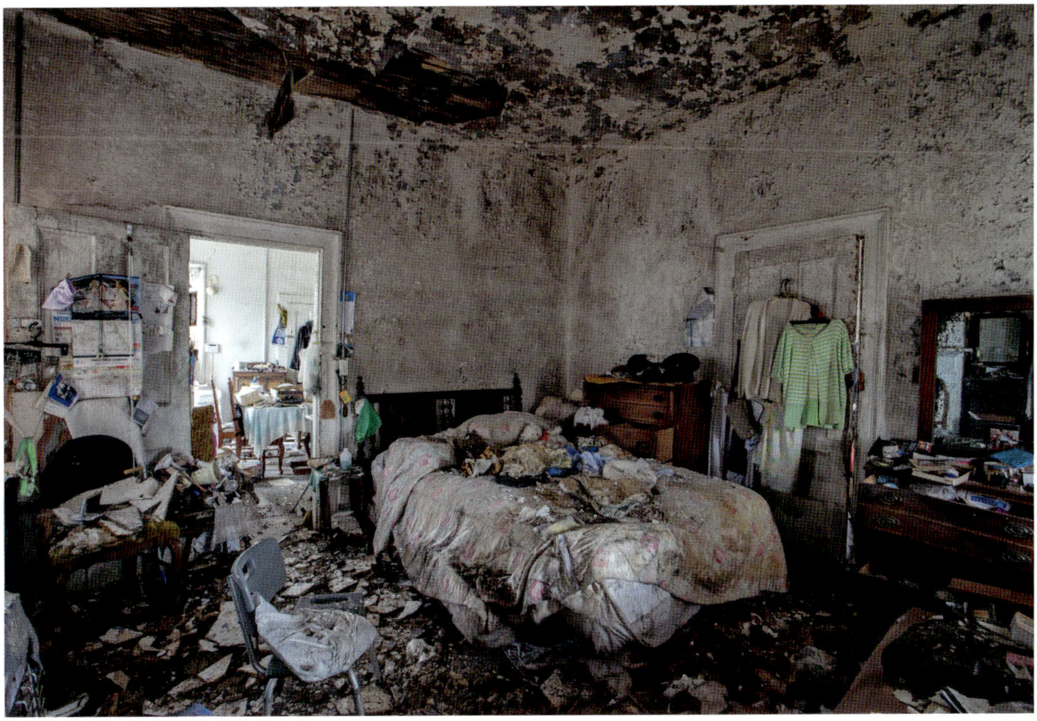

His wife continued to live in the home until she passed away in 2004. The upstairs rooms remain filled with the family's personal belongings.

3

THE CRAFTSMAN

In the early 1900s, Gustav Stickley began the publication of his influential magazine *The Craftsman*. The magazine was devoted entirely to the construction and interior design of the Arts and Crafts movement. Stickley was an architect himself, as well as a furniture maker. He was also an ardent proponent of the Arts and Crafts philosophy that advocated for a revolt against the presumed evils of the Industrial Revolution—mass-produced, shoddy goods—and a return to handcraftsmanship. Working with architect Harvey Ellis, Stickley designed 221 house plans that he published in *The Craftsman*. Before World War II, Arts and Crafts-style architecture became one of the most popular styles of housing. Most Craftsman homes are smaller cottages, often referred to as bungalows, with a small front porch. However, in the southeast, these large-scaled Craftsman dwellings are quite rare.

The farmhouse was built in 1915 by an architect from Atlanta. Arts and Crafts homes were constructed in harmony with their landscape; wood was often stained or painted brown. A wide porch stretches across the length of the front supported by rock columns. The original covered entrance has since collapsed from decay. The elaborate stonework covers the exterior wall, chimneys, and porch columns. The roofline is accentuated by wide overhanging eaves. Inside, a central hall greets visitors as they enter the main entrance. During construction, the house became so popular that neighbors asked the builder to build homes for them too. One house had its staircase removed entirely and replaced with one identical to this one. Craftsman homes are best known for their warm woodwork and many rooms. Built-in cabinetry provides storage and makes the most of available space. The box beam ceilings add another level of elegance and show the builder took the time and expense to add the beautiful detailing. The house has sat unoccupied since the late 1990s. Vines and ivy have engulfed the home, almost completely covering portions of the exterior.

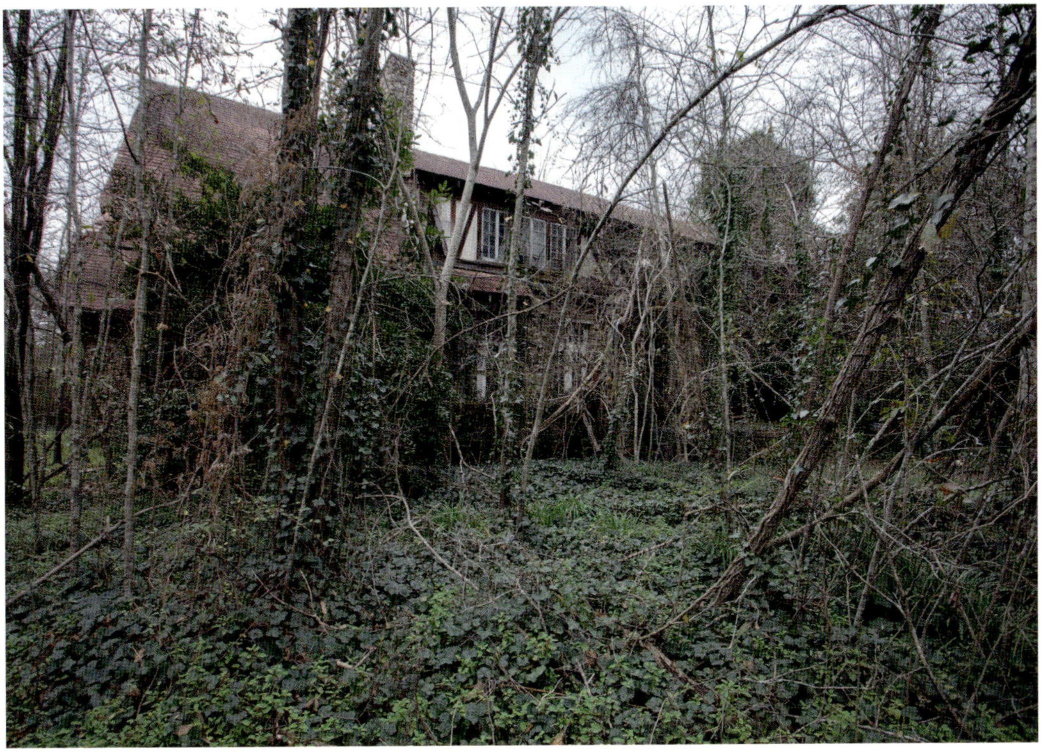

Surrounded by trees and dense greenery, the two-story farmhouse has been left to languish.

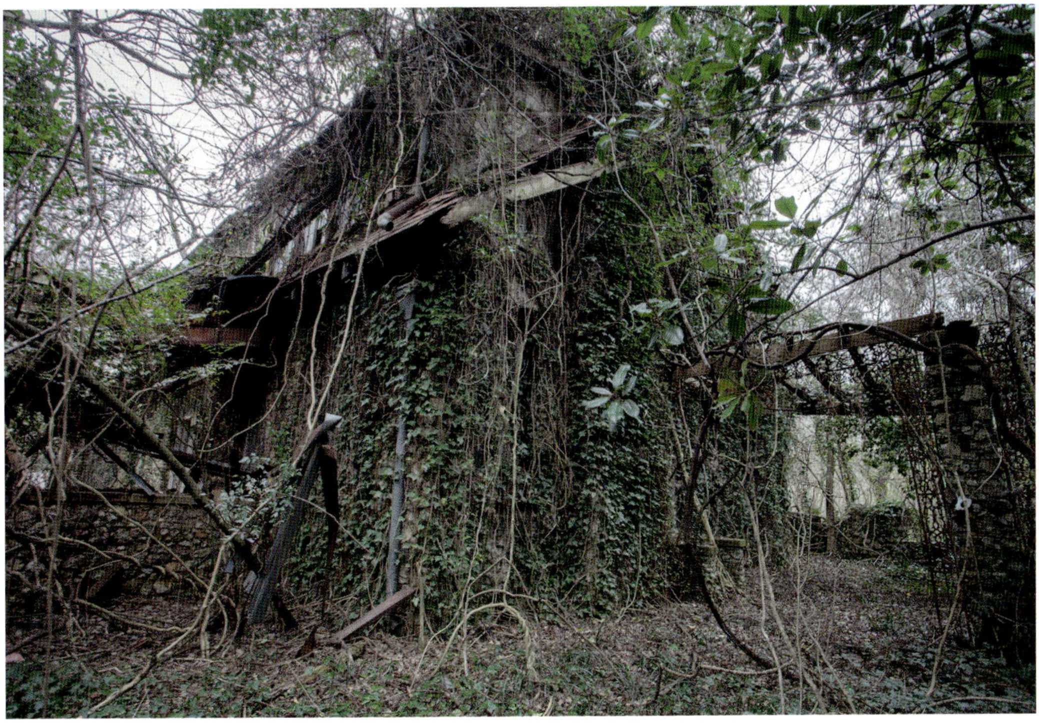

The house appears to be losing its battle with Mother Nature as vines and ivy envelop much of the exterior.

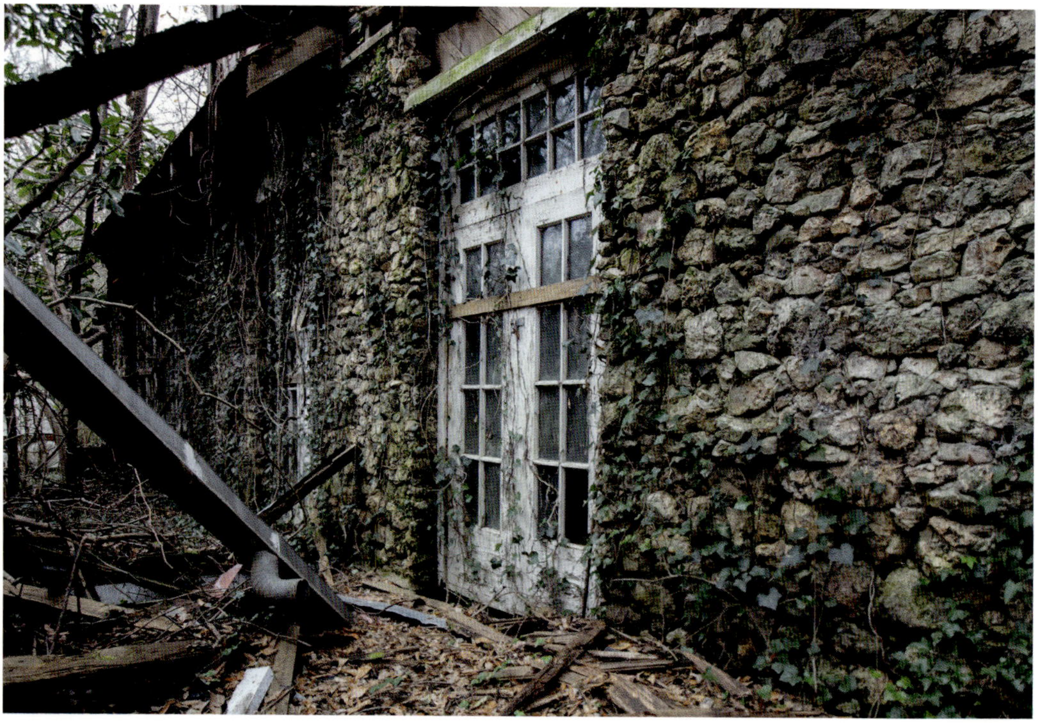

The roof over the porch is long gone and a set of French doors remains boarded.

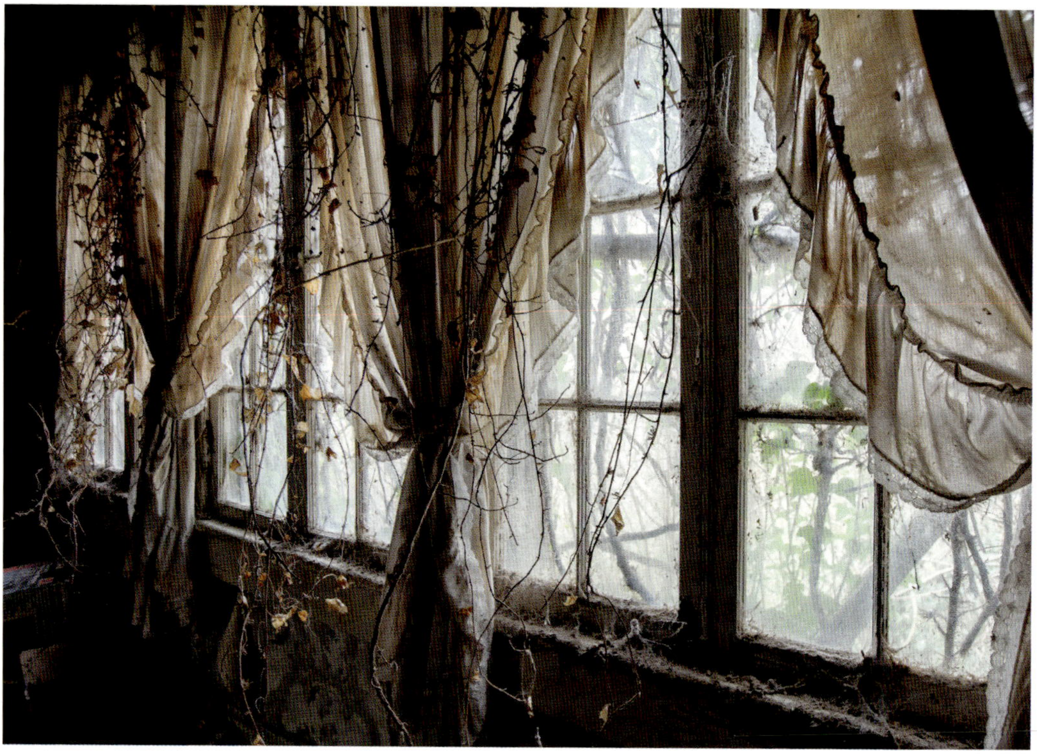

Vines stretch up the house and into the second-story windows.

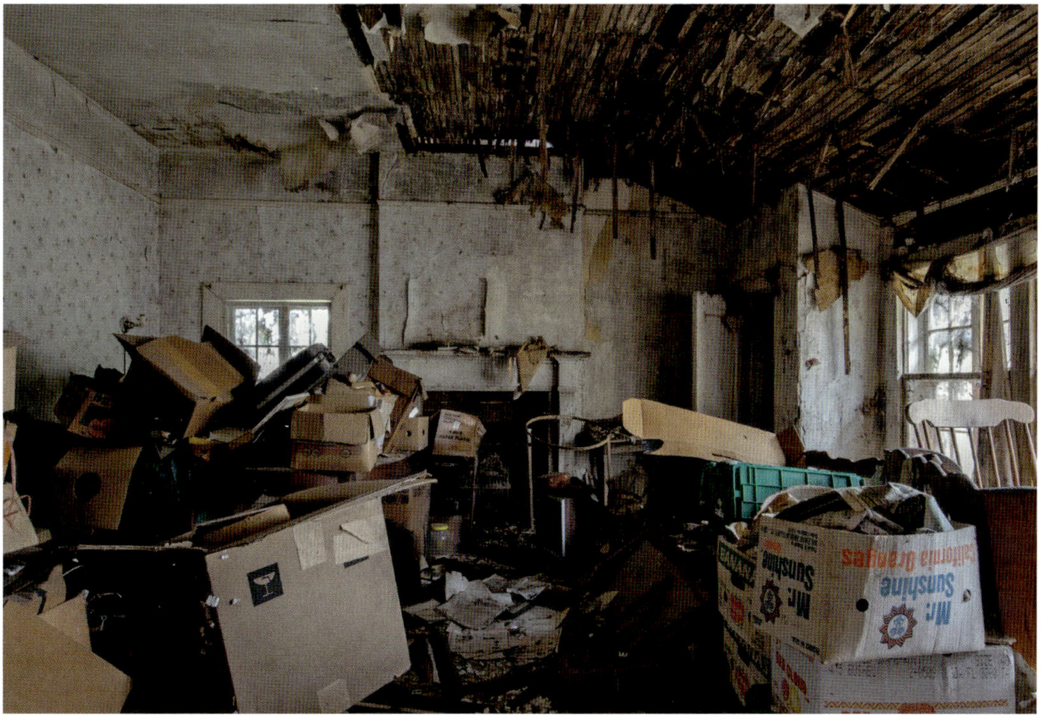

An upstairs bedroom full of belongings. A portion of the plaster ceiling has collapsed due to water damage.

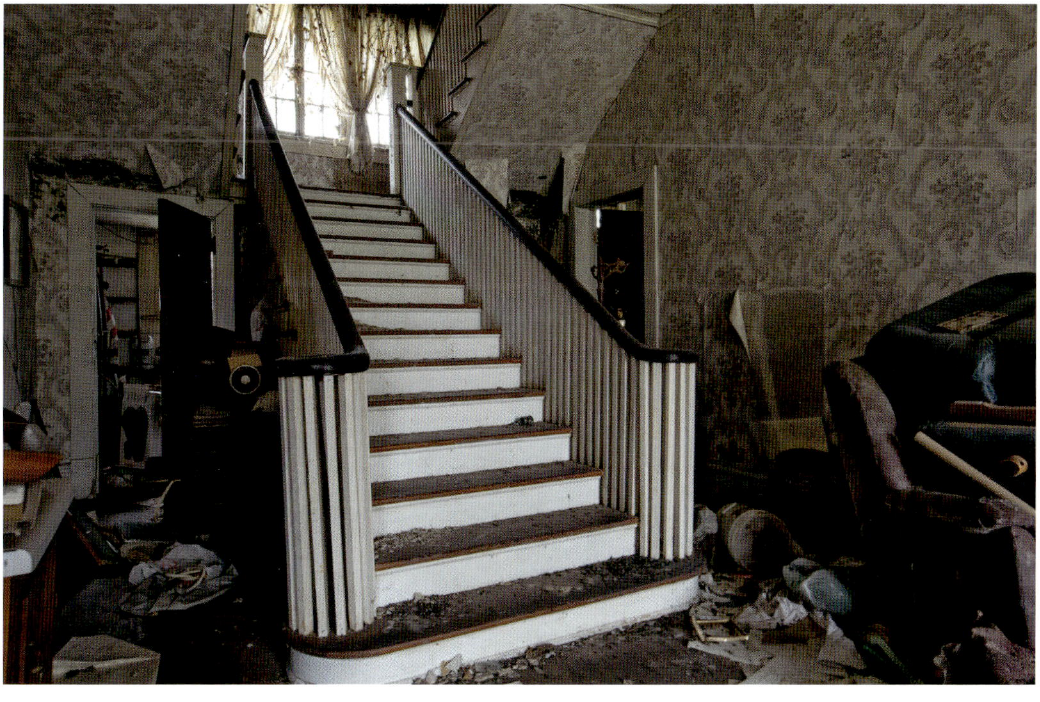

The house was so admired that neighbors are said to have asked the builder to replicate its staircase design in their homes. One homeowner even purportedly went as far as to rip out their existing staircase and replace it with a copy of this one.

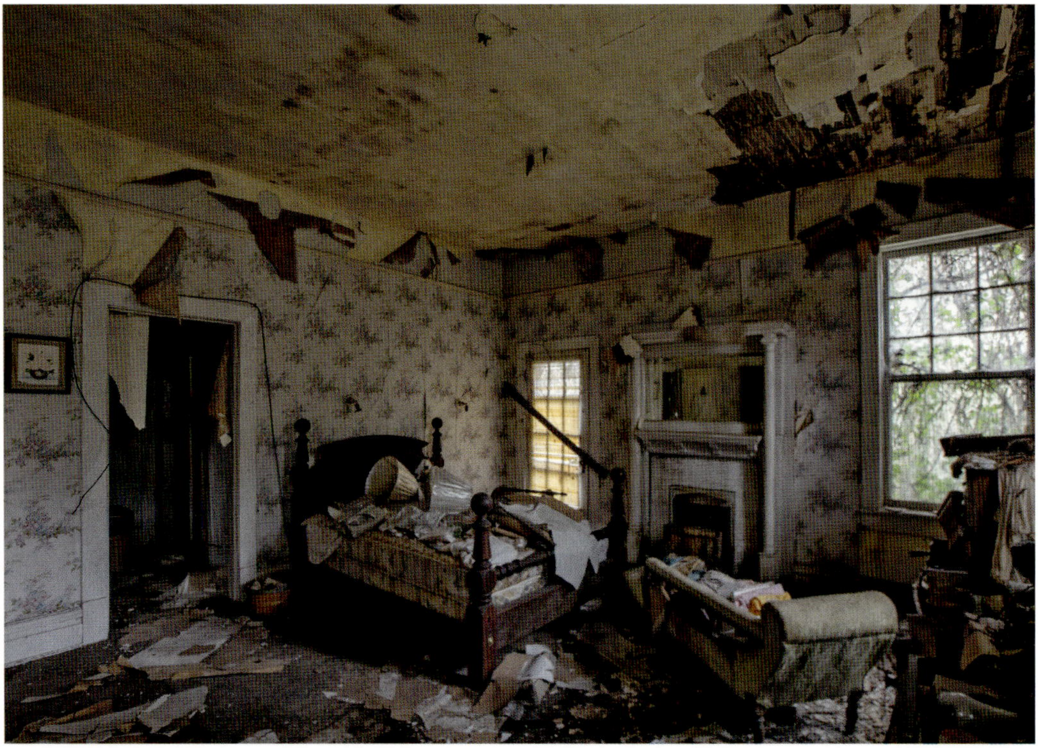

A downstairs bedroom.

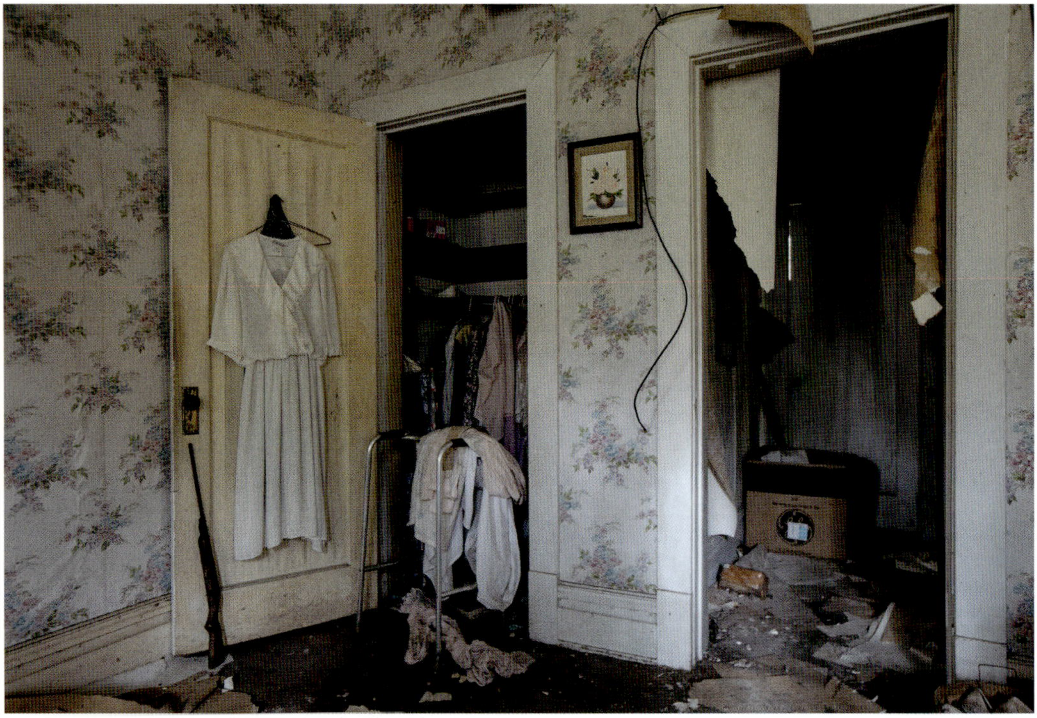

A rusty old rifle was discovered among the items in a closet.

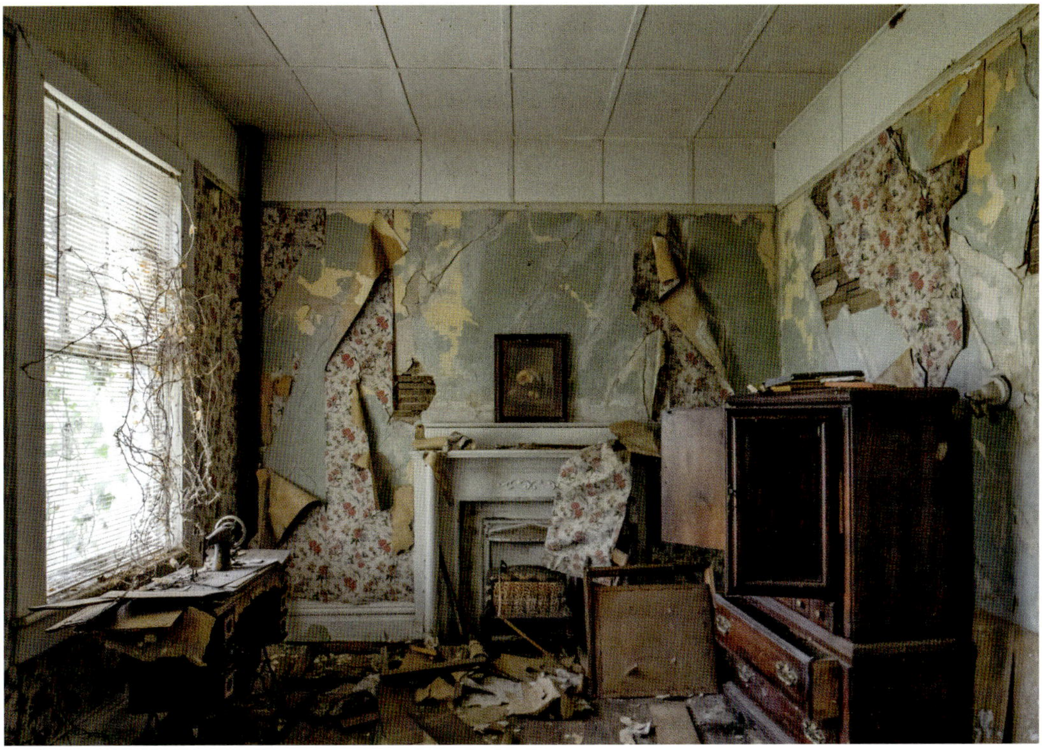

Wallpaper peels off the walls of a downstairs bedroom.

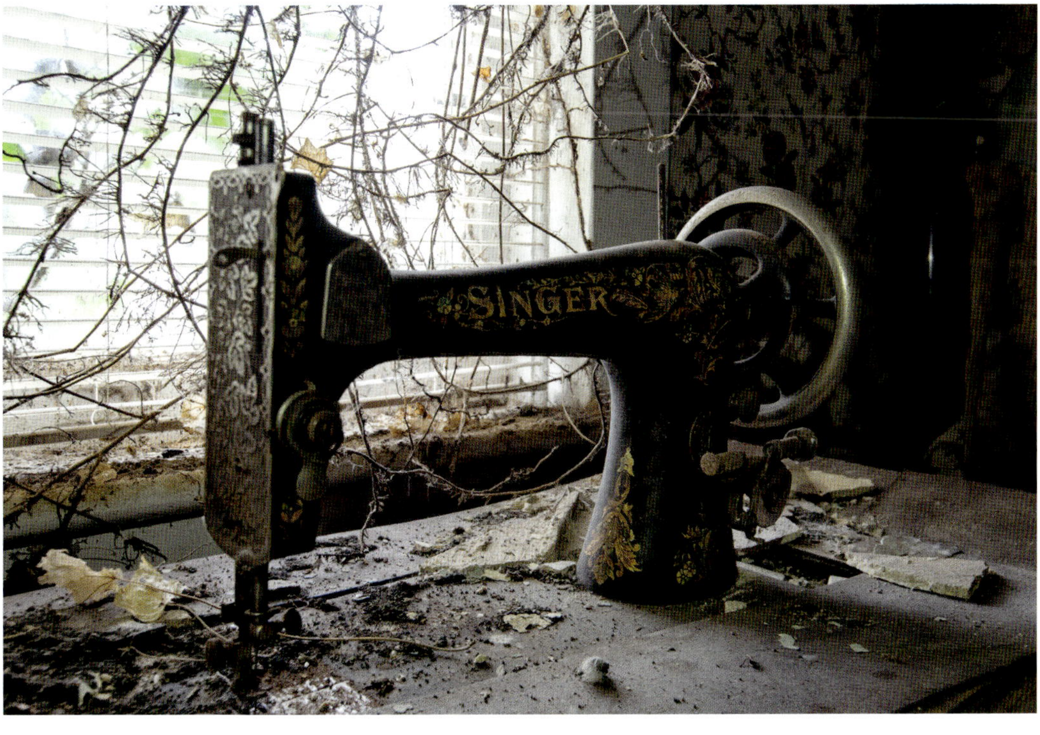

An old Singer sewing machine sits in front of a window. Vines have made their way inside through broken glass.

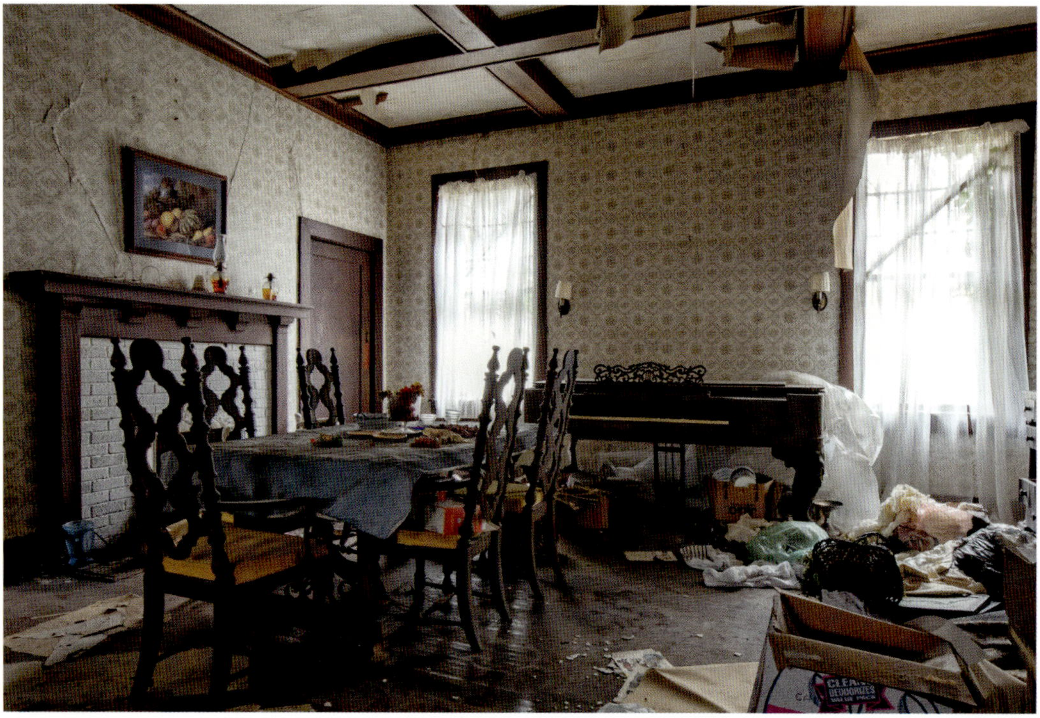

An antique table and chairs remain in the dining room next to a square grand piano.

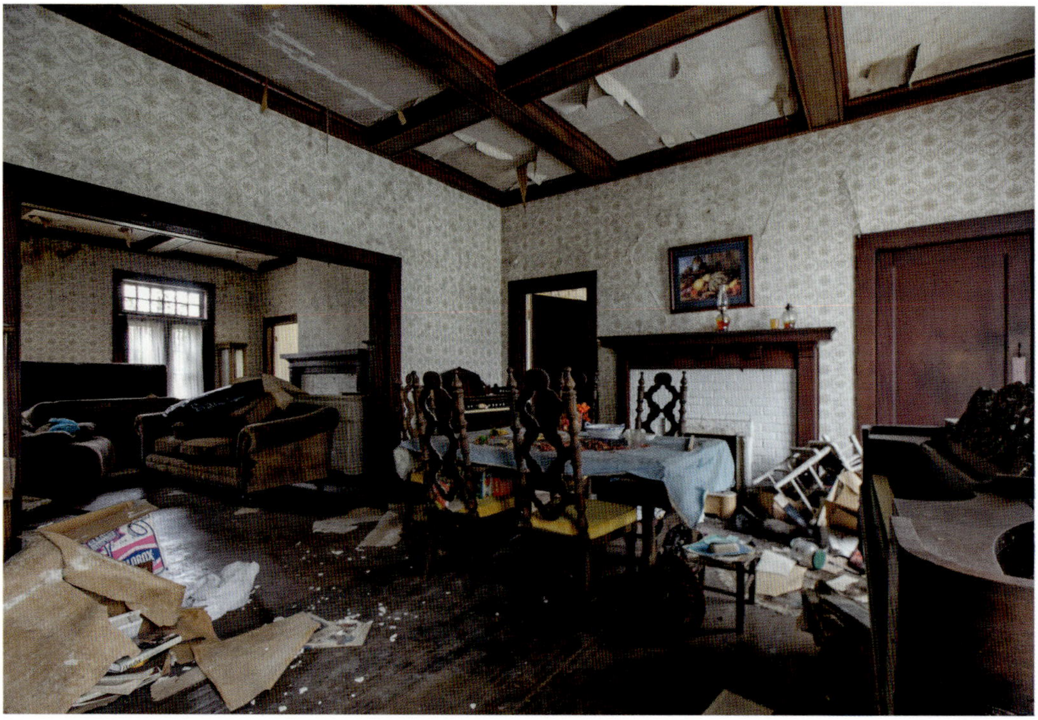

The formal dining room and parlor showcase some of the design elements that made the Craftsman style so popular, including exposed beams and fine wood paneling.

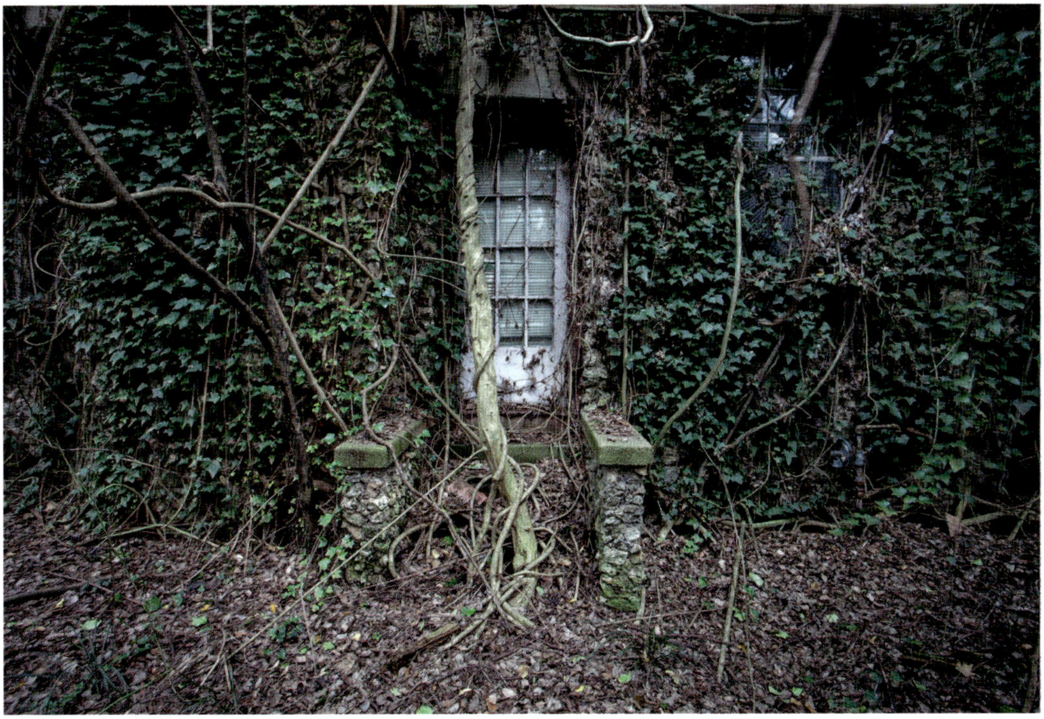

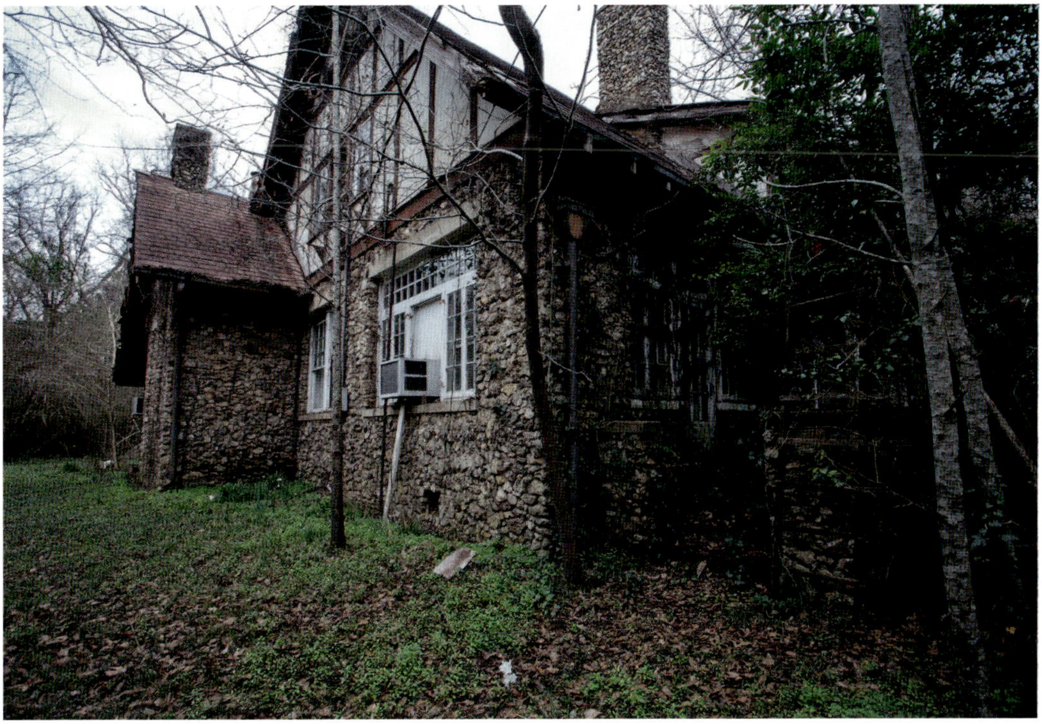

4

DRAKEFORD HOUSE

In 1870, the East Alabama Female College burned to the ground, closing shortly after. The property was sold to John Hamilton Drakeford, the founder and president of the City Bank of Tuskegee. He was the son of Thomas Drakeford, a Tuskegee merchant known as the "oldest and most successful merchant in Macon County." Drakeford built this highly ornamental home on the site of the former college as a gift for his new bride.

Completed in 1892, the house has a late Victorian-era design with an asymmetrical façade, dominant front-facing gable, overhanging eaves, and polygonal tower. The eclectic style is typical of the late Victorian period. Certain elements of the home, for example, the main entry transom and sidelights, suggest a much earlier Greek Revival style. Over the years, several additions were made to the home, including a second-story screened-in porch and a solarium downstairs. The Drakeford House is one of eight historic homes that were added to the National Register of Historic Places in 1985 as a part of the North Main Street Historic District. These particular homes paved the way for future development.

In 2018, the out-of-state owner contacted Tuskegee University and wanted to know whether architecture students could develop a proposal for what to do with the aging home. While the owner never attended the college, his mother, brother, and nephew are all alumni. With faculty oversight, the students created plans to turn the home into a bed and breakfast or a wedding venue. After students submitted proposals to the owner, he awarded the top three students with a scholarship. He also told the faculty that he had funding to renovate the house and use it as a lab for learning about historic preservation and restoration. In what was planned as a two-year project, students would observe and assist contractors as they renovate the house. Due to liability concerns, students cannot work as laborers, but they are responsible for the architectural drawings and conducting historic research.

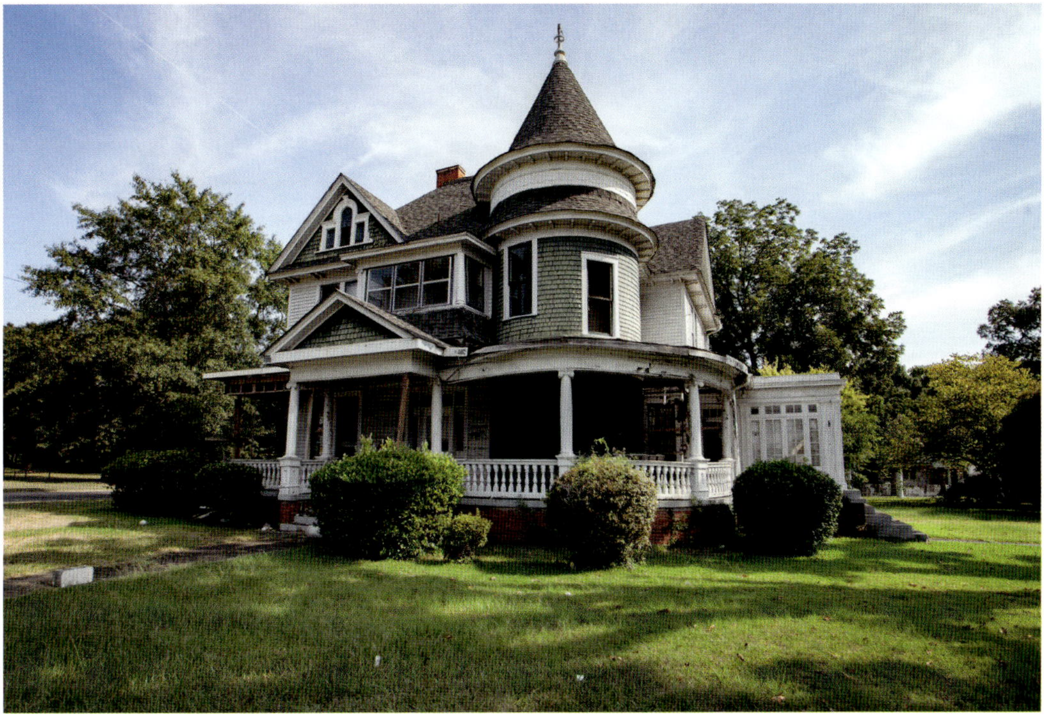

The Drakeford House is a contributing property to the North Main Street Historic District.

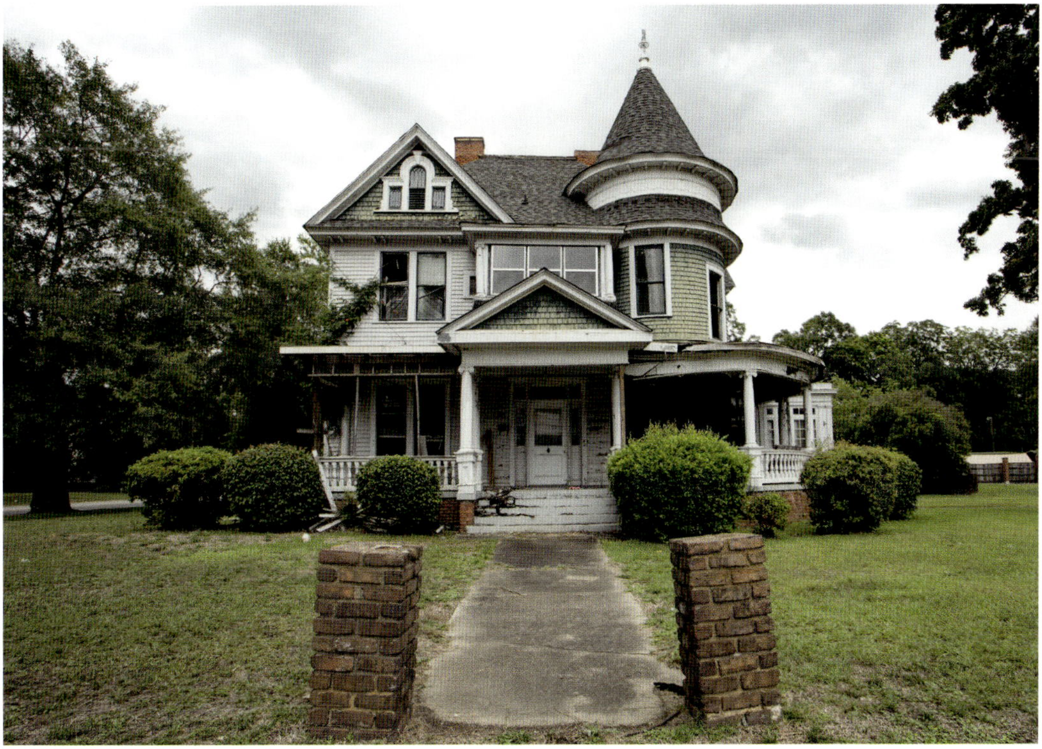

The home and seven others were added to the National Register of Historic Places in 1985.

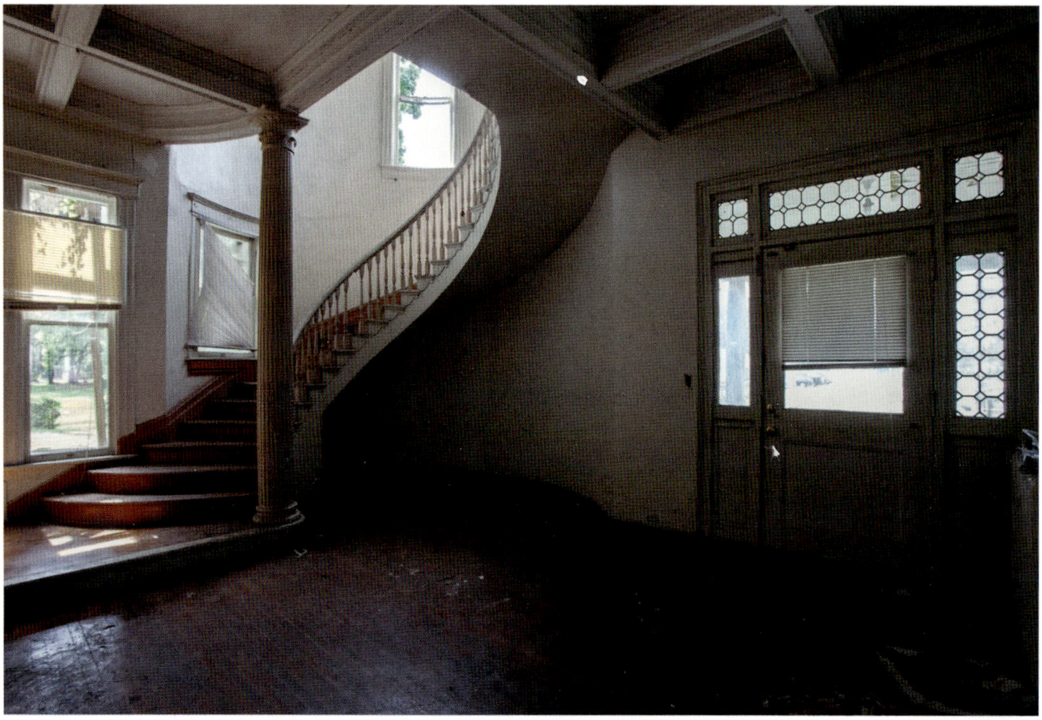

The foyer and spiral staircase inside the Drakeford Home.

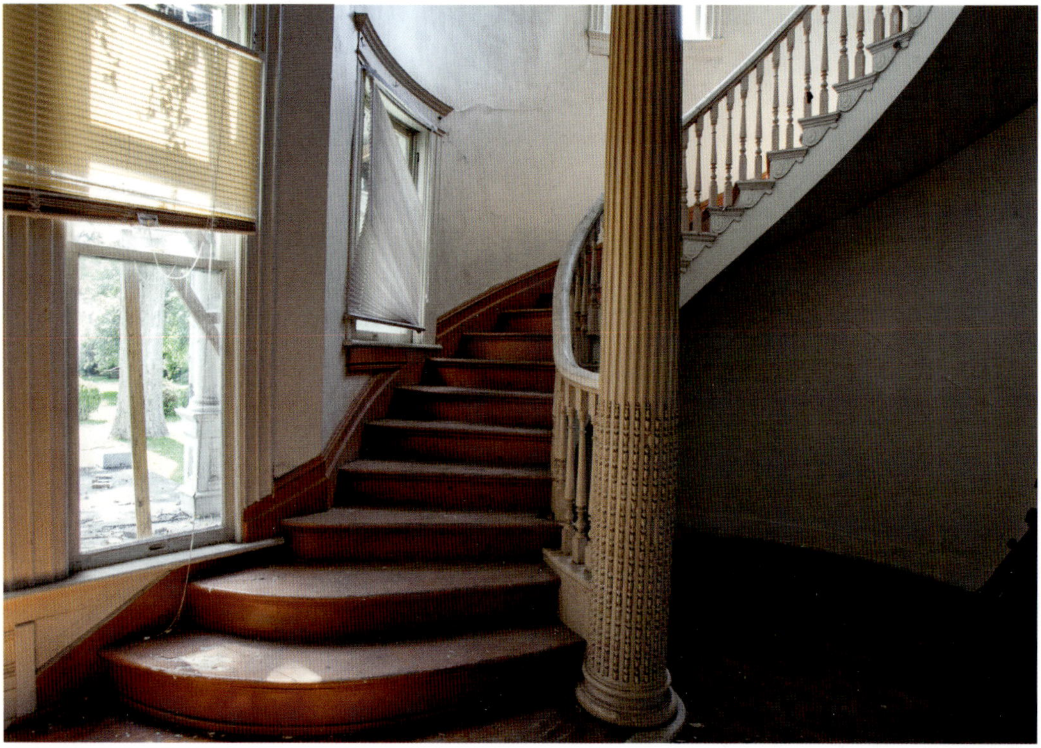

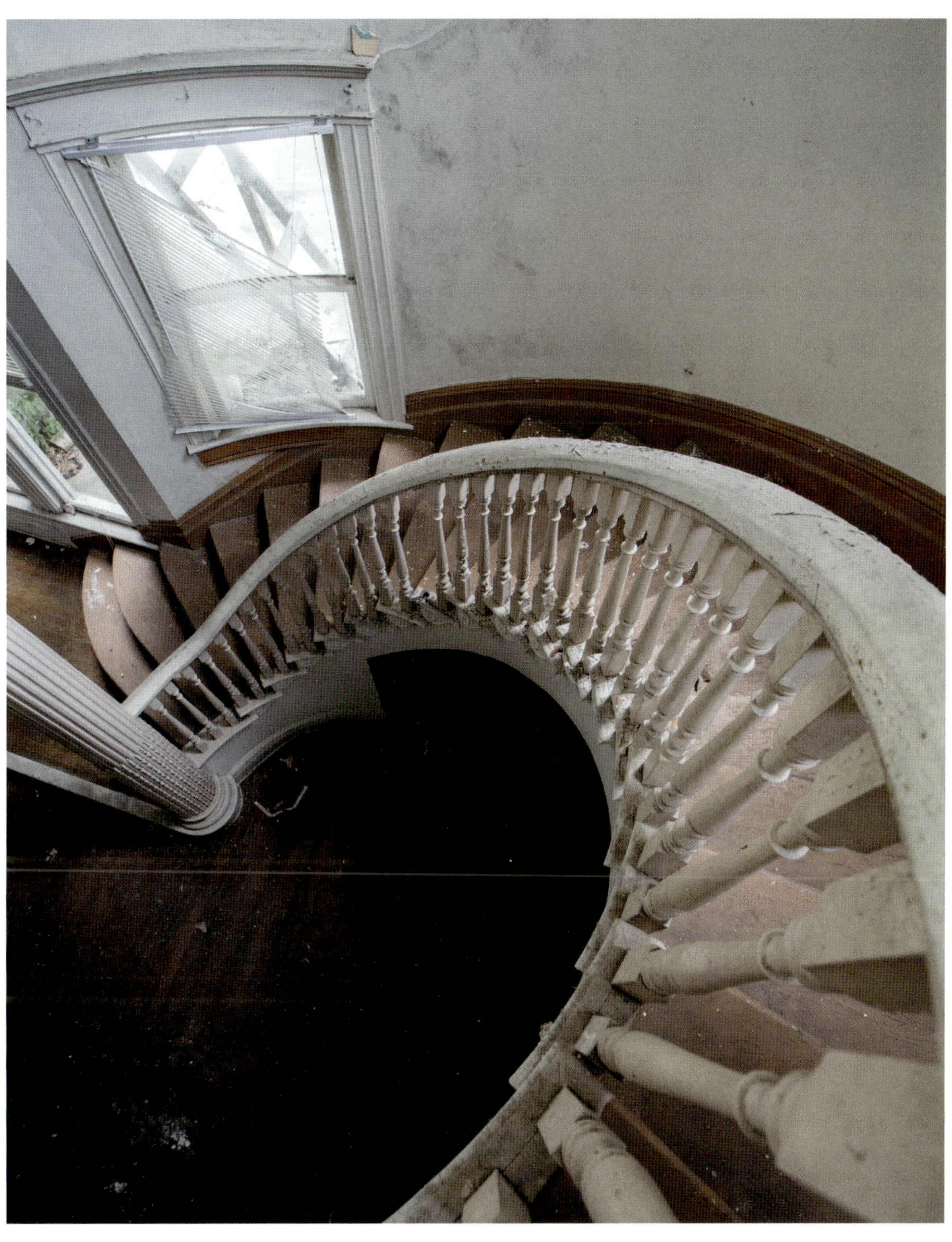

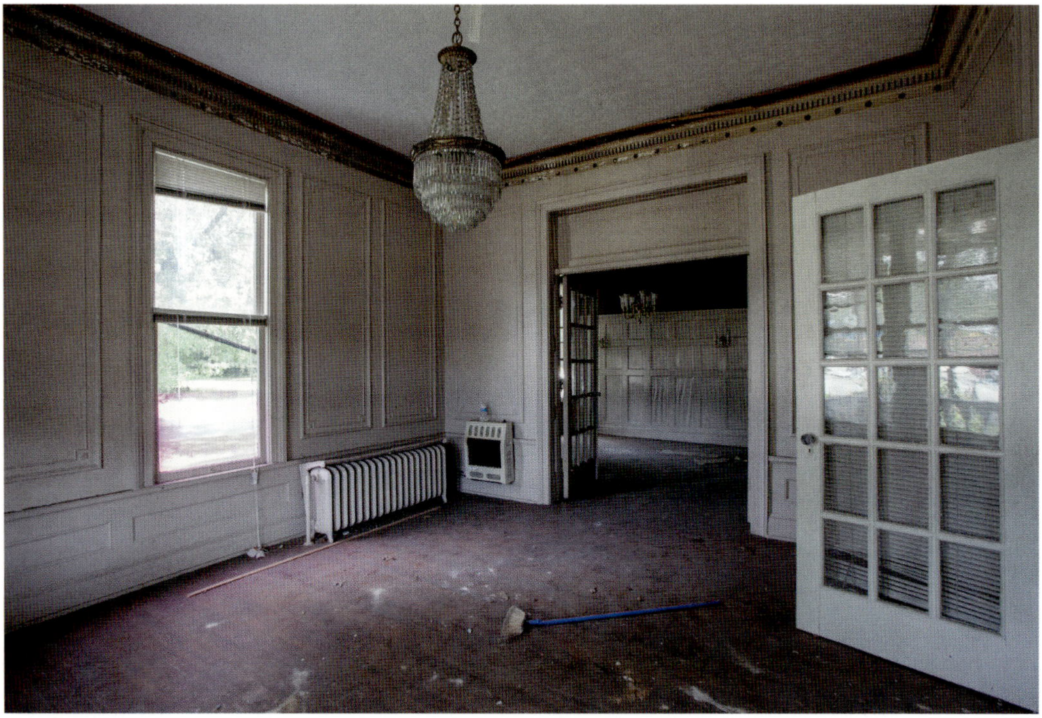

The home was occupied by John. H Drakeford, a successful businessman primarily active during the early twentieth century. He was the founder and president of the City Bank of Tuskegee.

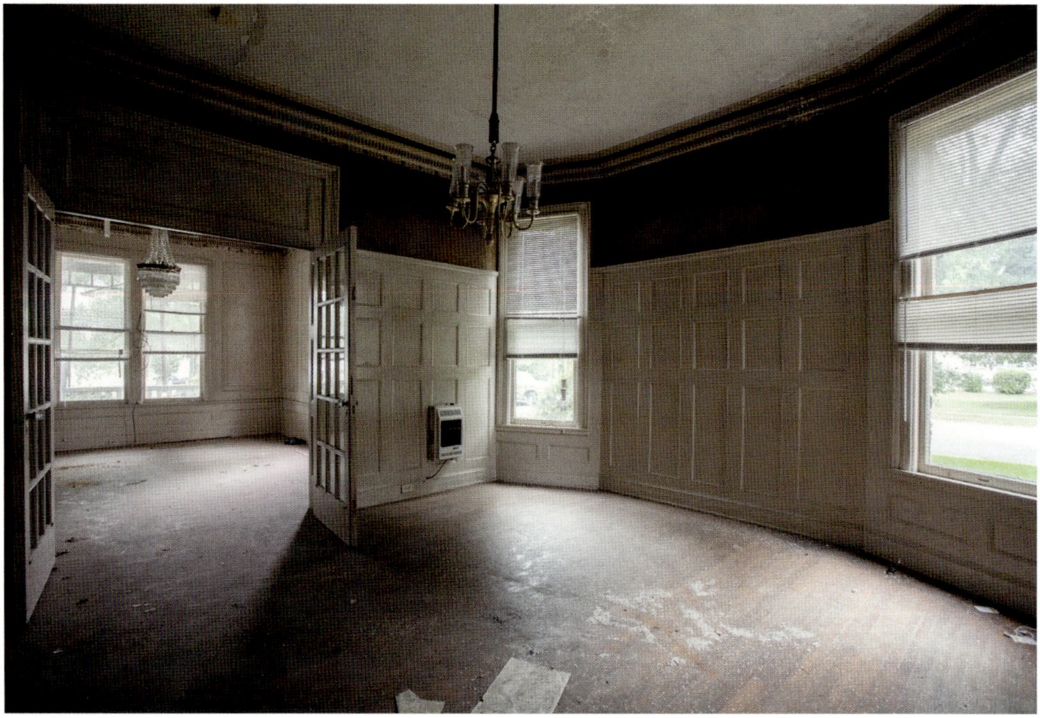

The Drakeford family was known to host many parties in the formal dining room.

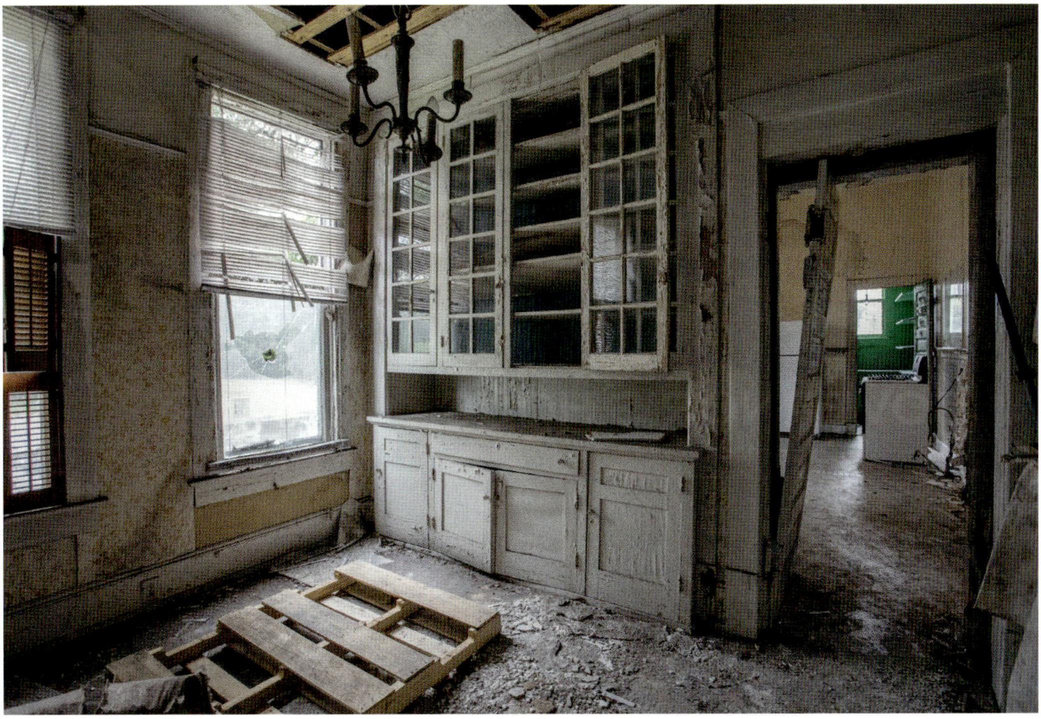

A built-in cupboard next to the kitchen.

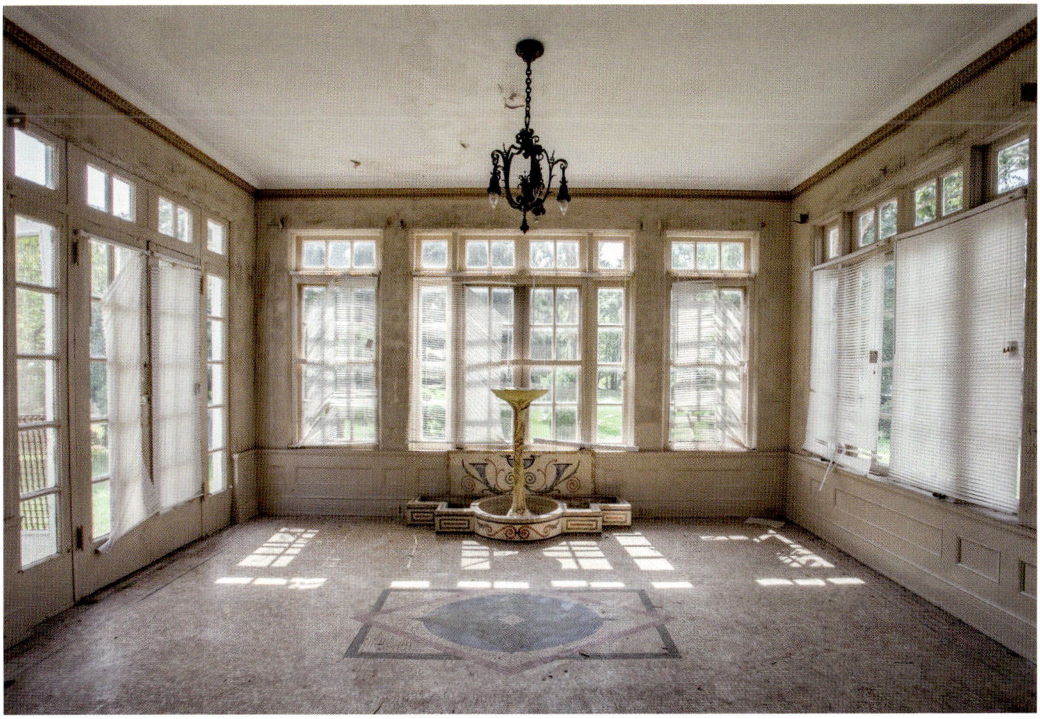

The downstairs solarium was a later addition to the house.

5

GOVERNOR'S HOUSE HOTEL

uilt in 1965, the Governor's House Hotel was once a premier landmark in Alabama's capital city of Montgomery. The hotel featured 197 guest rooms, six meeting rooms, and a large banquet hall totaling over 19,500-sq. feet of meeting and convention space. The Governor's House had all of the luxuries of a private country club with outdoor activities including swimming, golf at a nine-hole golf course, and horseback riding. The hotel even had a restaurant and lounge—the Rotunda Restaurant and Filibuster Lounge. One fascinating feature of the hotel was the custom-built outdoor swimming pool in the shape of Alabama.

During the 1960s, the Governor's House Hotel quickly became one of the top convention centers in Montgomery. The hotel hosted all sorts of famous people and events. Former Alabama Governors George Wallace and Fob James both held their campaign election parties in the Alabama Room. Politicians were frequent guests in the Rotunda Restaurant. However, the guest list was not limited to only government officials. Many famous actresses and actors were also known to patronize the hotel. In 1990, Whoopi Goldberg was a guest at the Governor's House while she filmed the movie *The Long Walk Home.*

By the 1990s, the Governor's House Hotel was showing its age. Amenities like the horse stables and golf course were long gone. The area around the property was in a steady decline, and the hotel went through a re-branding as an economy-class hotel. Visitors complained of mold in the rooms and unsanitary conditions. The Governor's House had passed its heyday and was a mere shadow of its once glorious self. Before permanently closing, only a third of the building was in use.

According to news reports, city officials are confident the area may regenerate itself and would entertain the idea of abating some property tax to get a developer to renovate the old hotel. In April 2019, Montgomery firefighters responded to reports of a two-alarm fire at the property. There was no power to the building, ruling out electrical issues that could lead to fires. Due to its secluded design, the site is a magnet for the homeless and vandals. Several rooms appear to be occupied with makeshift doors in place. Numerous fires have been reported since the building first went up for auction in 2010.

In 2018, a sale was pending on the property, but it never materialized. Today, the Governor's House Hotel remains for sale. The site now belongs to the state of Alabama through a tax lien. The Department of Revenue owns the property, and anyone with $166,000 can take possession of this famous Montgomery landmark.

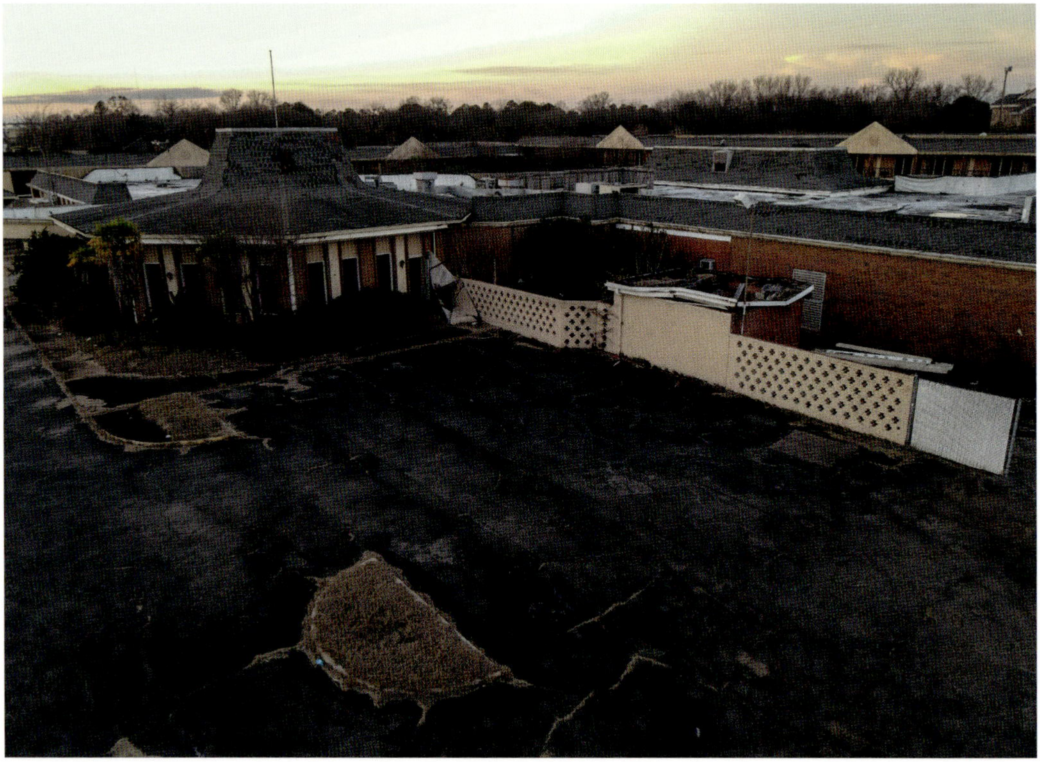

Today, the Governor's House is labeled as an eyesore. Years of vandalism and neglect destroyed the hotel.

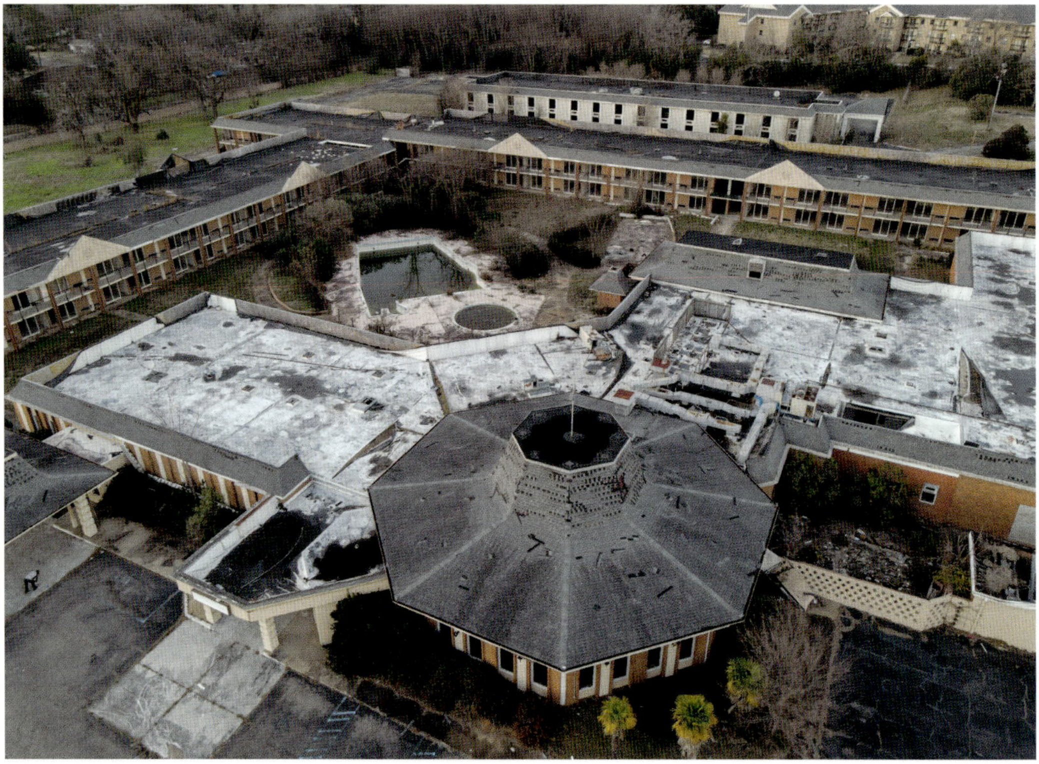

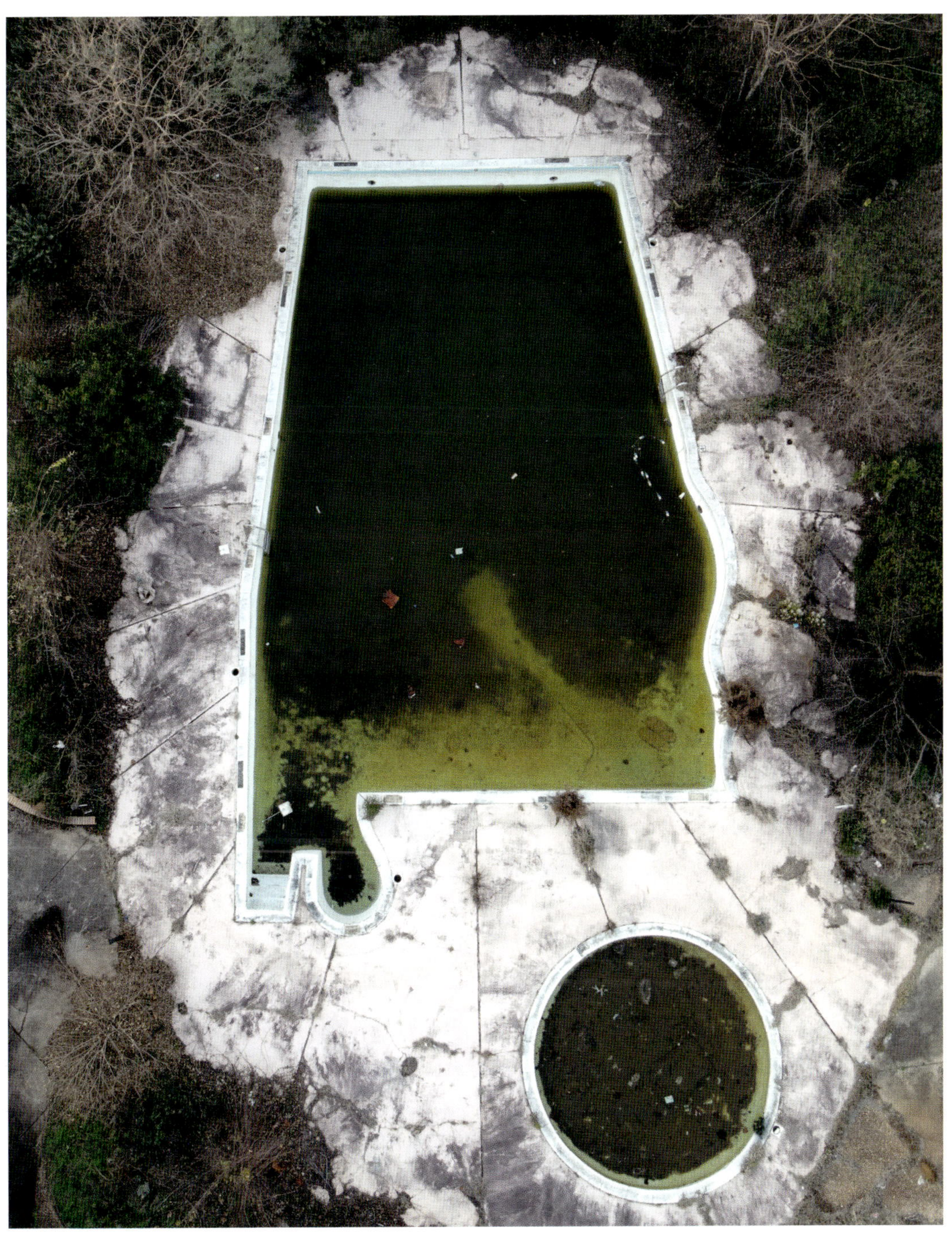

A custom Alabama-shaped pool was once the centerpiece of the property.

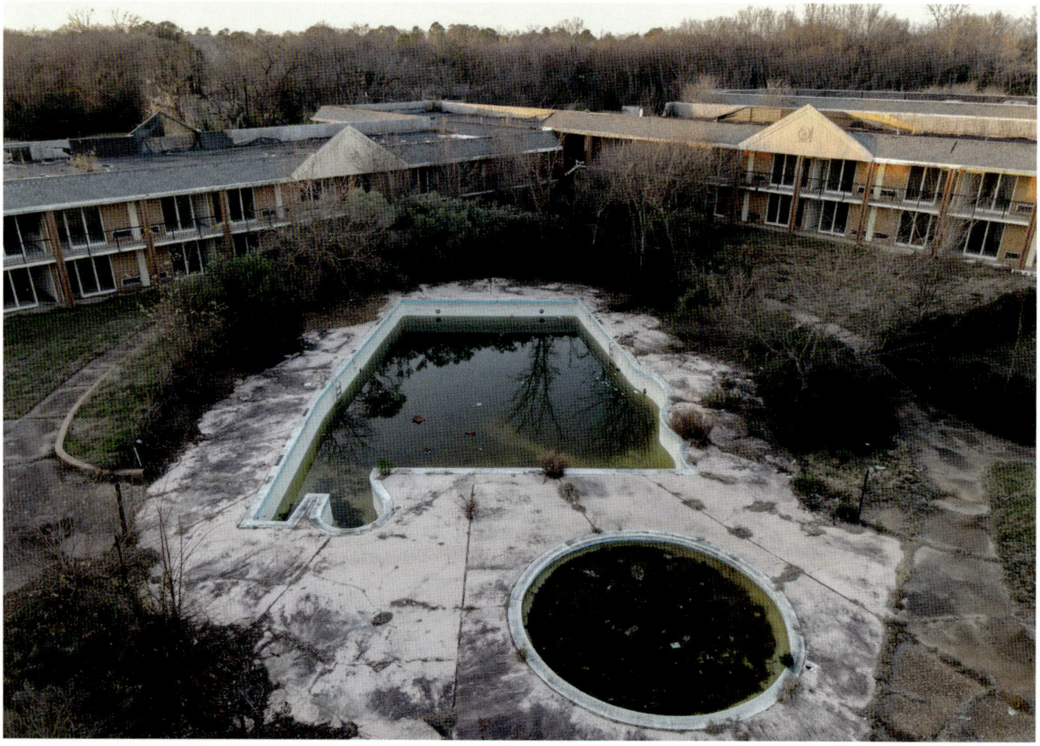

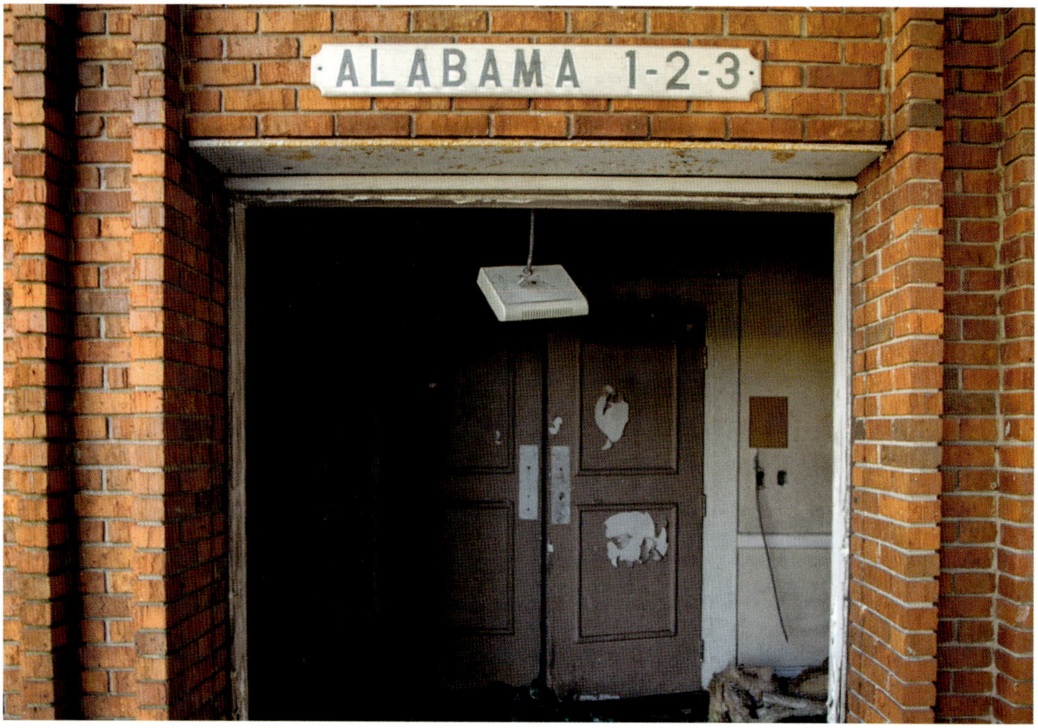

In the hotel's heyday, election parties and events were held in the Alabama Room.

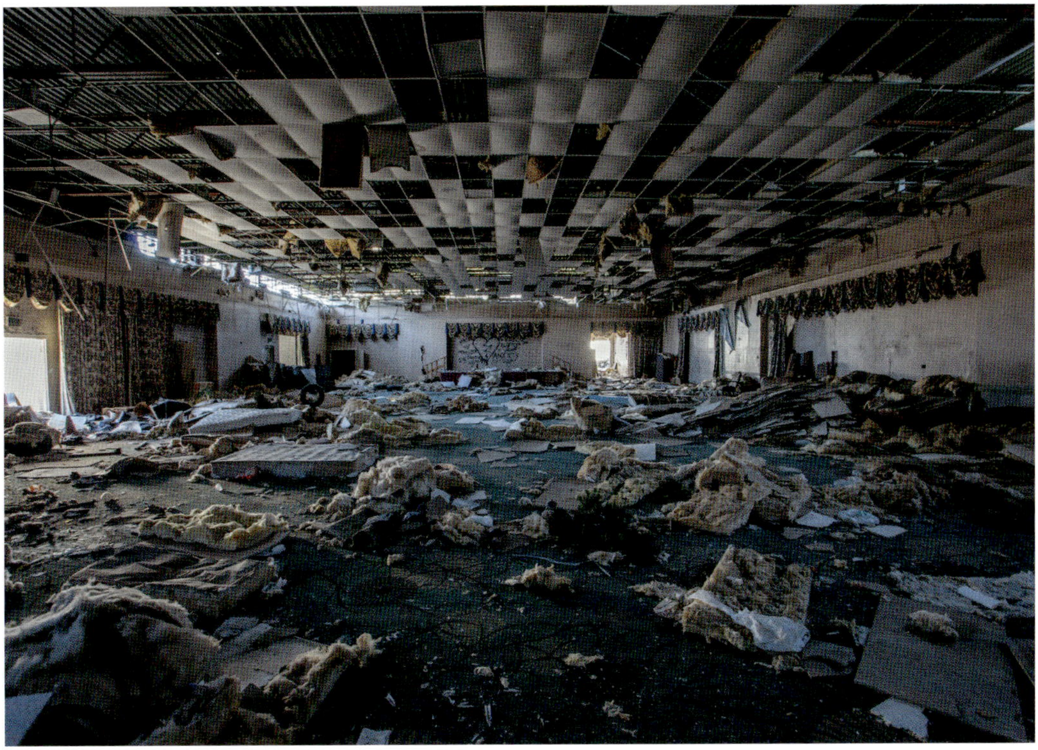

After years of sitting abandoned, the Alabama Room is filled with trash and debris and ceiling tiles.

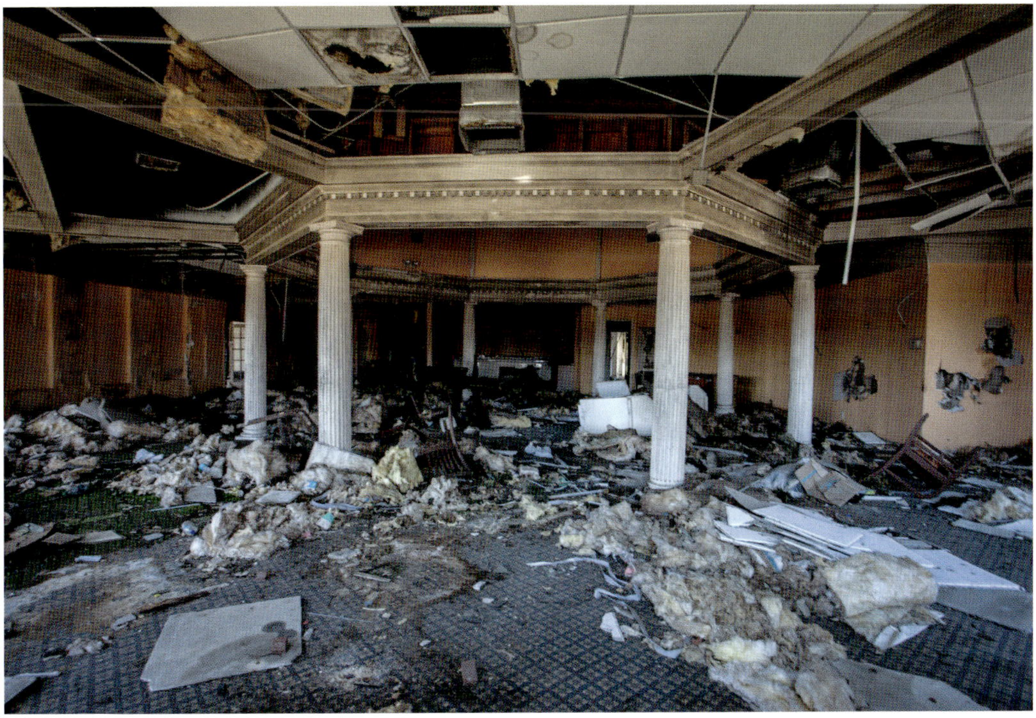

6

HOUSE OF ROCK

Behind a gated driveway in Irondale sits a nearly 9,000-sq. foot ranch-style home that was once the residence of Mildred and Norris Underwood. Built in 1963, the estate is constructed of Bessemer Grey brick and features five bedrooms, five baths, two kitchens, multiple living areas, and a large vaulted addition with an indoor swimming pool. There is even a room dedicated to housing the owner's pet birds, complete with large windows, a dirt floor, and an open skylight for the birds to fly up to the second floor. At one time, the grounds were meticulously landscaped with a Japanese-themed garden in the backyard. There were four koi ponds surrounded by various plants and trees. According to neighbors, the owners had many visitors who would come to just enjoy the garden, which is said to have rivaled the Birmingham Botanical Gardens.

Norris Underwood was born on May 13, 1926. He served in World War II in the U.S. Navy alongside his twin brother, Horace. Both were aboard but unharmed when transport ship LST-6 was sunk by mines in the River Seine, France, in late 1944. Norris and Mildred founded and operated Irondale Fabricating Company, which conducted wrought-iron construction throughout Alabama. They built jails and bomb shelters across the state, as well as such high-profile projects as the scrolling sign atop the Two North Twentieth Building in downtown Birmingham. Even after he retired, he managed many Irondale industrial and retail properties.

Norris and Mildred celebrated fifty-nine years of marriage before Norris passed away at the age of seventy-nine in March 2006. Sadly, Mildred passed away a few years later in August 2012. The house was left to their daughter who listed it for sale, but due to the house's size and location, finding a buyer proved difficult. By 2018, the property had fallen into foreclosure and was left abandoned. In 2020, the property was sold to a new owner who began renovations shortly after acquiring the home.

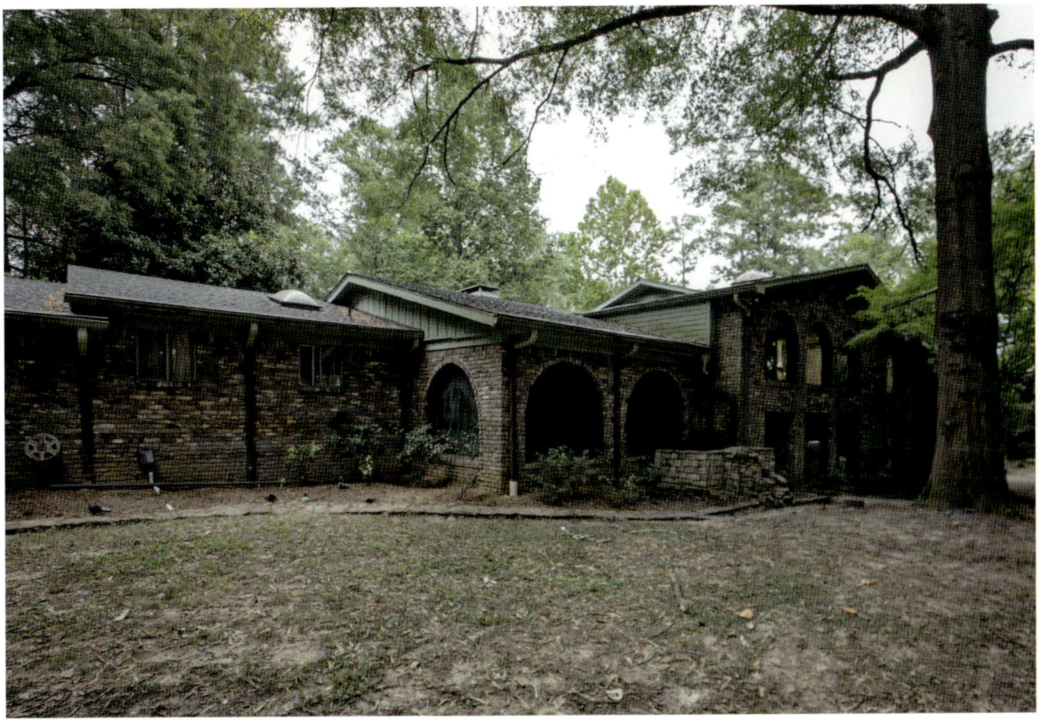

Eccentric design details are plentiful inside this 1960s ranch-style beauty.

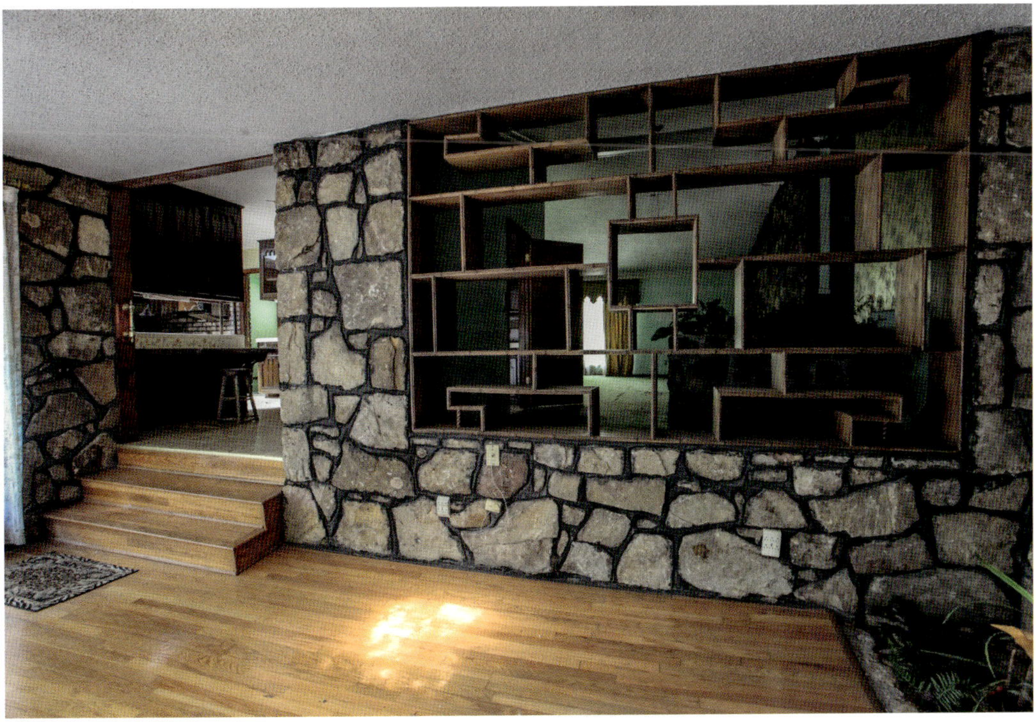

Stepping inside the home, its crowning glory is the profusion of distinctive Bessemer Grey bricks on the exterior and some interior walls.

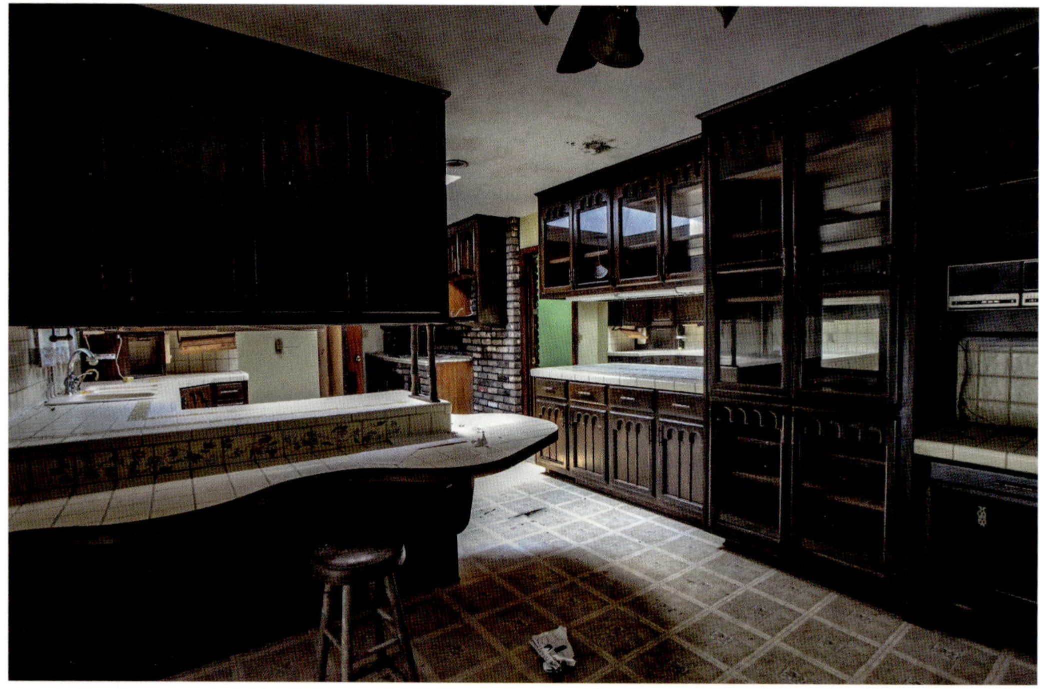

The open-plan kitchen with a breakfast bar would have been perfect for gathering the family around, although the heavy wooden units look outdated today. There are two fully furnished kitchens at each end of the house.

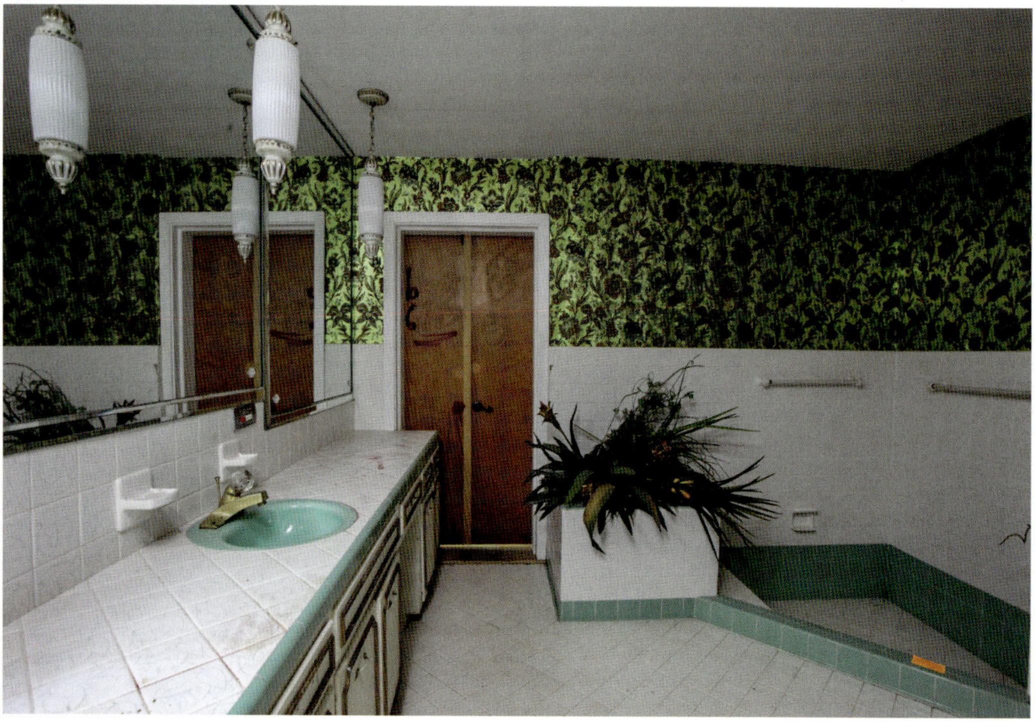

Shimmering wallpaper and what looks like a sunken bath marks this bathroom as a luxurious space. It is one of five in the home that would have been used by the lady of the house, Mildred Joy Underwood.

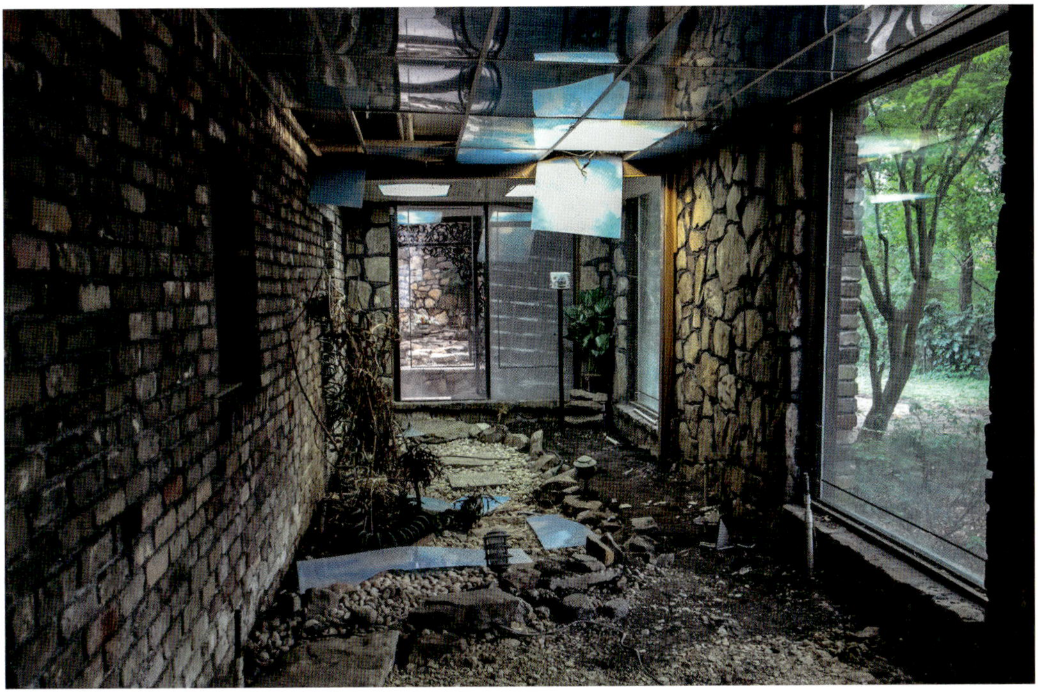

The couple decided to bring nature indoors by creating a room within the property to house their many pet birds. The aviary has huge windows, a dirt floor, and an open skylight so their feathered friends could fly up to the second floor, making it much more like a luxury avian palace than a mere birdcage.

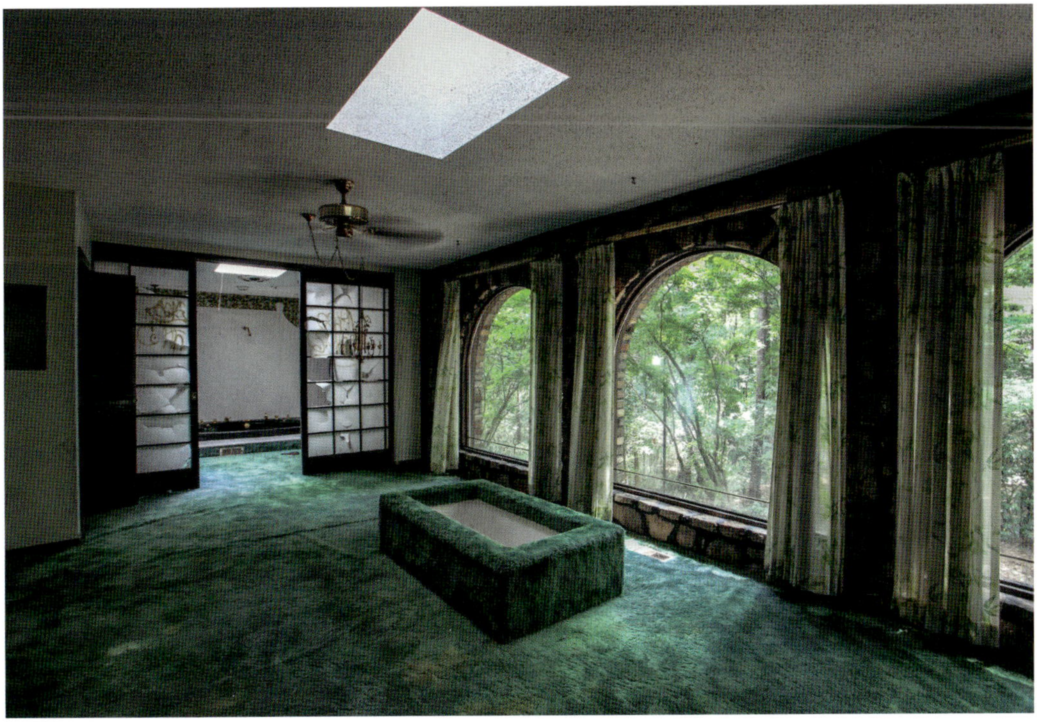

The second-floor room above the aviary, the cut-out in the floor allowed the birds to fly throughout the house.

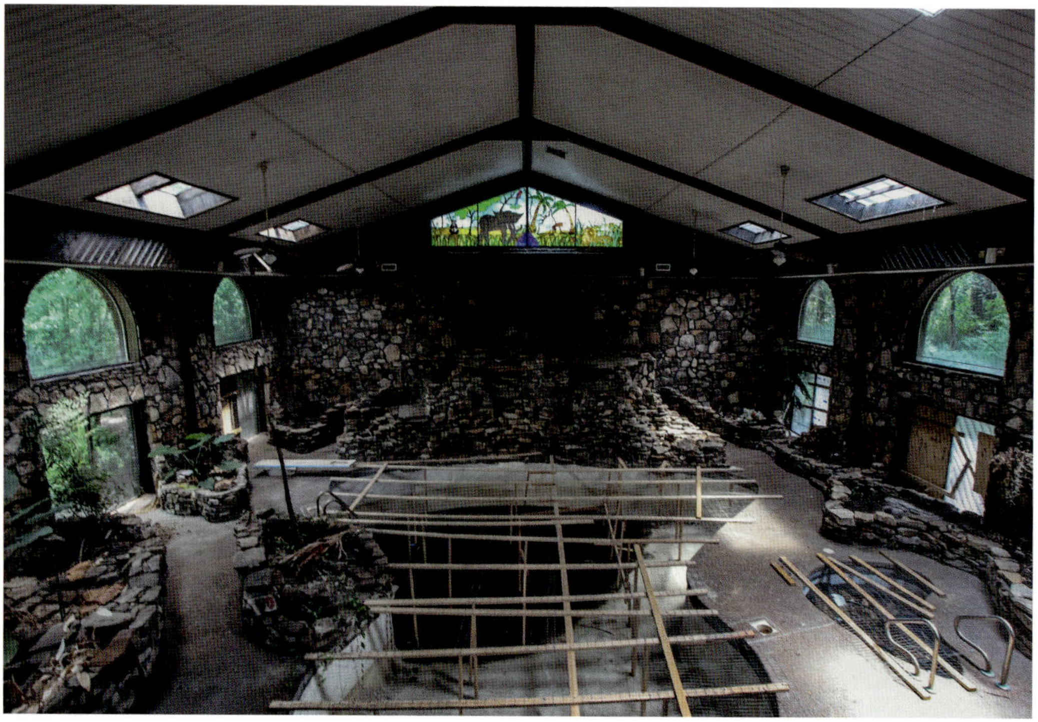

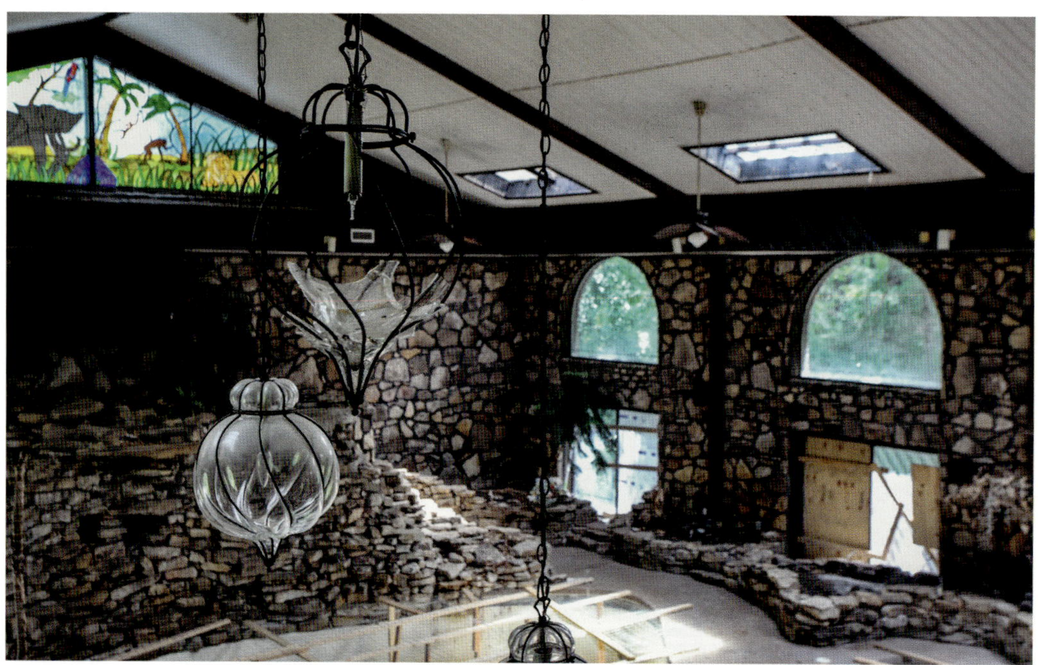

Perhaps the biggest surprise inside this fascinating property is a massive, vaulted 1970s addition to the house. This indoor pool area is set up like a tropical paradise with exotic indoor plants dotted around.

The attention to detail in the pool room is stunning, with elegant wrought-iron hanging lights resembling miniature bird cages. You can also see a colorful stained-glass window on the far wall depicting exotic wildlife, including a parrot, monkey, lion, and elephant.

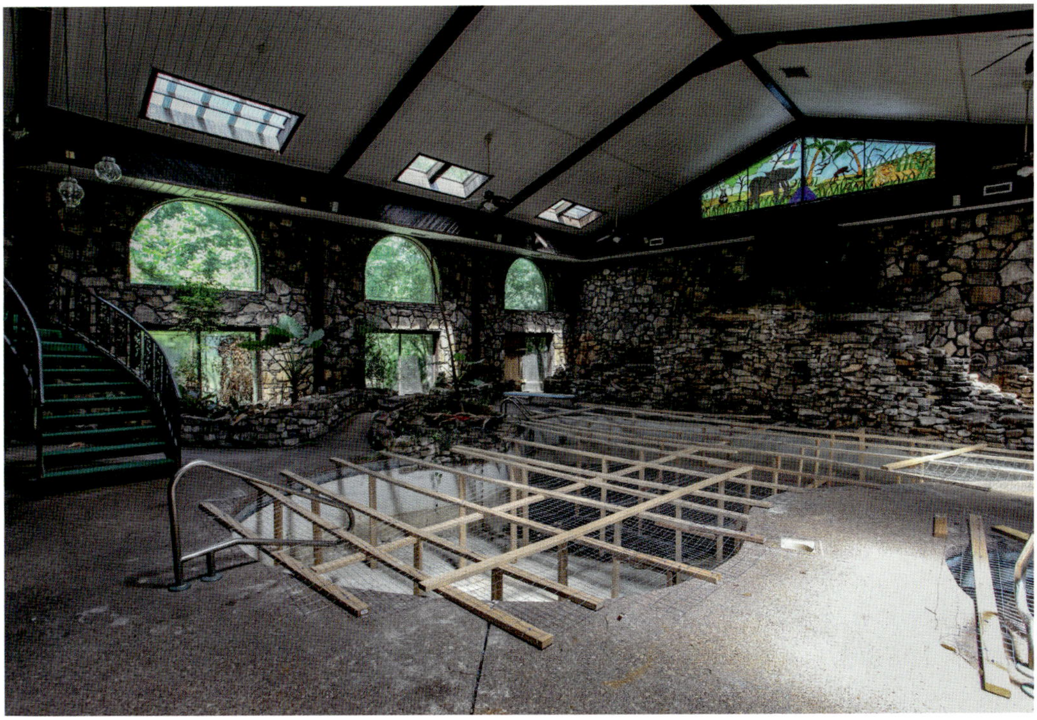

At one end, the rocks were stacked to form a waterfall so that guests could jump off the top into the pool.

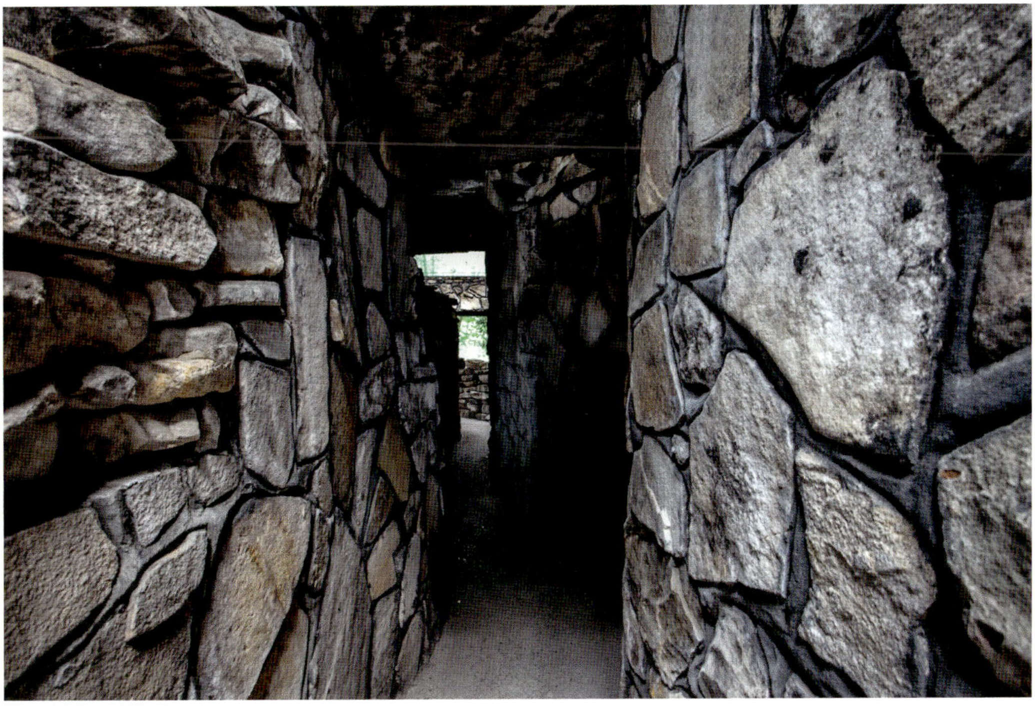

Filled with added extras, there was a grotto shower hidden behind the waterfall too.

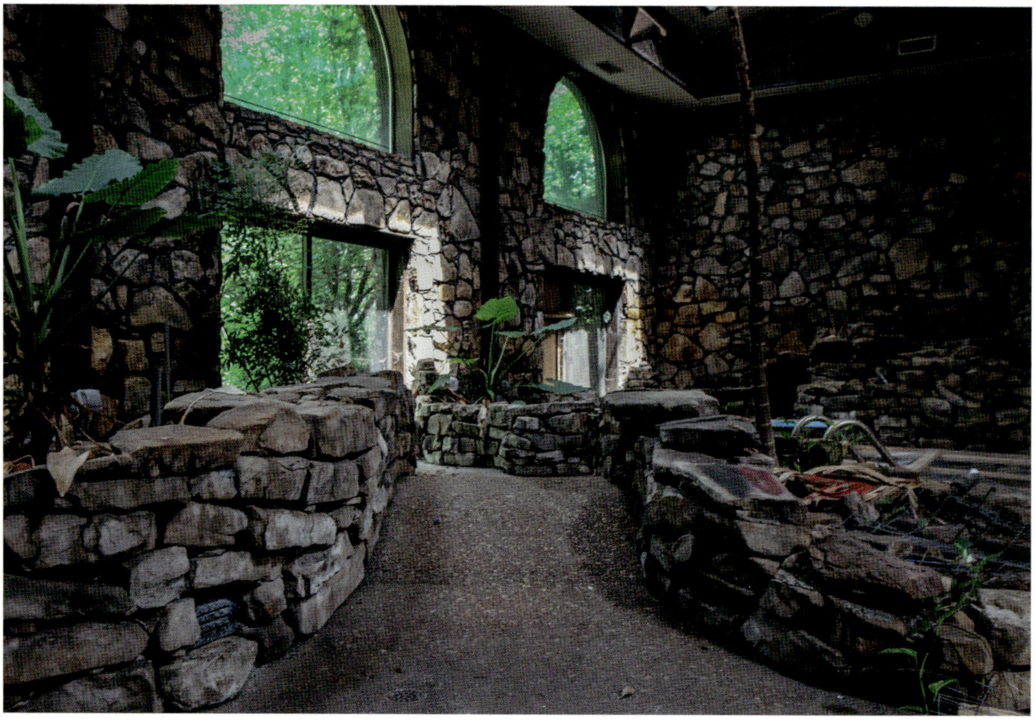

Leaving the pool room, you step outside through the sliding glass doors into the almost 3 acres of private land.

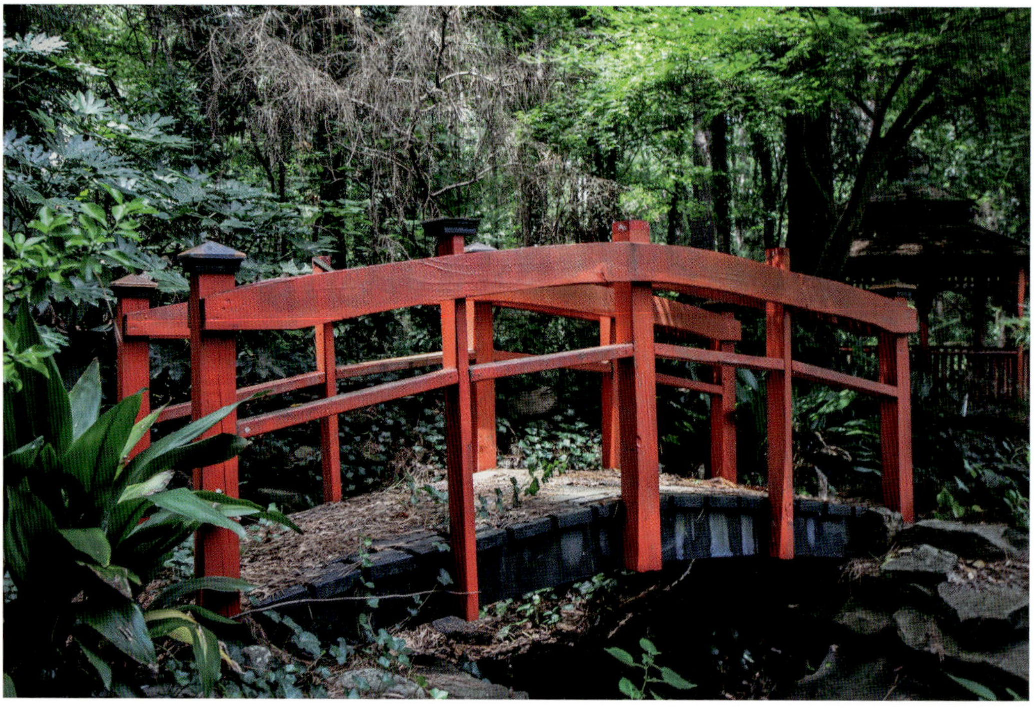

These grounds are what the house became most known for because they were magnificently landscaped into a series of Japanese-style gardens as well as four koi ponds, a red Japanese-style bridge, and a matching gazebo.

7

JEMISON CENTER

The Jemison family settled near Tuscaloosa, Alabama, in the 1830s and became one of the wealthiest and most influential families in the state. Robert Jemison, Jr., was a Confederate senator, businessman, and entrepreneur. His business empire grew to encompass toll roads and bridges, a grist mill, a sawmill, livery stables, a hotel, and six plantations totaling over 10,000 acres. Jemison was one of the leaders who built support for the Alabama State Hospital for the Insane, later renamed Bryce Hospital, which opened in 1861 in Tuscaloosa.

After his death in 1871, Jemison's largest plantation, known as Cherokee Place, was bequeathed to the state of Alabama Board of Mental Health. By the 1920s, Bryce had become severely overcrowded. Satellite institutions were created nearby to help relieve the pressure, such as the Alabama Home for Mental Defectives (later known as Partlow State School). In 1939, the former site of Cherokee Place was transformed into the State Farm Colony for Negroes. The building known as the Jemison Center was constructed a short drive from the main campus, named for Jemison's generosity. Before the Jemison Center was built, African-American patients were housed in the lofts of the barn at Bryce Hospital.

The approach to treatment at Bryce followed the concept that patient work was an important component of mental healthcare. Patients housed at the Jemison Center would tend the fields around the property. This was a part of the self-sustainability of Bryce as well as a way to feed a large number of patients with limited state funding. By the 1960s, the concept of patients remaining in the hospital for long periods of time, while at the same time working productively, became a subject of public concern. Many citizens felt that the hospital retained patients as a source of free labor.

In 1970, the Jemison Center made headlines after a journalist from the *Tuscaloosa News* visited the facility and reported on the abhorrent conditions:

Human feces were caked on the toilets and walls; urine soaked the aging floors; many beds lacked linens; patients were sleeping on the floor. One small shower served 131 male patients; the 75 female patients only had one shower too. Most of the patients at Jemison were highly tranquilized and appeared to have not bathed in days. All appeared to lack any semblance of treatment. The stench was almost unbearable.

Conditions at the Jemison Center and Bryce Hospital in Tuscaloosa led to a landmark lawsuit—Wyatt *v.* Stickney. At that time, Bryce Hospital had over 5,000 patients living in intolerable conditions that the *Montgomery Advertiser* compared to a "concentration camp." Wyatt and his aunt testified about the improper treatment designed to only make patients more manageable. In 1971, the lawsuit was expanded to include patients at Alabama's other inpatient mental health facilities. The resulting court-ordered agreements formed the basis for federal minimum standards for the care of people with mental illness who reside in institutional settings known as the Wyatt Standards. The standards are founded on four criteria for evaluation of care: humane psychological and physical environment, qualified and sufficient staff for administration of treatment, individualized treatment plans, and minimum restriction of patient freedom.

After thirty-three years, the case of Wyatt *v.* Stickney came to a conclusion. Through a tenure of nine Alabama governors and fourteen state mental health commissioners, the case was the longest mental health case in national history. The state of Alabama estimates its litigation expenses at over $15 million.

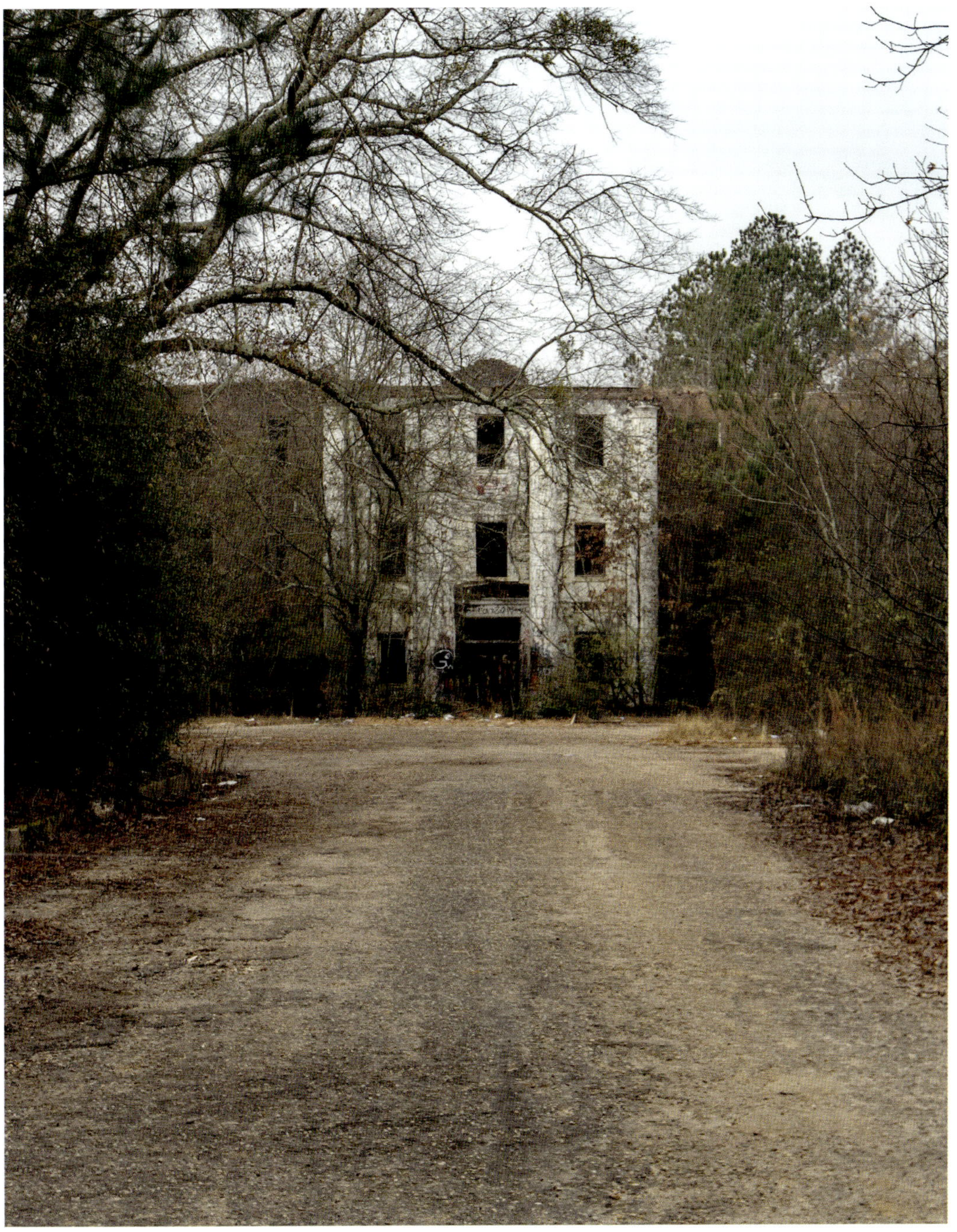

The former Robert Jemison Plantation went by several names, including the Crab Apple Plantation and the Cherokee Plantation in Northport.

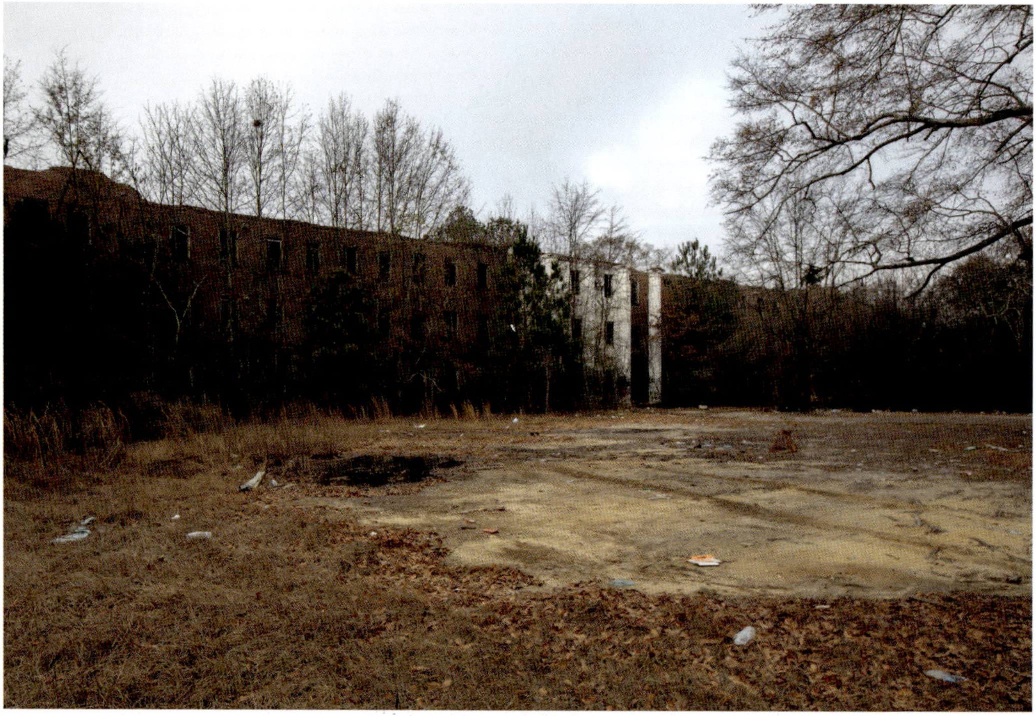

During the segregated era of the 1920s, the former plantation became the State Colony for the Negro Insane, later renamed the Jemison Center, an extension of Bryce Hospital for African-American patients.

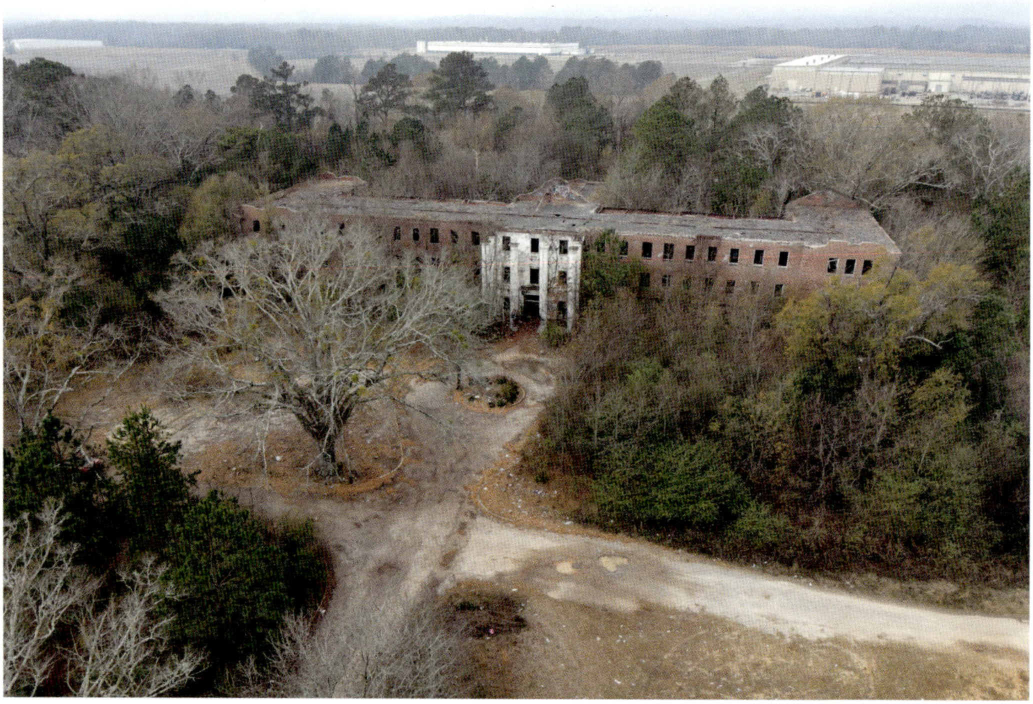

Patients performed farm and domestic labor as part of their treatment.

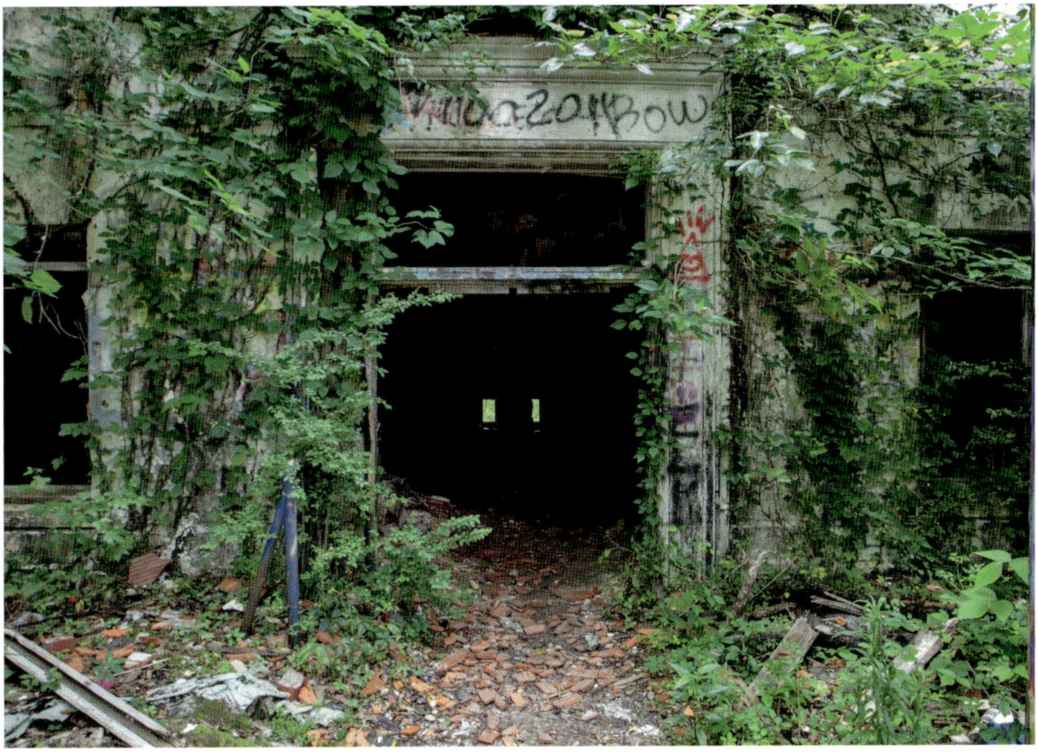

The main entrance to the asylum is now covered in overgrowth.

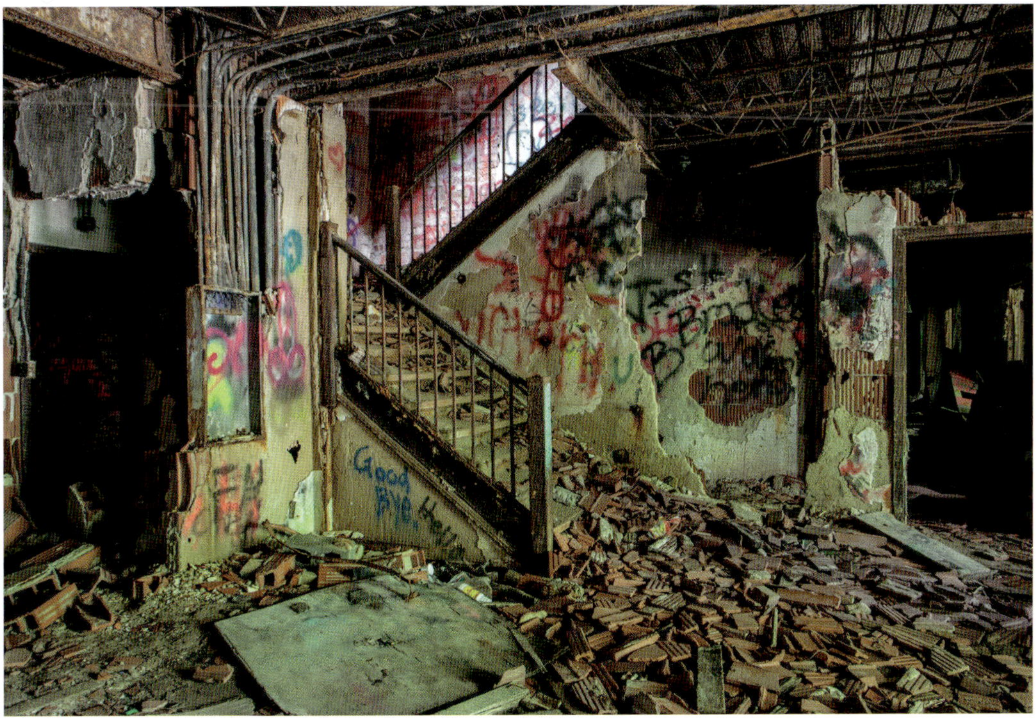

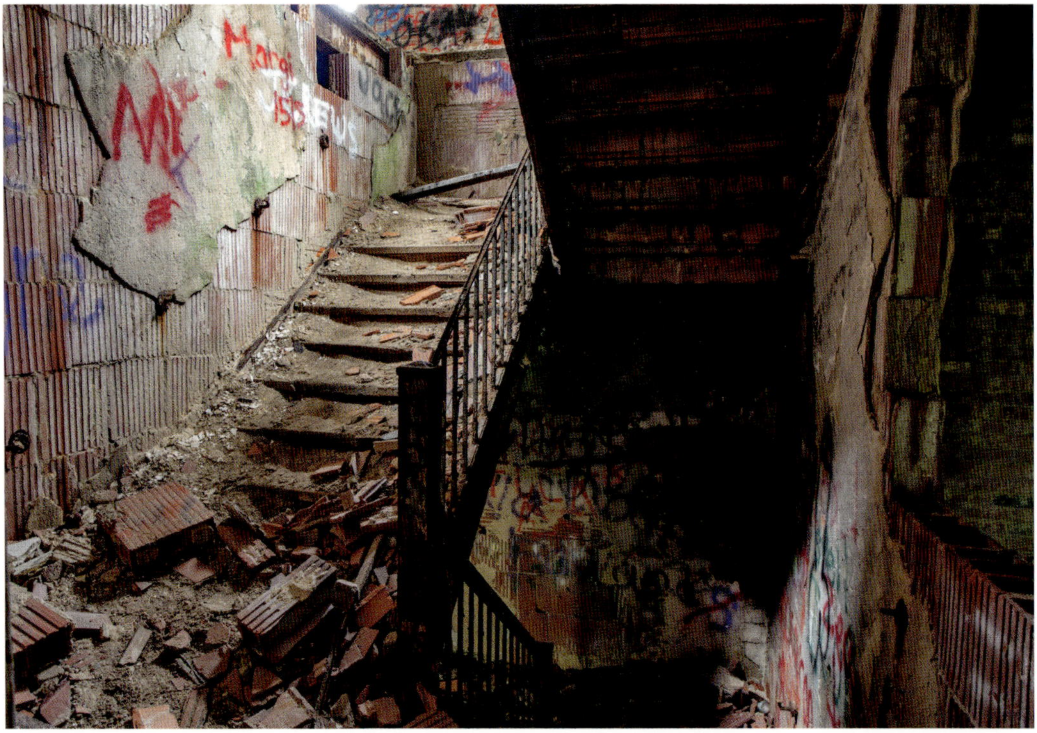

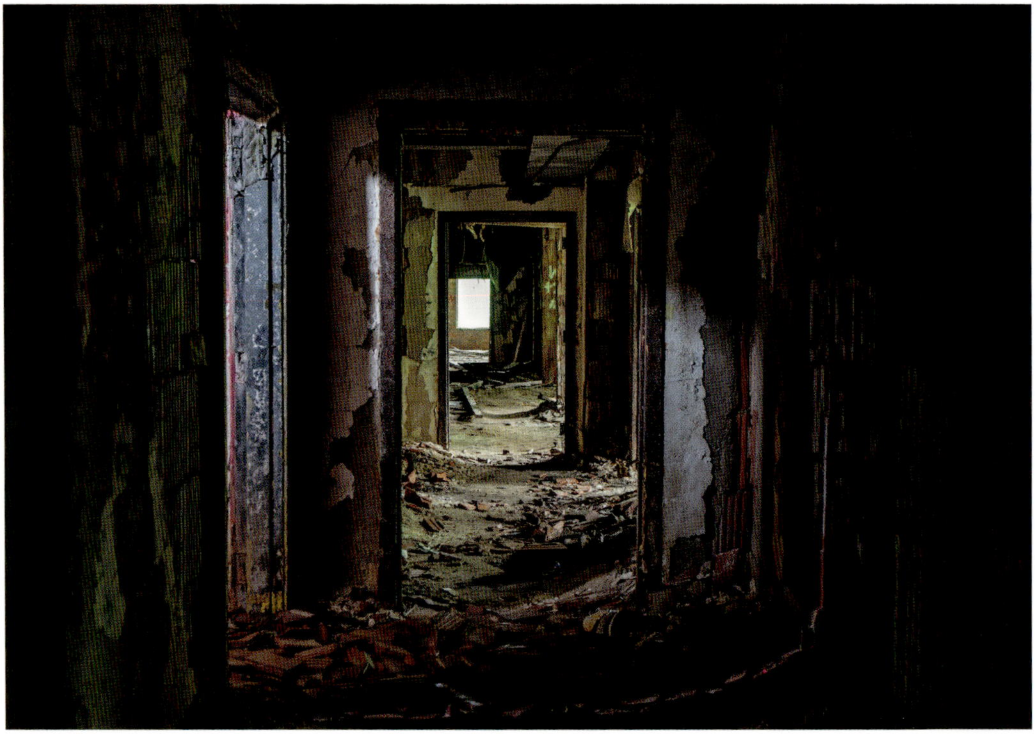

The hallways inside the Jemison Center are dark and littered with debris.

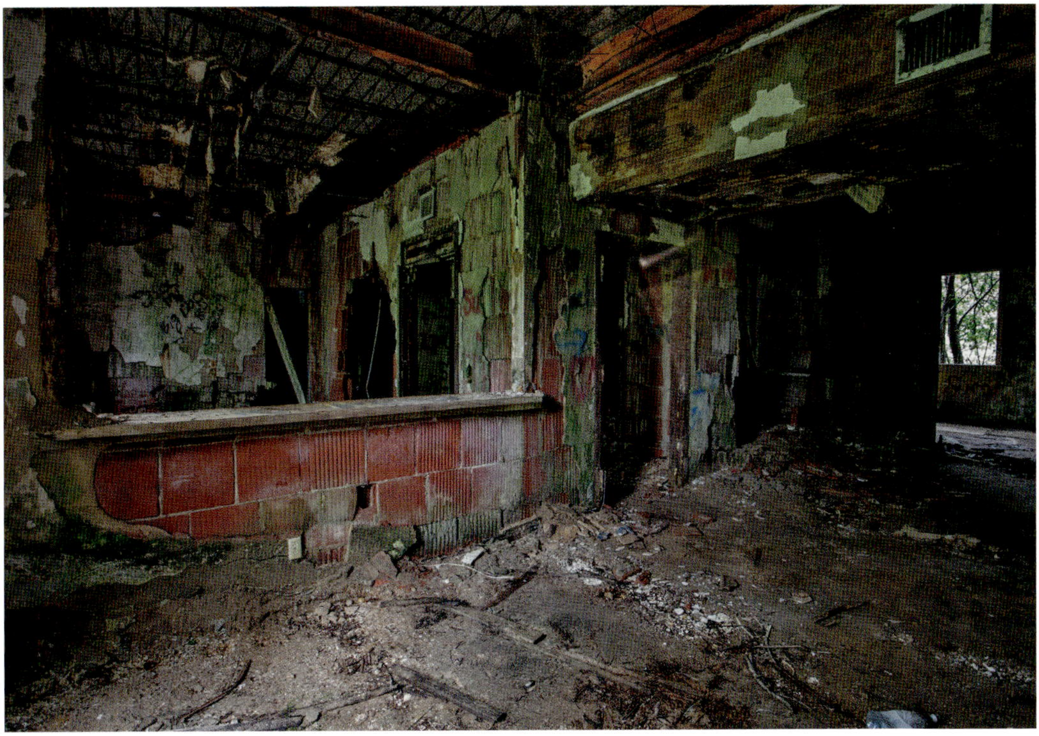

What is left of a nurses' station inside a ward.

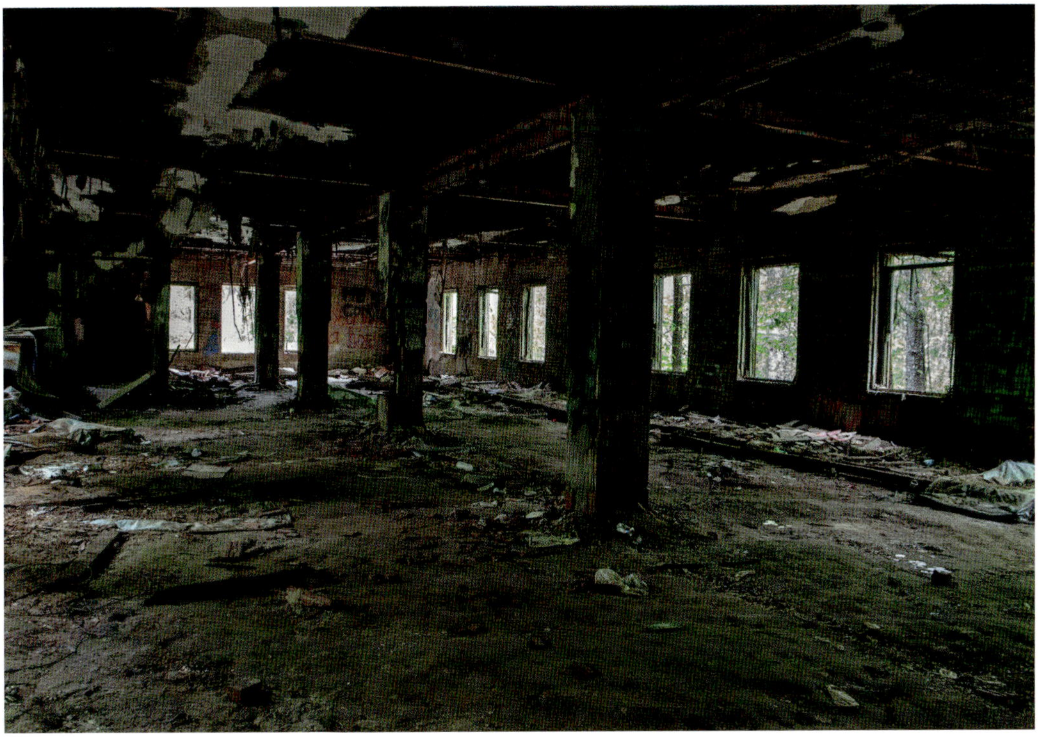

A patient ward inside the Jemison Center.

8

MID-CENTURY MASTERPIECE

Constructed in the 1960s, this mid-century modern home was once a Southern showpiece. The house was designed by prominent architect John Randal McDonald and holds the distinction of being the only one built in Alabama. McDonald—who studied under Louis Kahn, Ludwig Mies van der Rohe, and other modernist masters at Yale University in the 1940s—designed hundreds of structures throughout his decades-long career, continuing to practice until his sudden death in 2003. At one point, he became well known for delivering the stylings of Frank Lloyd Wright at a comparatively affordable price. McDonald also reportedly designed homes for celebrities, such as Mickey Mantle, James Garner, and Maureen O'Hara.

Designed as affordable informal living, the living room, dining room, and kitchen are combined into one open space. The terrazzo floors, exposed brick, and an abundance of skylights help bring the outside elements indoors. The home has a host of unique features including a partially flat roof, narrow hallways, no ceiling lights, and the most prominent feature—a sunken hearth fireplace.

Sweeping lines give the two-bedroom, two-bath 1,500-sq. foot home a much larger feel. The children's rooms are in the center of the house and are divided by a folding door that makes separate rooms for sleeping and opens into a large daytime play area. The master bedroom has sliding doors to the porch on one side and sliding closet doors on the other. In the rear of the property, a 1960s Chevrolet Corvair belonging to the previous owner rests nearby a large inground swimming pool. After the owner died, the property remained unoccupied for years. After sitting abandoned for quite some time, the property was sold in March 2021 to investors who plan to turn the house into an Airbnb.

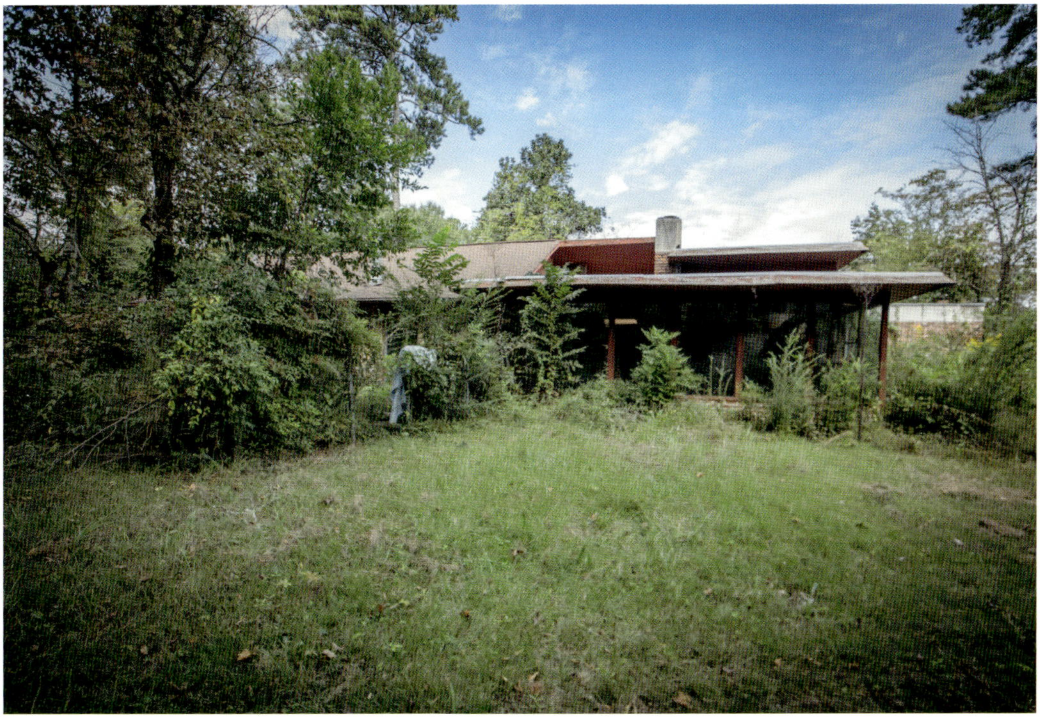

This house is the only one in Alabama built by famed architect John Randal McDonald.

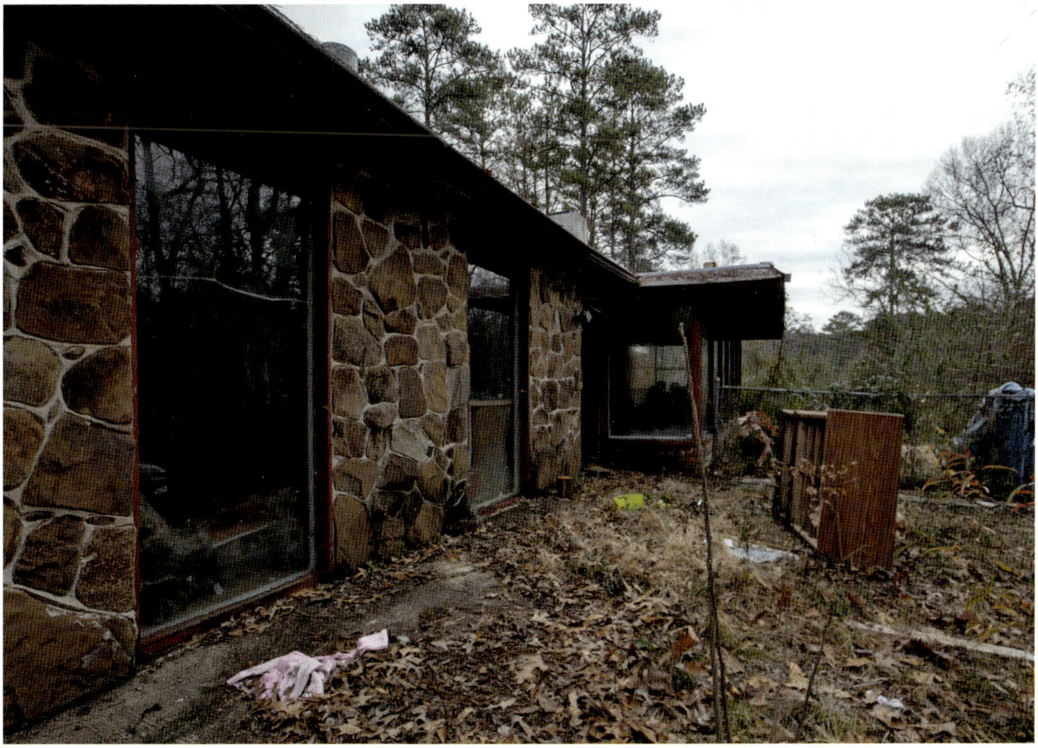

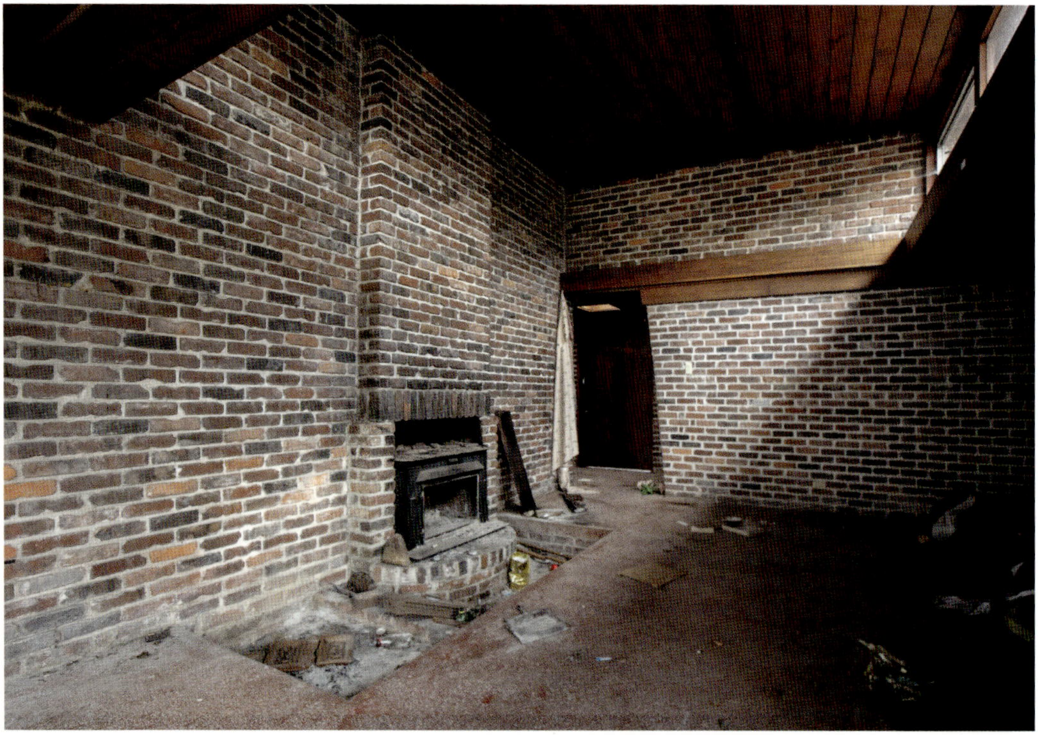

The living room is highlighted by a sunken hearth fireplace with close seating for fire gazing.

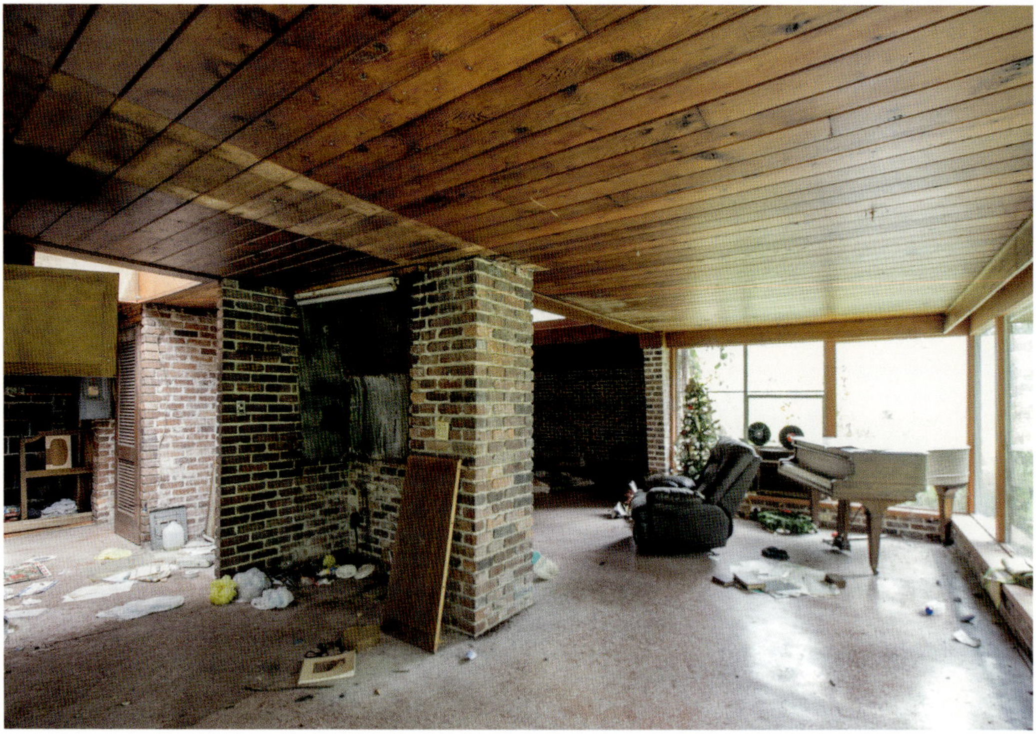

The living room overflows into a large music room in the back of the house.

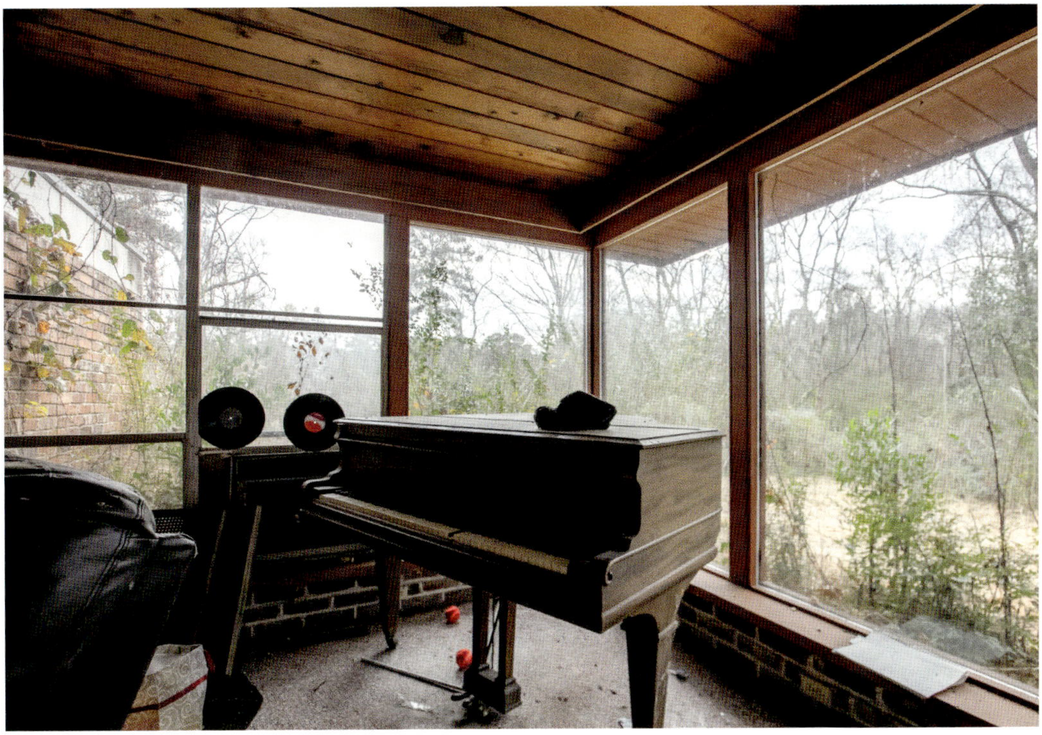

A piano sits near a wall of windows in the music room in the rear of the house.

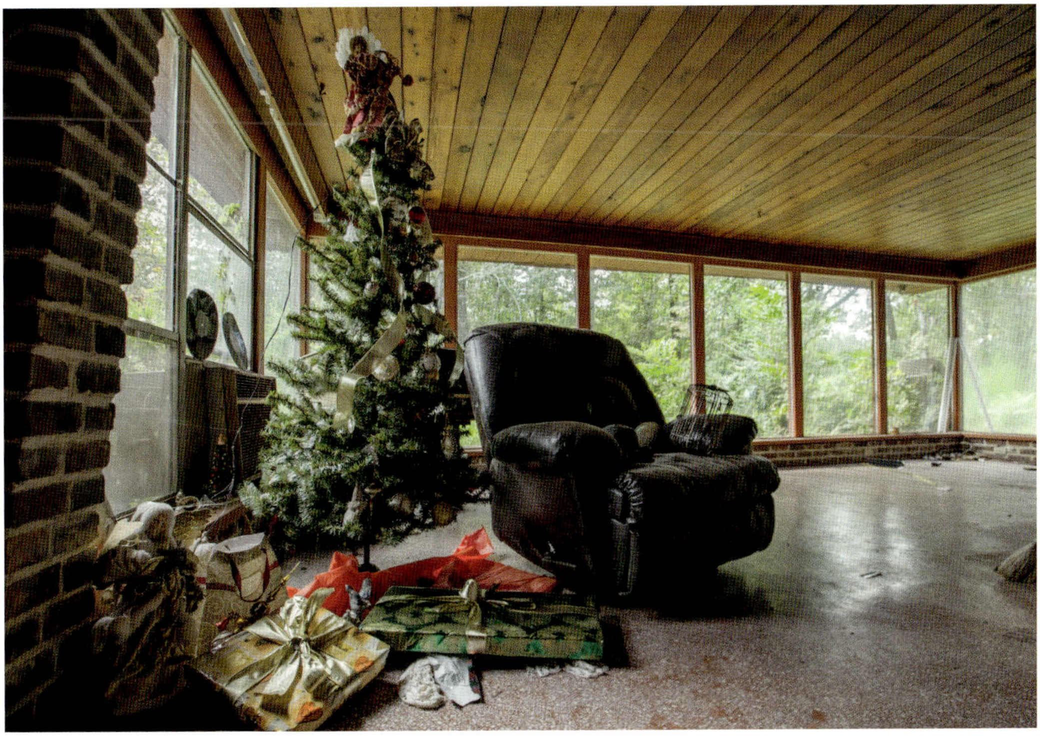

A decorated Christmas tree still stands next to a wall of windows in the living room, complete with wrapped presents.

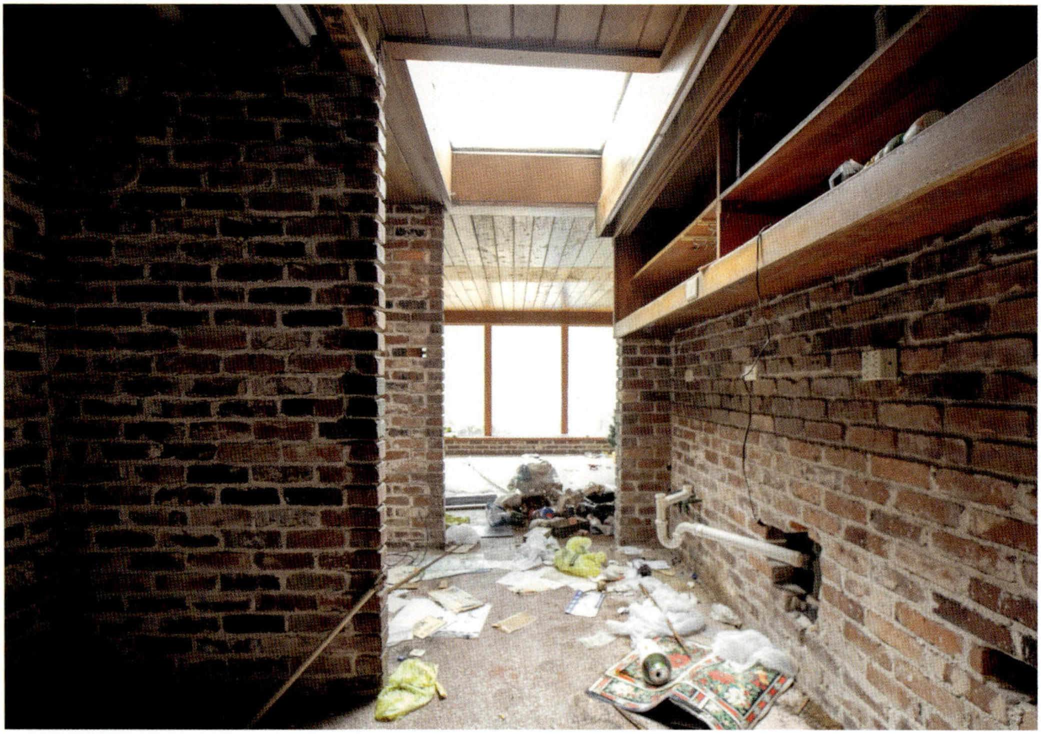

The galley kitchen features an overhead skylight and is quite small compared to the rest of the space.

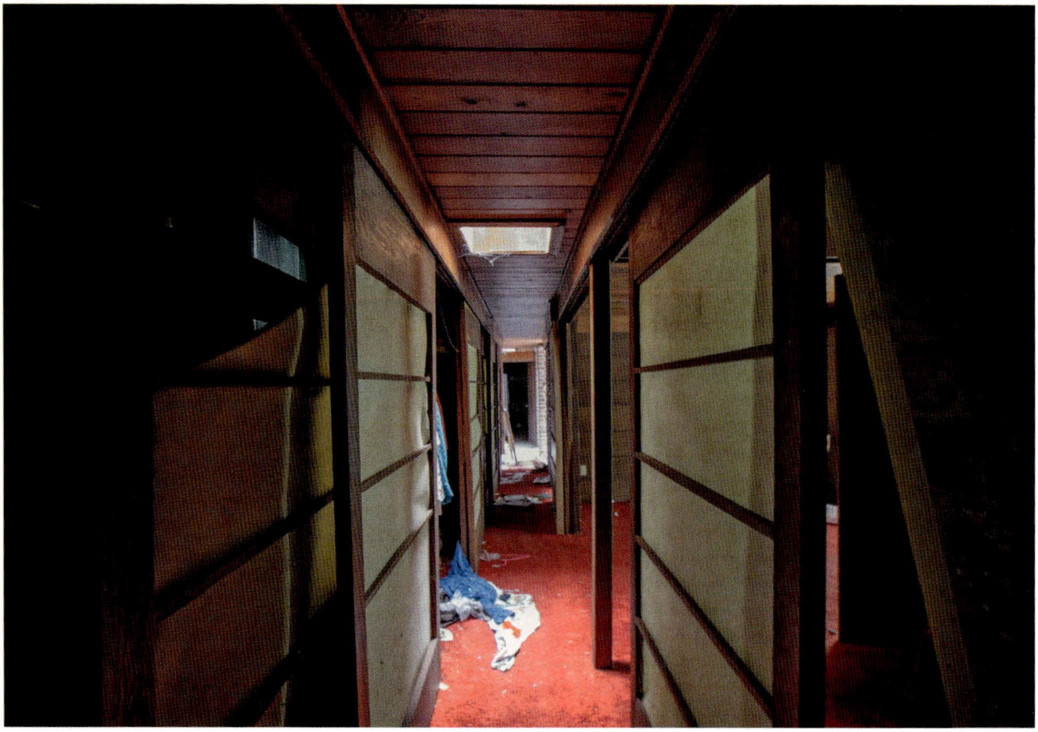

The hallway of the home is lined with Japanese-style sliding doors that conceal storage.

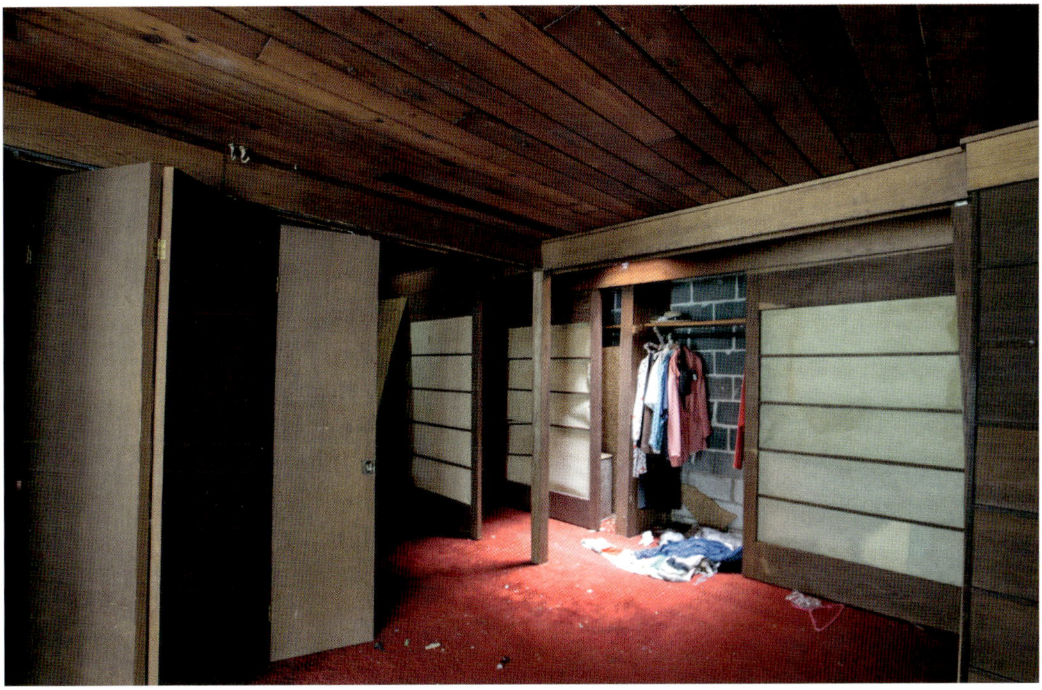

The children's room is situated in the middle of the house and can be partitioned off with both sliding doors from the hallway and a folding door in the middle of the room.

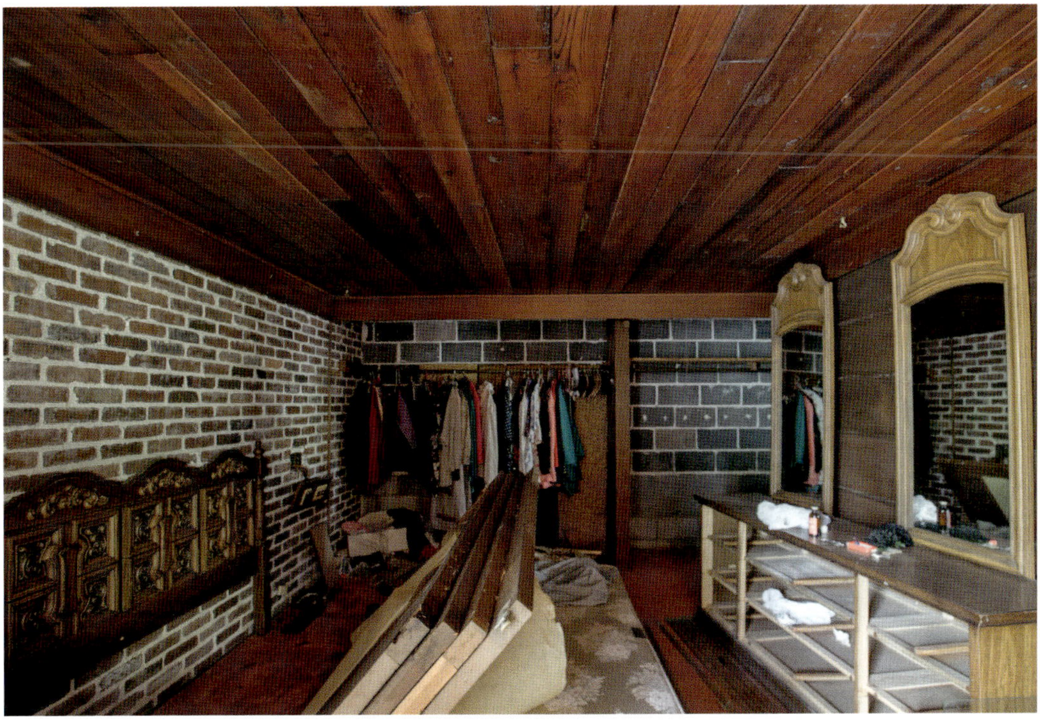

The master bedroom is located at the end of the hallway. Notice there are no overhead lights in any of the rooms; McDonald excluded them in the design of the home.

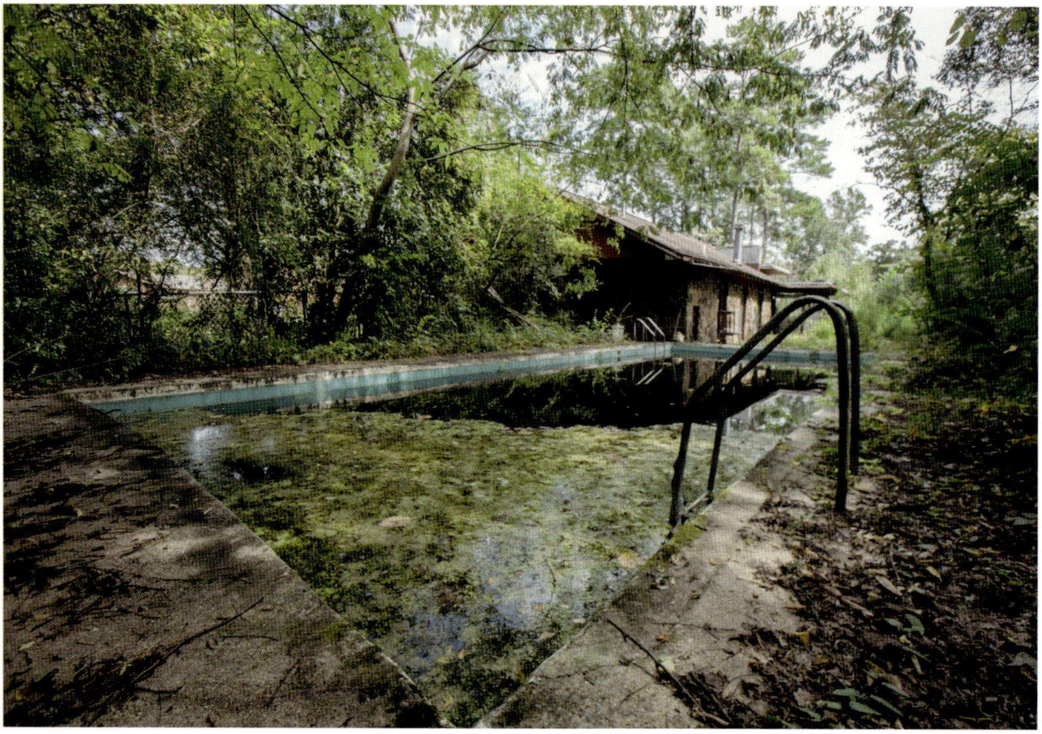

A large pool in the backyard has become more like a pond for wildlife.

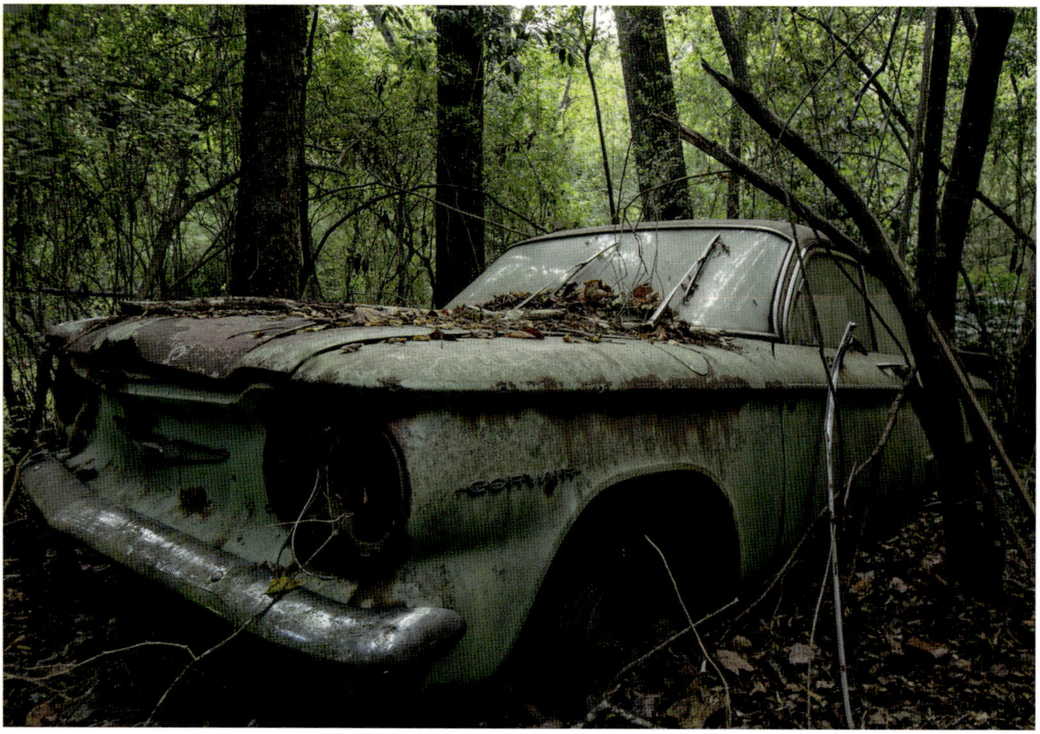

A Chevrolet Corvair rests behind the home next to a collapsed shed.

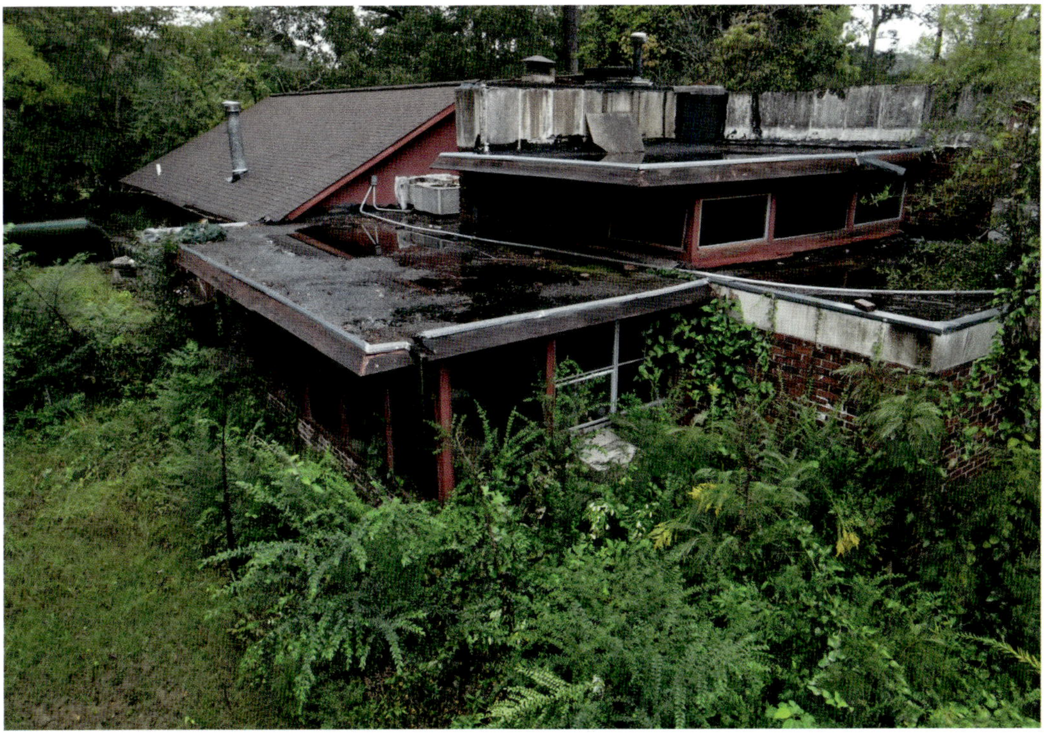

The home made the *Birmingham News* when it was built and was called "an unusual dream home."

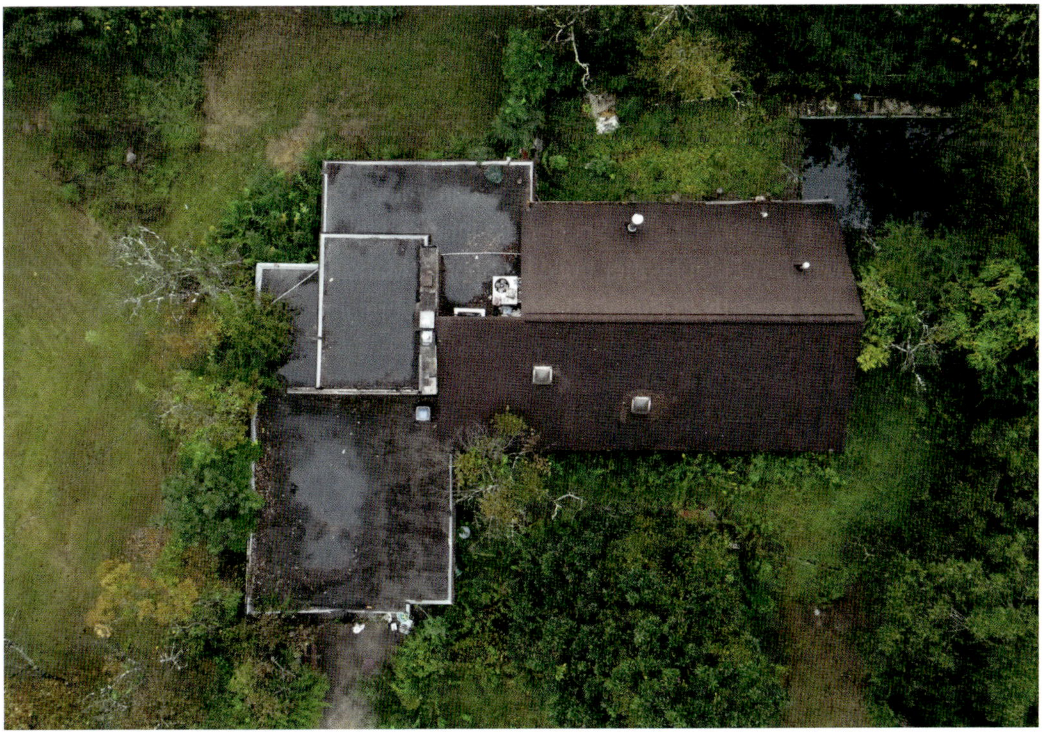

A drone shot of the McDonald house shows its partially flat roof.

9

MOULTHROP HOUSE

Situated atop a high bluff overlooking Lake Eufaula are the ruins of the Moulthrop family home and the Shorter Cemetery. The bluff was home to the early settlers of Eufaula in the 1830s and 1840s. General Reuben Shorter and his wife Mary Butler Gill Shorter settled on this property in 1837, which at the time consisted of approximately 100 acres. General Shorter owned thousands of acres of rich cotton land on both sides of the Chattahoochee River between Eufaula and Columbus, Georgia.

By the 1850s, the settlers on the bluff discovered that water-borne diseases—typhoid, yellow fever, and diphtheria—were killing off many of the people that lived close to the river. This resulted in a migration of the settlers to what would later become downtown Eufaula. However, even after the death of General Shorter in 1853, the Shorter family stayed on the property, which was inherited by one of his sons, Eli Sims Shorter, Sr., who was a U.S. congressman. After the death of Congressman Shorter in 1879, his son, Eli Sims Shorter, Jr., inherited the property but eventually moved to downtown Eufaula after building Shorter Mansion. Eli Shorter, Jr., sold the surrounding property to Robert H. Moulthrop but retained ownership of the 5 acres where the Shorter family cemetery is located.

Constructed in 1899, the Moulthrop family home was designed by John Adams and constructed by Alabama State Senator Robert H. Moulthrop. The house is believed to be a mixture of Imperial Revival since it has a tower and Queen Anne architecture. There are four bedrooms upstairs and one downstairs. The first floor had a dining room, living room, and large covered porch. Also on the land was Doc's House, home of the caretaker, a grist mill, a storage house with two rooms, and a shed built to work on Ford Model Ts.

State Senator Robert H. Moulthrop wrote the Equal Education Bill in Alabama. He fancied visiting Italy every year. He was born in a small cottage in Quitman County,

Georgia. He was a brick manufacturer from 1899–1902. He served as an alderman of the city of Eufaula from 1894–1900 and a member of the city board of education for many years. Moulthrop was a Democrat and a member of Eufaula's executive committee, a member of the Protestant Episcopal Church, a mason, and a Knight Templar. Fannie Dale was the home's early nanny. She was a daughter of slaves and worked for $3 a week as a nanny. Quite a few children and family members were born in the Moulthrop home.

In June 2020, the land surrounding the house was cleared. The home and 25 acres were re-purchased by an LLC group with family ties. The group plans to restore the house to its prominence. There are several plans, including a venue for weddings or other events, and building cottages on the property for guests. The group is optimistic, hoping to have it ready by Thanksgiving 2021 for family members to gather.

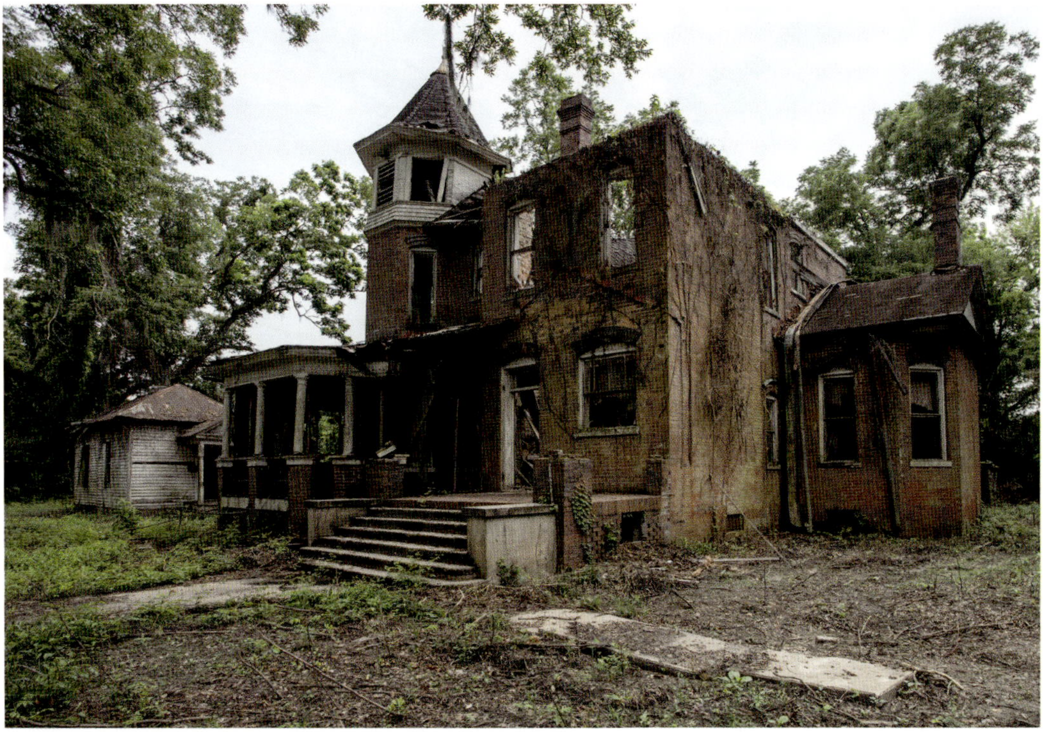

The Moulthrop House is believed to be somewhat of a mixture between Imperial revival (since it has a tower) and Queen Anne.

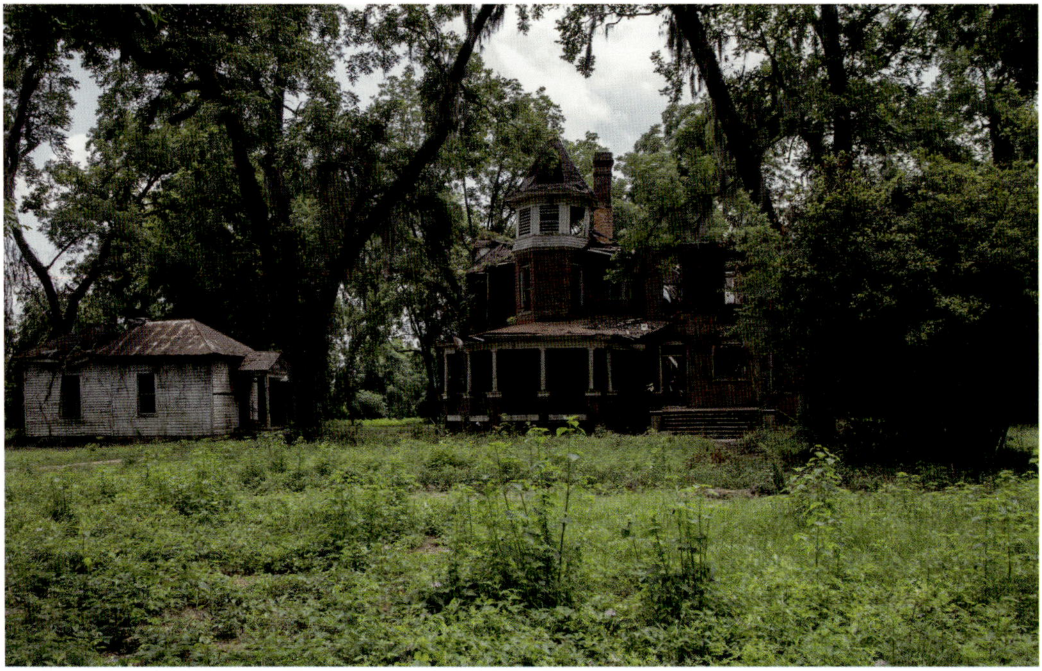

In 1884, Alabama State Senator Robert H. Moulthrop purchased land from Eli Shorter that connects with the Shorter Cemetery. The home and 25 acres were re-purchased by an LLC group with family ties.

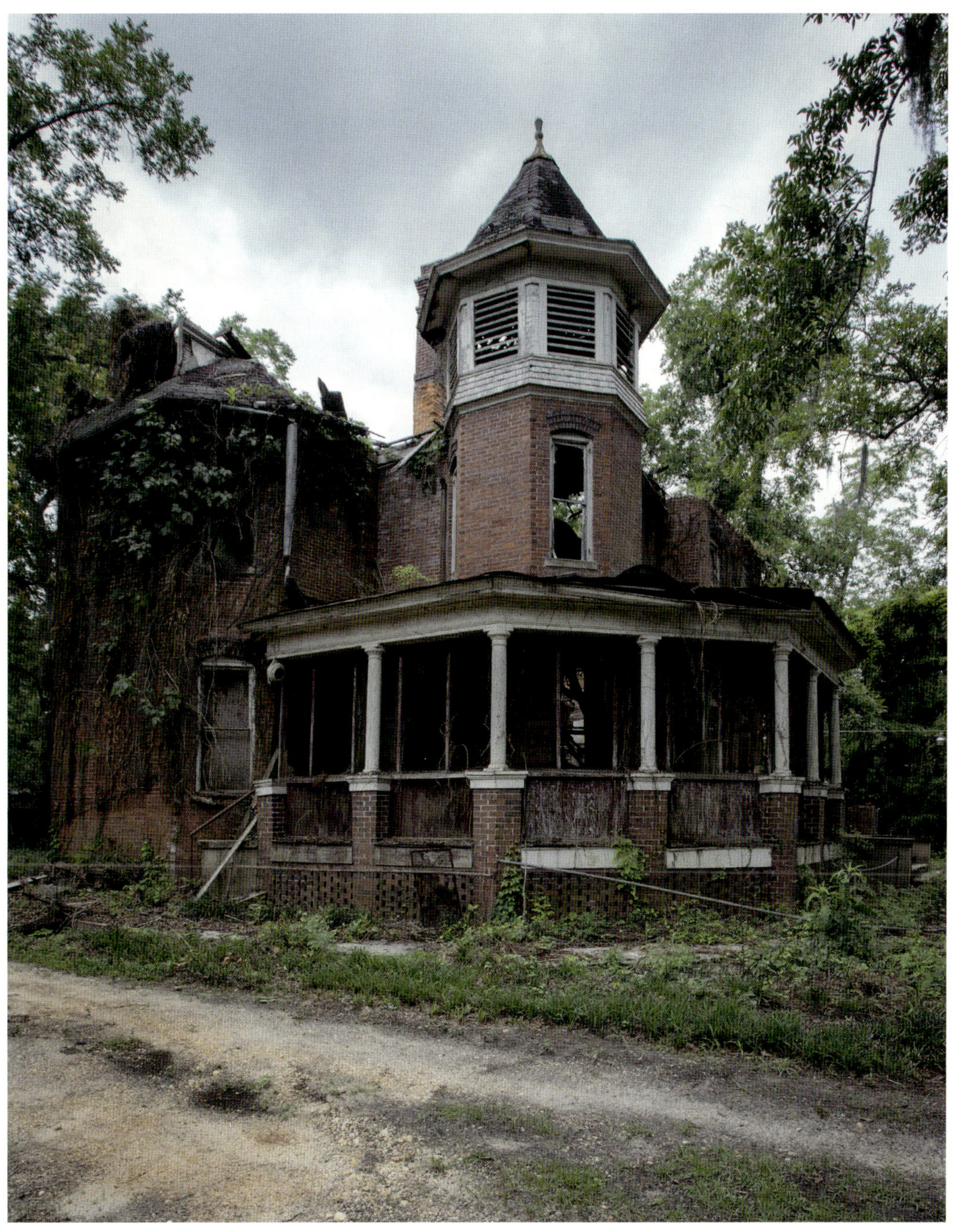

The Moulthrop House is located in Eufaula on a private drive straight off Riverside Avenue.

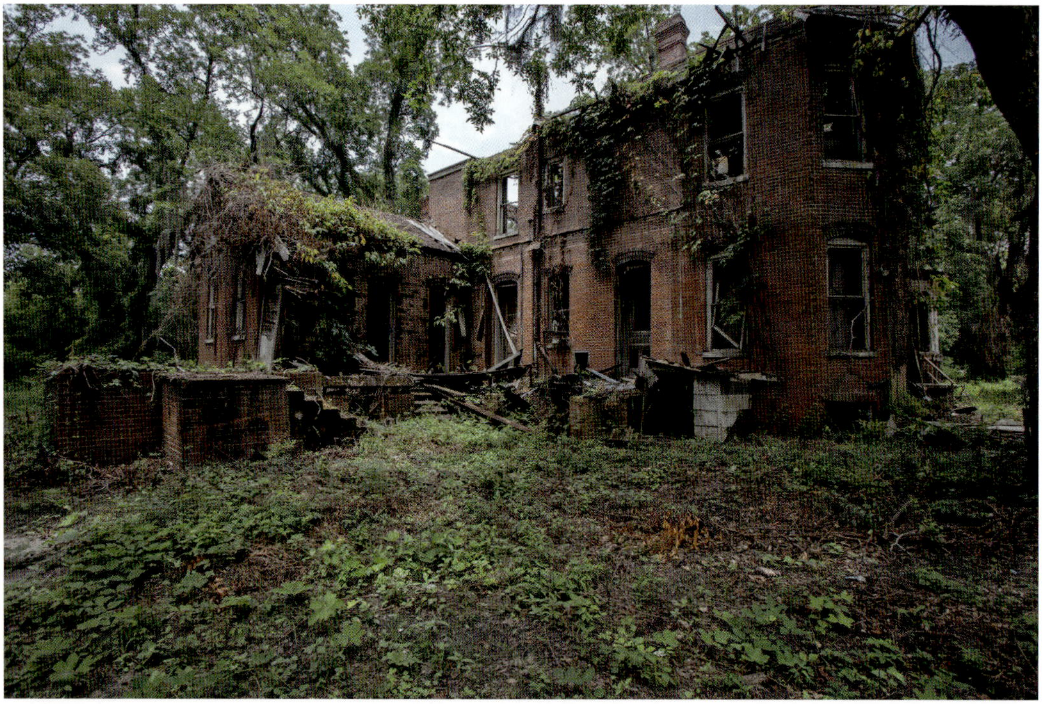

When the river was flooded and Lake Eufaula was built in the 1960s, the Moulthrops lost about 14 acres of land to the lake.

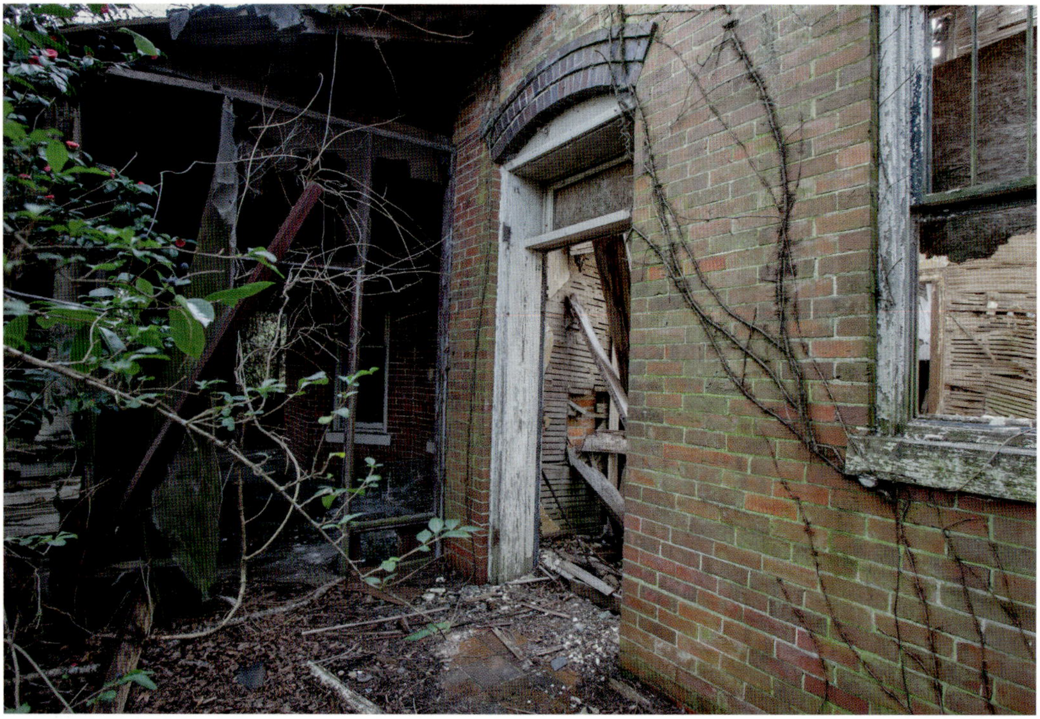

The bricks, which were used as deep as six thick on the house, were made by Moulthrop and Son Company. On a clear day on the lake, circular kilns can be seen in the water.

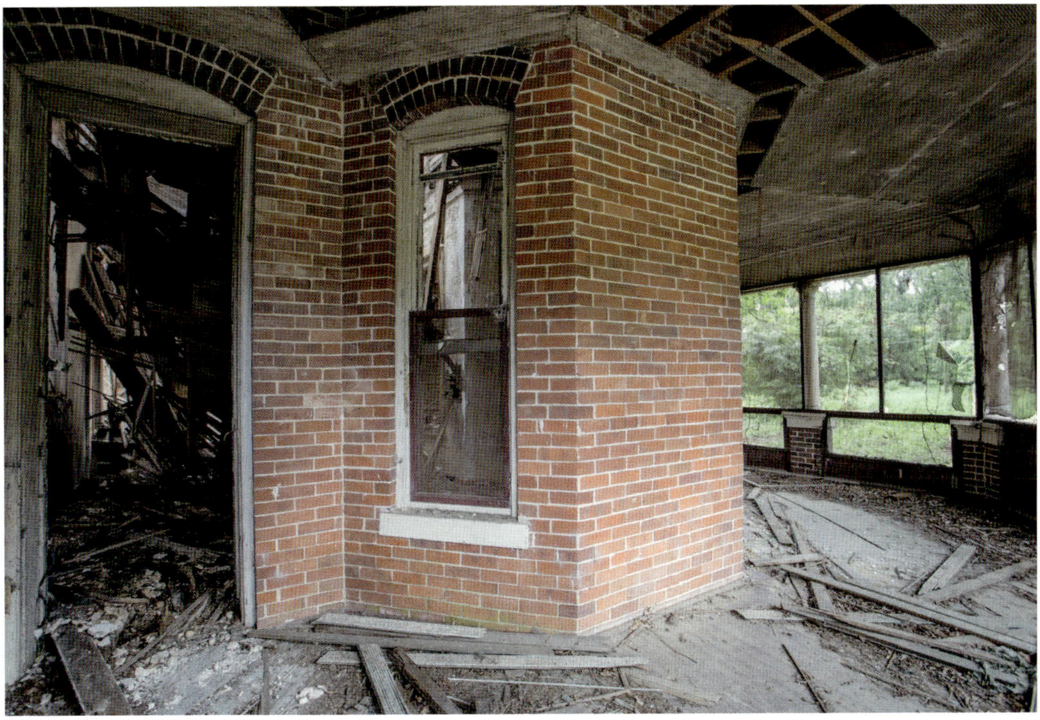

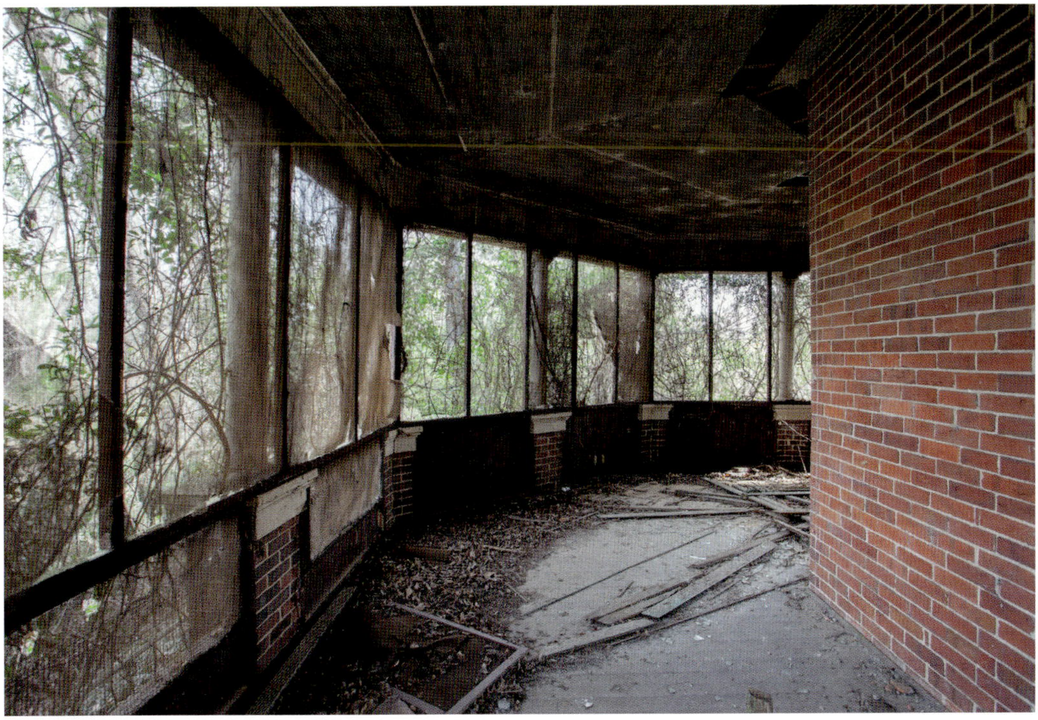

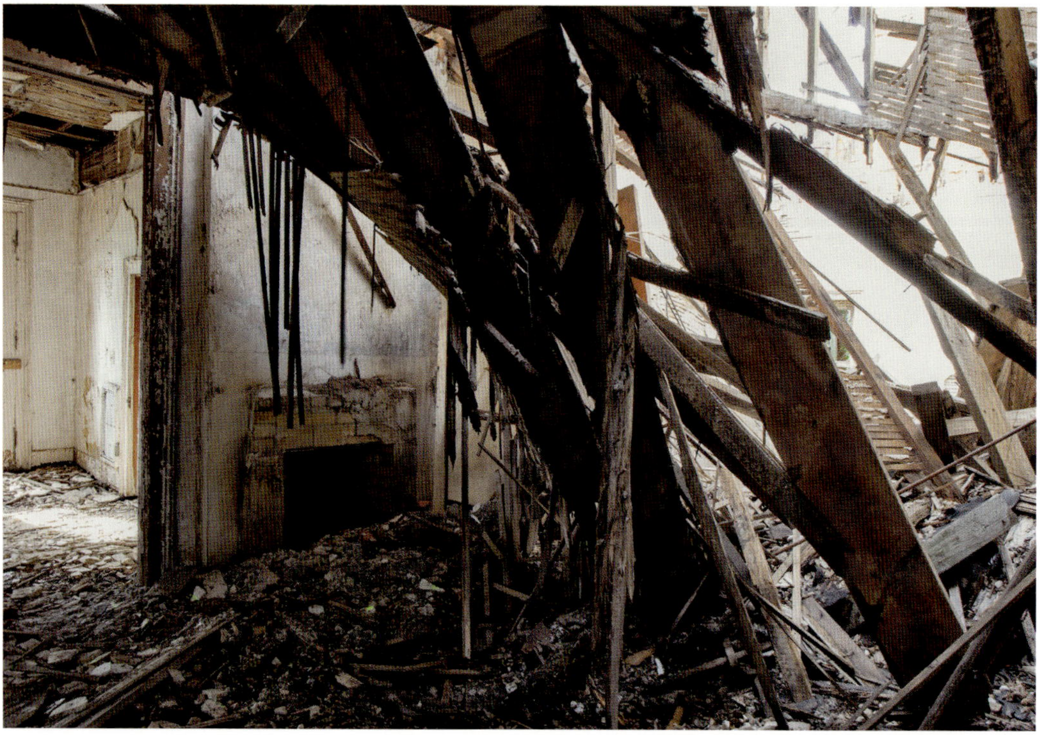

The house originally had four bedrooms upstairs and one downstairs with a living room, dining room, and porch.

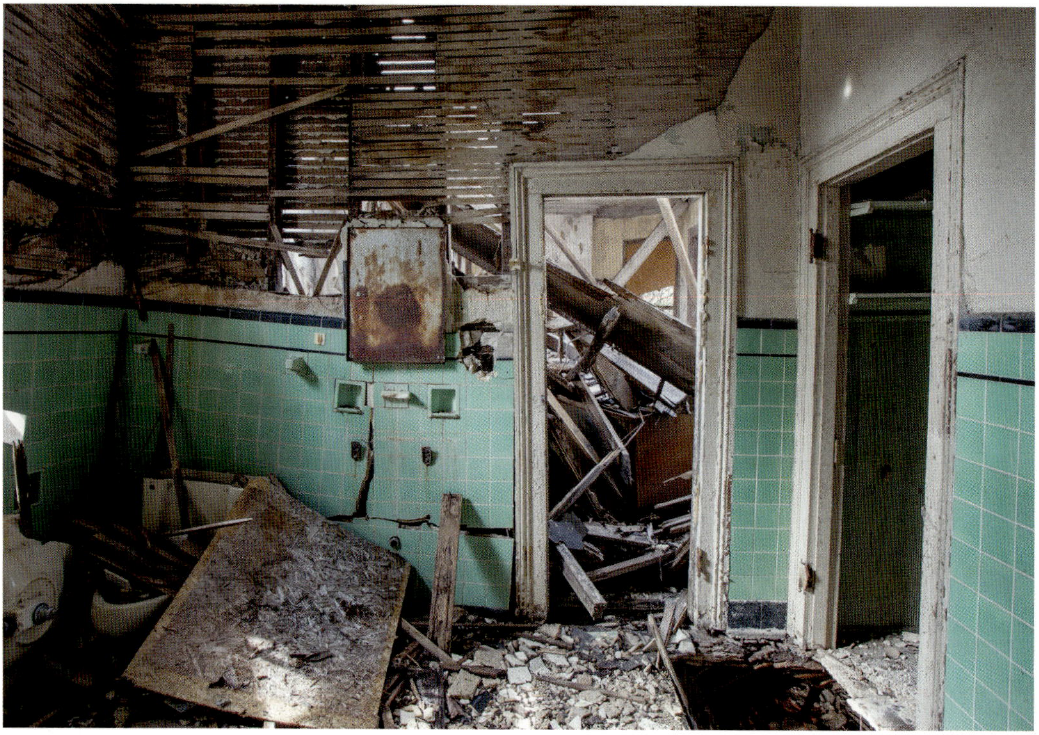

What is left of a tiled bathroom on the rear of the house.

10

OUTLAW HOUSE

During the early twentieth century, the Outlaw House was one of the few large period revival dwellings constructed in rural Mobile County. Built in 1914, the house was designed by the famous architect George Bigelow Rogers, who designed many local landmarks including the main branch of the Mobile Public Library, Bellingrath House, and the Van Antwerp Building. The house is considered to be one of Alabama's finest examples of the Spanish Colonial Revival subset of the Colonial Revival Movement. With thick stucco walls, arched doorways, overhanging eaves, roof brackets, and solid massing, the home conveys a certain Mediterranean flair.

In 1918, archive records from the newly formed FBI (then known as the Bureau of Investigation) identify an agent by the name of G. C. Outlaw based in Mobile. According to reports, Outlaw investigated a threat made by the Ku Klux Klan against the leader of a multicultural group. With the white supremacist organization pervasive in the South, Outlaw would have been on the front lines of the fight against the KKK.

Before World War I came to a close in 1918, reports also show that Outlaw investigated anti-war sentiments among shipyard workers in Mobile. George likely acquired the house for his family soon after he left the FBI—the last records of his career date back to 1919—at which point he began pursuing a completely different profession altogether. In 1920, George Cabell Outlaw, who still went by the moniker G. C., was instrumental in the creation of Morrison's Cafeteria with his business partner, James Arthur Morrison, who helped develop the cafeteria dining concept, which was unique at the time and would later become synonymous with the South. The public quickly accepted the idea of self-serve home-style cooked food offered at a modest price. Their first self-serve restaurant opened its doors in Mobile, but they went on to launch cafeterias in over 150 locations across the South.

Rumored to have won the house in a poker game, Outlaw moved his wife and two sons into the palatial property in 1925. According to censuses from the time, George Cabell Outlaw shared the remote property with his wife, Mayme; their sons, George Cabell Junior and Arthur; a cook by the name of Hattie Durham; and Hamp Samuels, their house boy. With its spacious wings, the vast home would have had more than enough room for the small household.

When George Outlaw acquired the property, the house included 120 acres of land. He used the fruits from his business empire to make some innovative renovations to the new family home. He created a lake on the estate—now known as the G. C. Outlaw Dam—by diverting the flow of a natural spring. He used the dam to generate power for the house, and it became the first in the area to have electricity and a telephone, while an oil furnace in the basement provided heat. The lake covers over 17 acres and is up to 14 feet deep. A stone wall lines the edge of the lake. At the southeastern corner, stone steps lead down to the water. Several stone birdbaths were situated around the lake. George Outlaw was also instrumental in bringing power to other houses in the area.

In 1940, change was in the air for the Outlaws as George moved his family into the city and away from their rural retreat. At the age of twenty-five, his youngest son, Arthur, began working as an auditor in the family business. The father and son duo continued to work together until his father's death in 1964. In the 1960s, Arthur Outlaw renovated the old Outlaw home, restoring the heritage features and introducing modern touches to the dated interior. All the while, he was climbing the rungs of the family business, eventually rising to the post of vice-chairman of the board and director of Morrison Restaurants, alongside serving as the mayor of Mobile from 1967 to 1968.

With Arthur at the helm, his father's empire had a staggering net worth of $221 million at its peak (around $372 million in today's money). During the 1980s, Arthur Outlaw lived in the house until conflicts with him being mayor of Mobile and living outside of the city limits forced the family to vacate the property and move within the city limits. Today, they use a portion of the land for hunting and tree farming. According to tax records, the property is still owned by the Outlaw family. Family and friends still use Outlaw Lake today. There are currently no plans to renovate the house.

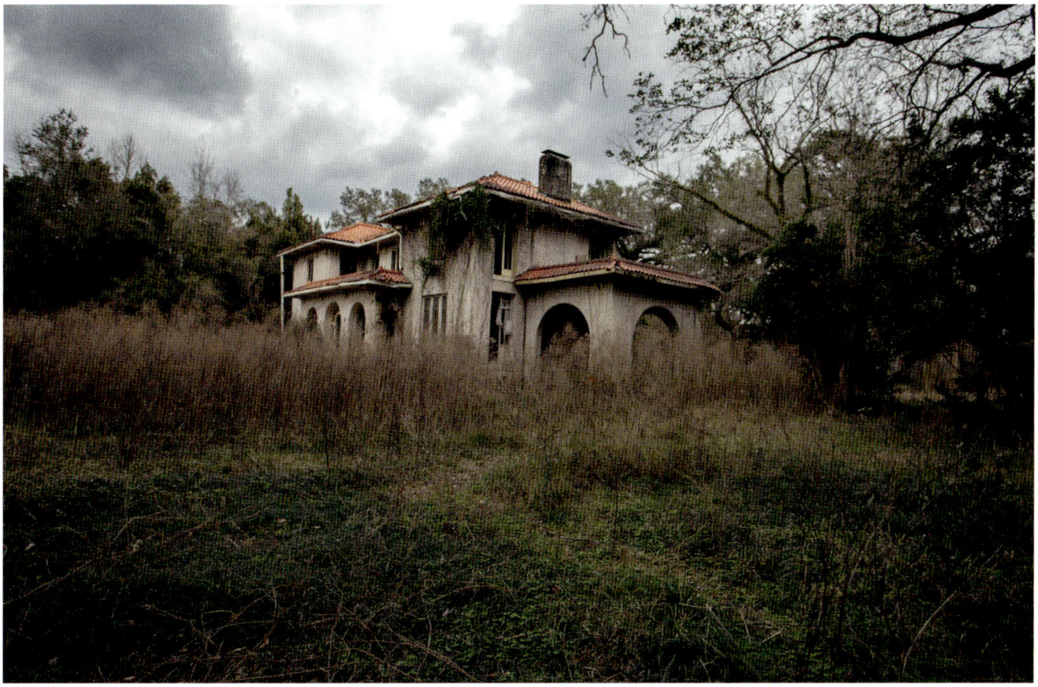

In the early twentieth century, the Outlaw House was one of the few large period revival dwellings constructed in Alabama.

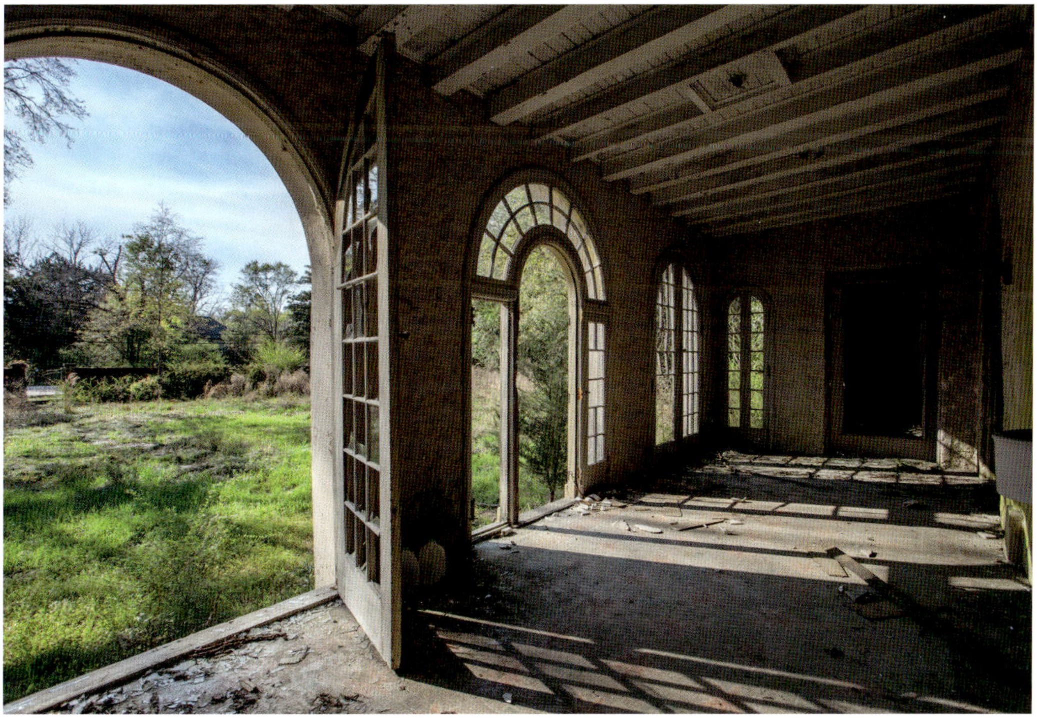

Designed by renowned architect George Bigelow Rogers, the home boasts thick stucco walls, arched doorways, and overhanging eaves in a Mediterranean style.

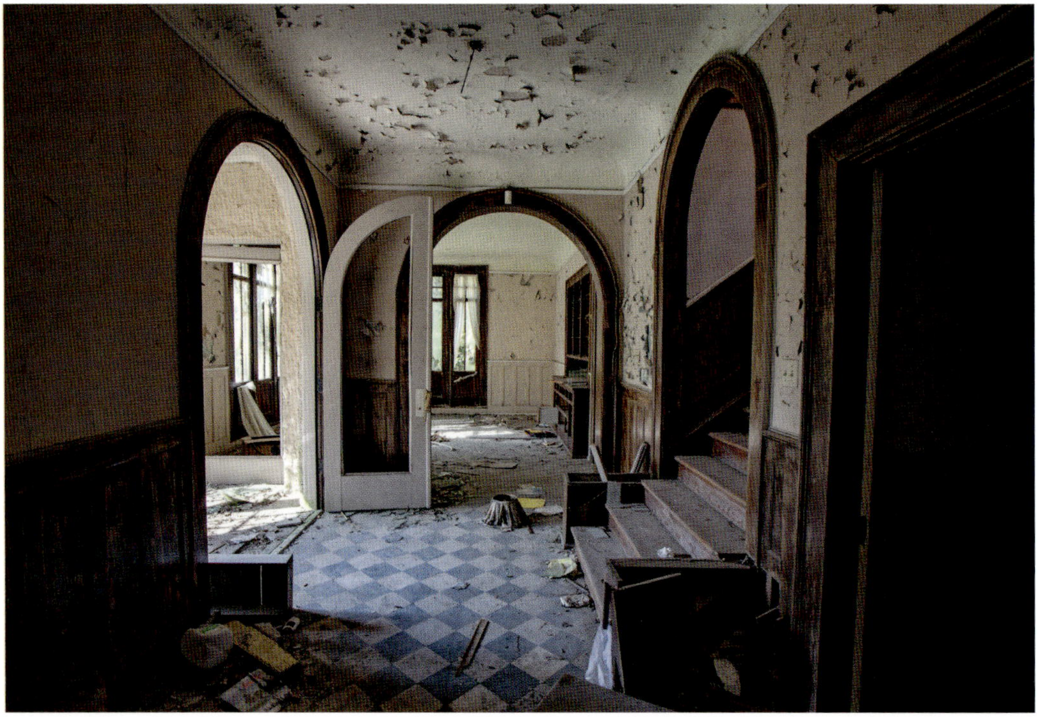

Rogers designed private residences and commercial buildings throughout Mobile, including the city's first skyscraper.

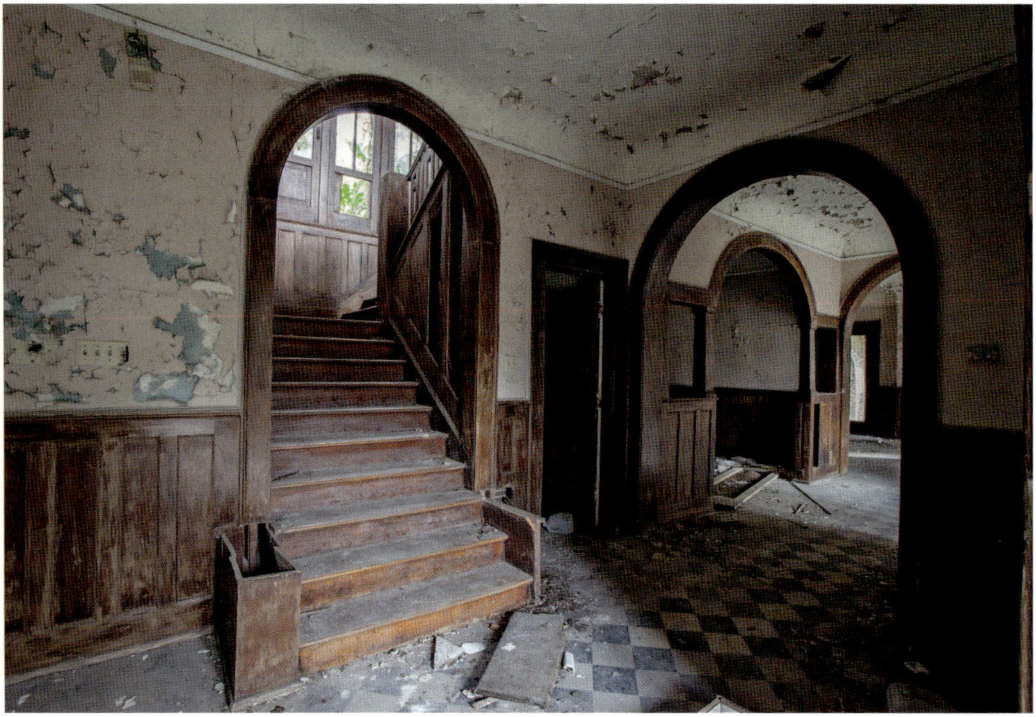

Outlaw acquired the property in 1925. Since there are no records of the sale of the home, it is suspected that he won the property in a poker game.

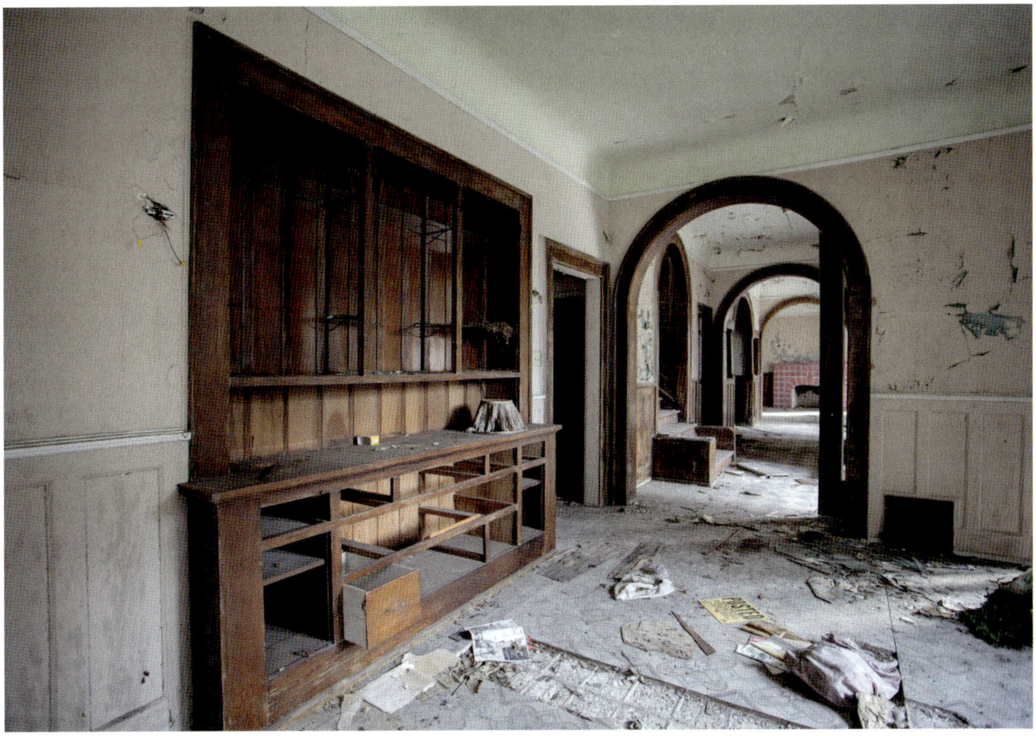

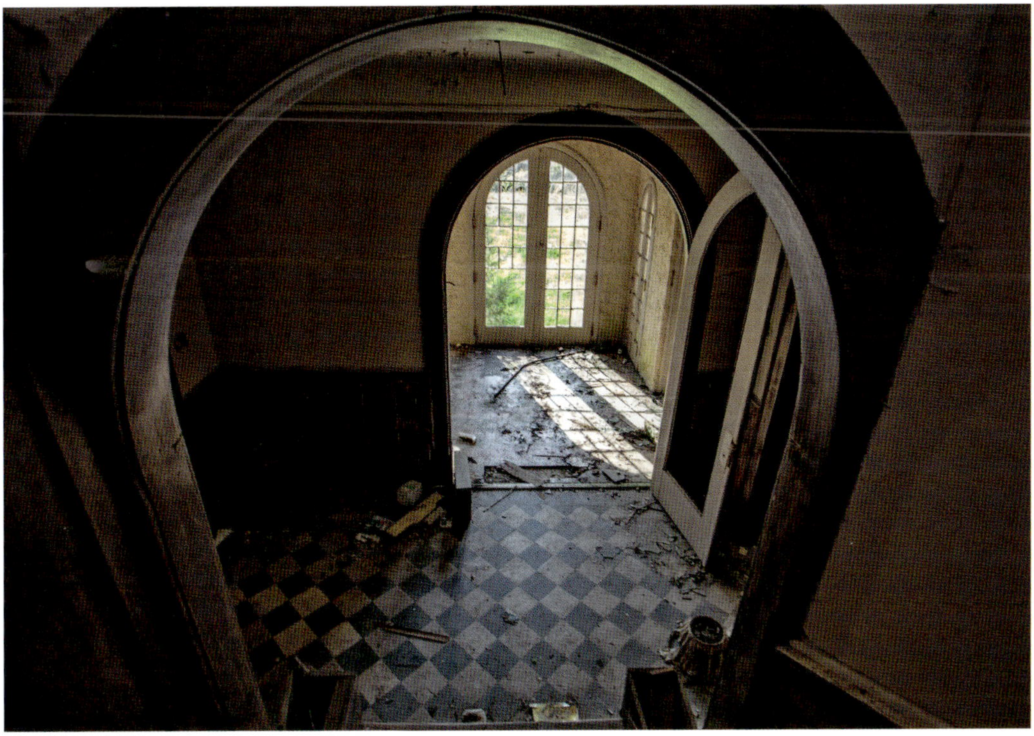

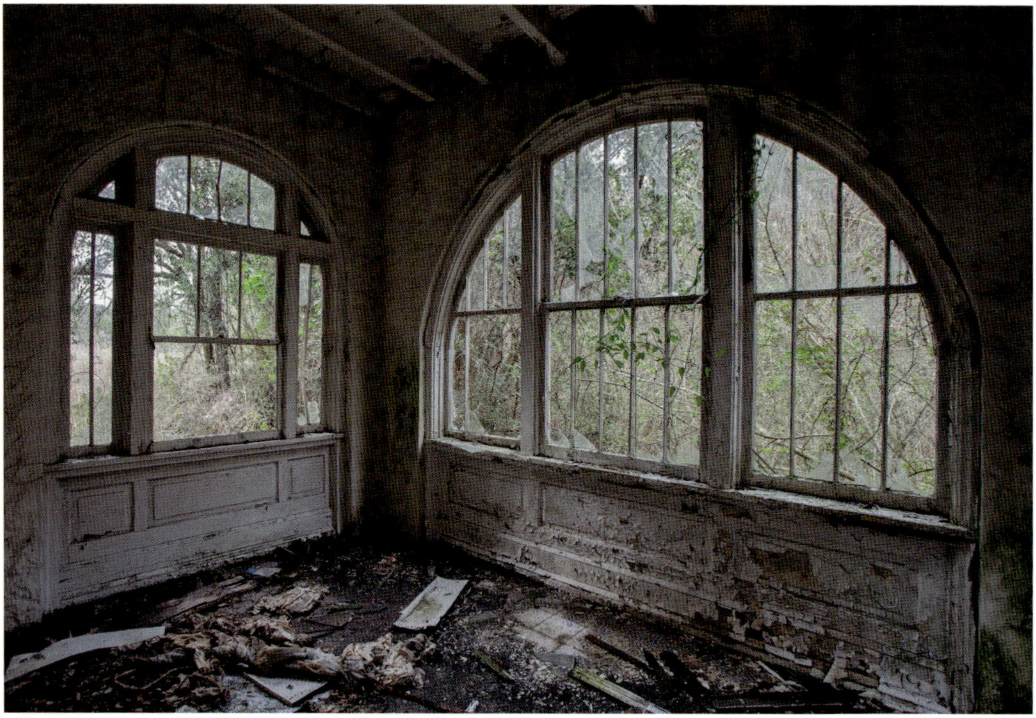

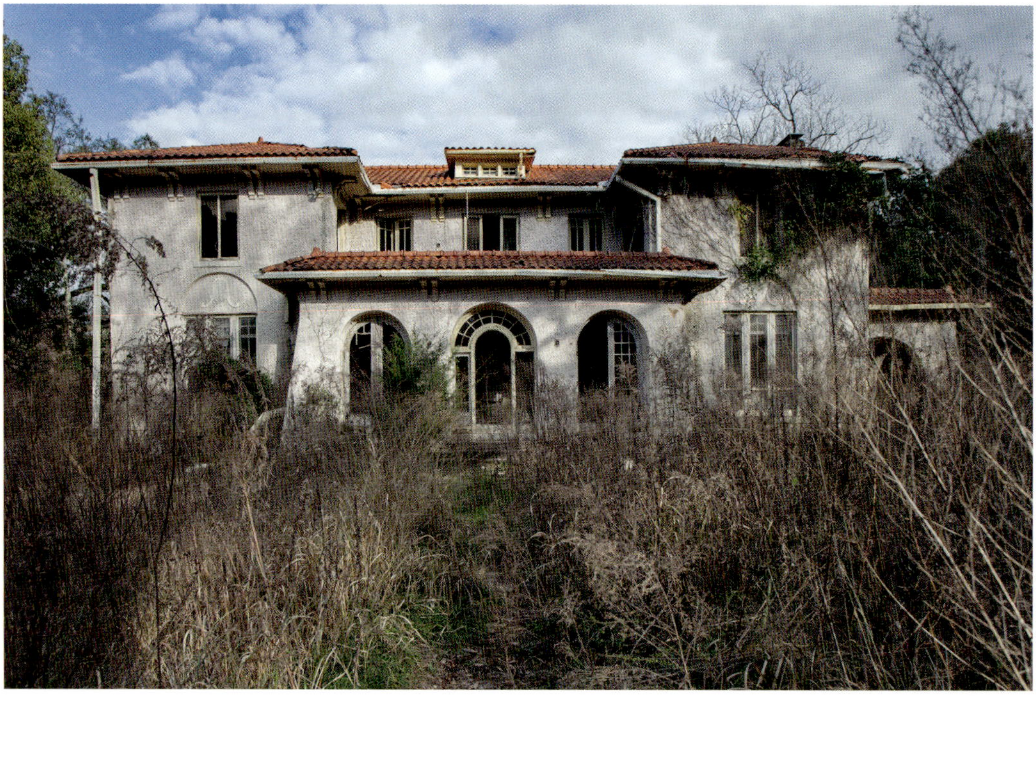

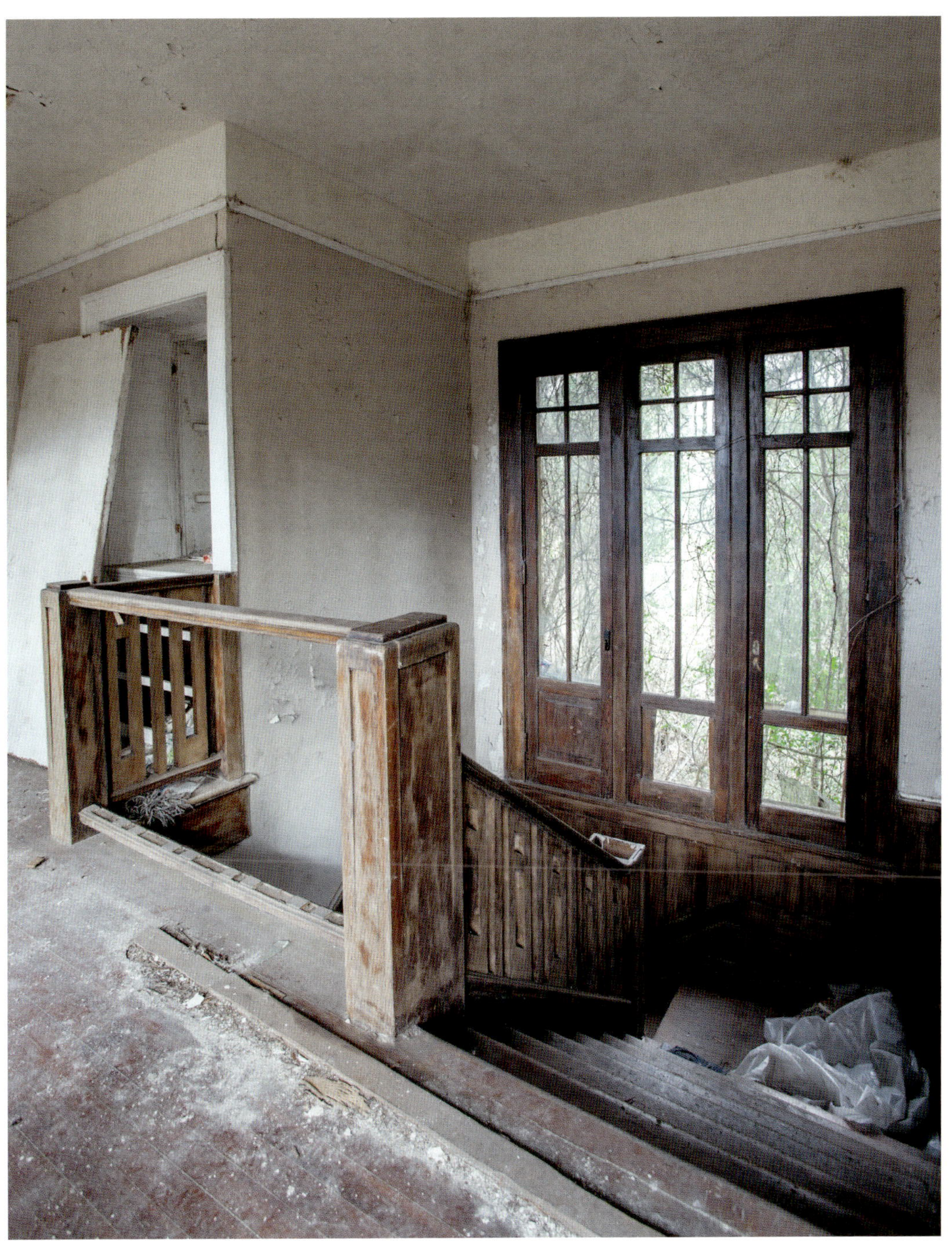

11

SEARCY HOSPITAL

The Mount Vernon Arsenal and Searcy Hospital complex is unlike any other collection of structures in the United States. Located in Mobile County, Mount Vernon Arsenal was established in the early nineteenth century and was in almost continuous occupation for over 200 years. The settlement that became the town of Mount Vernon arose near Fort Stoddert, which was built on the Mobile River by the federal government in 1799 to protect what was then the nation's southern border. From 1800 to 1811, Fort Stoddert was the main military structure there, being the southernmost terminus of the Federal Road. In 1807, former vice-president Aaron Burr was incarcerated at the fort after his arrest for treason. In 1811, the U.S. Government built the Mount Vernon Cantonment (a military encampment) 3 miles inland because yellow fever had broken out too often at the fort. After a visit in 1814, President Andrew Jackson ordered the Mount Vernon Arsenal to be built at the site of the cantonment.

In 1828, Congress authorized the construction of the Mount Vernon Arsenal as one of fourteen to be built nationwide as part of the first effort to create a unified national defense. The arsenals were to be used to manufacture and store arms and munitions. Construction of the arsenal began in 1830 on the main building with a turret and several surrounding buildings in a horseshoe layout. The arsenal buildings were completed in 1836, enclosed by a 12-foot-high brick wall.

In January 1861, Mount Vernon Arsenal was seized by the Alabama militia by order of Governor Barry Moore and turned over to the Confederacy, who occupied the site for the duration of the Civil War. At the time, the arsenal was outfitted with only seventeen men and their commander, General J. L. Reno. At the end of the Civil War, control of the arsenal reverted back to the federal government.

The Mount Vernon Arsenal was later converted to barracks where it became associated with the late nineteenth-century social movement to reform and provide humane treatment for Native Americans and served as the administrative head-quarters for Apache Village. In 1886, after decades of fighting to keep control of Apache land, Geronimo became the last Indian leader to formally surrender to the United States. Apache leaders Geronimo, Naiche, and Mangus, along with more than 400 Chiricahua Apache followers—men, women, and children—were brought to Mount Vernon from Fort Marion in Florida in 1887. It would become their home for the next seven years. The Apaches first lived in tents and later in cabins, creating a small village. Dr. Walter Reed was in charge of the barracks as post surgeon, and the Apache had few restrictions. They were free to roam and hunt as long as they were back to their assigned area by dark. They were technically "prisoners of war," although they had not been charged with or tried for any crimes, causing some Indian historians to describe them as early "political prisoners."

Each time the Apaches were forced from their land and moved northward towards the United States, Geronimo led retaliation raids on local villages. Many white settlers considered him a murderous savage, but to his people, Geronimo was the embodiment of a fierce warrior. He had earned their respect. According to historians, Geronimo's raids increased in intensity after authorities attacked his village and killed his mother, wife, and three children. Due to the bloody raids that followed in both Mexico and the United States, Geronimo was wanted by the government for decades before he surrendered. He was previously imprisoned in 1877 but later escaped in 1881.

During his captivity at Mount Vernon, he had a designated cell in the basement of the arsenal, but he did not stay under lock and key behind its massive wooden door. The urban legend is the cell and large door were only used when General George Crook came to visit the barracks. Newspapers in Mobile published accounts of his visits, traveling by train from Mount Vernon, without an escort. The publicity made Geronimo somewhat of a celebrity to his former enemies. He also met with Theodore Roosevelt in an unsuccessful attempt to let his people return to Arizona. In his 1905 biography, Geronimo wrote the Alabama climate disagreed with the Apaches, and many were unhealthy while at Mount Vernon. According to Geronimo, so many Apaches died that he consented to let one of his wives go to New Mexico to live and take their two small children. This separation would have been equivalent to a modern-day divorce, so she married again soon after.

Geronimo never learned to write in English, although he learned to write his name while at Mount Vernon. Many of the young children were sent to school in Pennsylvania until two Catholic nuns started a school at Mount Vernon. The nuns often expressed their appreciation for Geronimo's support of the school and main-taining discipline. One of the teachers said she could not have conducted school without Geronimo's services. The school building is no longer standing.

While at Mount Vernon, the Apaches hunted and cooked over fires, and for the most part, they tried to live their lives as they did before captivity. Since Congress did not appropriate enough funding for food for the army, many of the Apaches were inducted so they qualified for rations. Geronimo was not among the inducted. They also buried their dead in secrecy to prevent military personnel from witnessing their traditions or the locations of their burial sites. Today, the locations of many of the gravesites have not been confirmed by archaeologists, but historians have clues to their whereabouts from writings left behind. Historians have located the sites of two Apache villages of log cabins and aspects of the Native American Graves Protection and Repatriation Act may be relevant to their management.

In 1894, the Apaches were relocated from Mount Vernon to Fort Sill, Oklahoma, where they remained captive until 1914. Although they had been told they would be confined for only two years, they were held captive for twenty-seven years before being assigned to a reservation. In 1909, Geronimo passed away at the age of seventy-nine after falling from his horse. After the Apaches left, the infantry no longer needed the site and it was decommissioned. In 1895, the 1,500-acre property was transferred from the federal government to the state of Alabama. It sat unused until the state appropriated $25,000 for a new hospital.

The Mount Vernon Hospital for the Colored Insane was established in 1900 on the former arsenal site near Mobile to care for mentally ill black patients. In its early years, Mount Vernon was described as a beautiful place where patients received expert care, although black people were still considered inferior and Searcy's facility needs were routinely put behind those of Bryce Hospital. Like Alabama's first superintendent Dr. Peter Bryce, Dr. James Thomas Searcy believed mental patients should be treated in bucolic surroundings and assigned farming and maintenance duties to give them a sense of purpose; soon, overcrowding and a lack of funding would raise concerns about standards of care at both Bryce and Searcy hospitals. Two years were spent renovating and re-purposing the old arsenal buildings constructed in the 1830s and the barracks built in the 1880s. In 1902, the staff and first patients arrived.

Similar to Bryce, Mount Vernon's facilities included a farm and other maintenance shops to run the hospital. Patients were given duties such as caring for livestock or harvesting crops. Some critics saw this as enforced manual labor, but according to staff accounts, the work was beneficial. Food grown on the farm was prepared and served at the hospital to staff and patients. It was not until a ruling in the Wyatt *v.* Stickney case in 1970 that farm operations ceased and courts ordered "a minimum standard of care." By this point, Searcy and Bryce were both severely overcrowded and underfunded.

During the early twentieth century, America saw the emergence of pellagra, a then-unknown disease caused by a diet deficient in niacin and protein. In 1906, fifty-seven patients died from a mysterious illness at the hospital. Dr. George H. Searcy noted an illness in some patients at Mount Vernon and later reported his findings and treatment to colleagues at the Medical Association of Alabama. Initially, the disease was a mystery, but it was later identified as one of the first major outbreaks of pellagra in the United States. The cause of the pellagra was unknown at the time, but one of the key observations was that it only struck patients, not the staff. Dr. Searcy conducted a study of patients and determined their cases were caused by ingesting moldy cornmeal, which was not fed to the nurses. This confirmed the initial hypothesis of other doctors. Searcy's study was one of the first intensive studies of the disease in the country. His contribution was vital in the overall discovery and treatment plan for the pellagra epidemic that was plaguing the nation.

In 1969, Alabama's mental hospitals were desegregated as mandated in the Civil Rights Act of 1964. It would be a few years before true integration occurred, but eventually, the hospitals were treating patients based on region and not race, with Searcy treating patients in south Alabama and Bryce treating those in central and north Alabama. As with most state-operated facilities, funding from the state dwindled over the years, which led to a reduced staff, resulting in substandard care and very little maintenance of the historic buildings. In the 1980s, the state funded construction of several modern wards at Searcy. The Mount Vernon complex was added to the National Register of Historic Places in 1988. The hospital operated with 400 extended-care and 124 intermediate-care beds.

However, by the twenty-first century, many of the buildings at Searcy were once again deteriorating. In 2012, Searcy Hospital permanently closed, the same year a smaller facility was built at Bryce and the old campus was abandoned. Searcy closed with little fanfare except for the faint protests by residents in Mount Vernon. The mayor of Mount Vernon said the closure cost the town 300 jobs and they still have not recovered.

The big changes were years in the making, as lawmakers pushed away from institutional care for the mentally ill. The state planned to direct patients to community-based programs although an investigation by the local news showed that many patients ended up in Alabama jails. There are several historic groups working to save Searcy Hospital, however little has been done. Altogether, there are about 1,800 acres with Searcy stretching across 150 of those acres. When the federal government deeded the property to the Alabama Department of Mental Health in December 2010, it placed a restriction on its sale: all the money must go back to mental health. The land has been surveyed but never appraised. No one has expressed interest in the property either. Preservationists would like to see the property transformed into a state park or museum.

So far, two buildings have collapsed, another damaged by strong winds, and many are covered in overgrowth. Most of the roofs have deteriorated and the oldest building, the main arsenal, is crumbling brick by brick. Of the twenty-three structures built for the arsenal during the first construction period in the 1830s, at least thirteen survive. The Alabama Department of Mental Health spends about $125,000 a year on 24/7 security and basic maintenance on the property and is working with the Mt. Vernon Historical Committee, the town of Mount Vernon, the Alabama Historical Commission, and the Alabama Department of Archives and History on a long-term plan for the site.

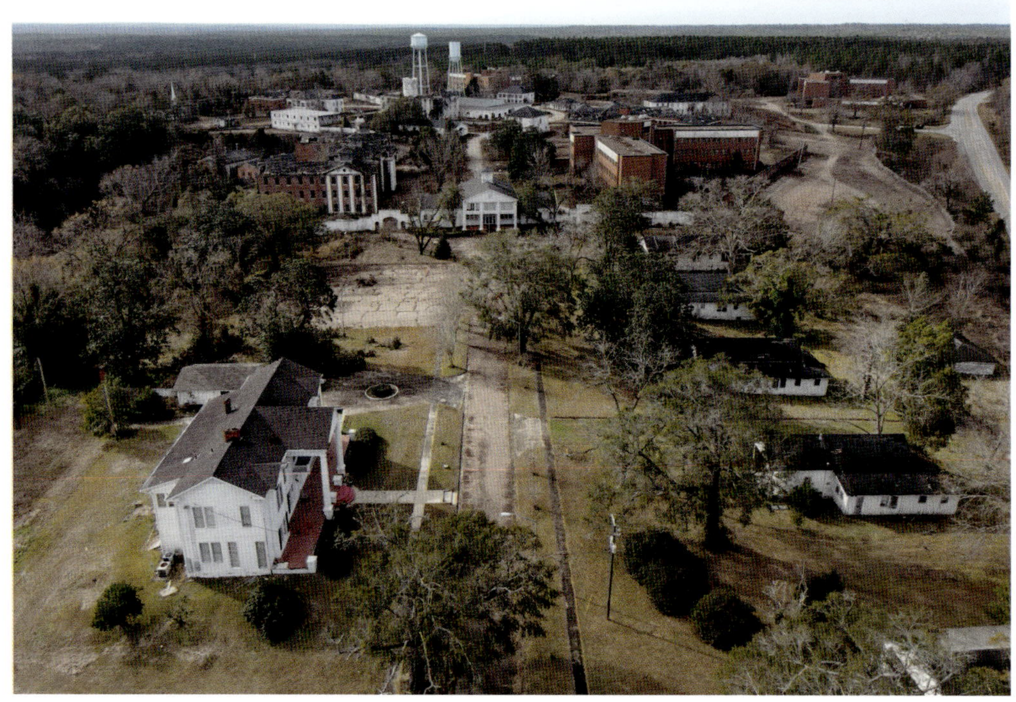

The structures at Mount Vernon span the entire life of the complex from 1830 to the present. In 2019, the National Trust for Historic Preservation listed Searcy Hospital among "America's 11 Most Endangered Historic Places."

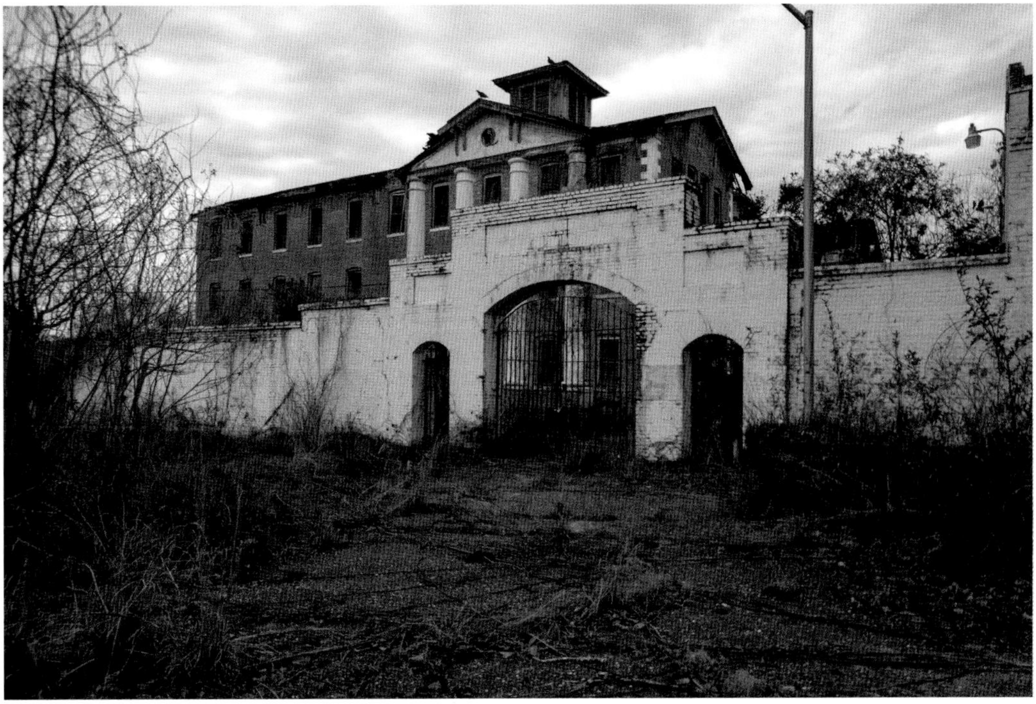

A 12-foot-high, 1-mile-long brick wall surrounds the original part of the complex.

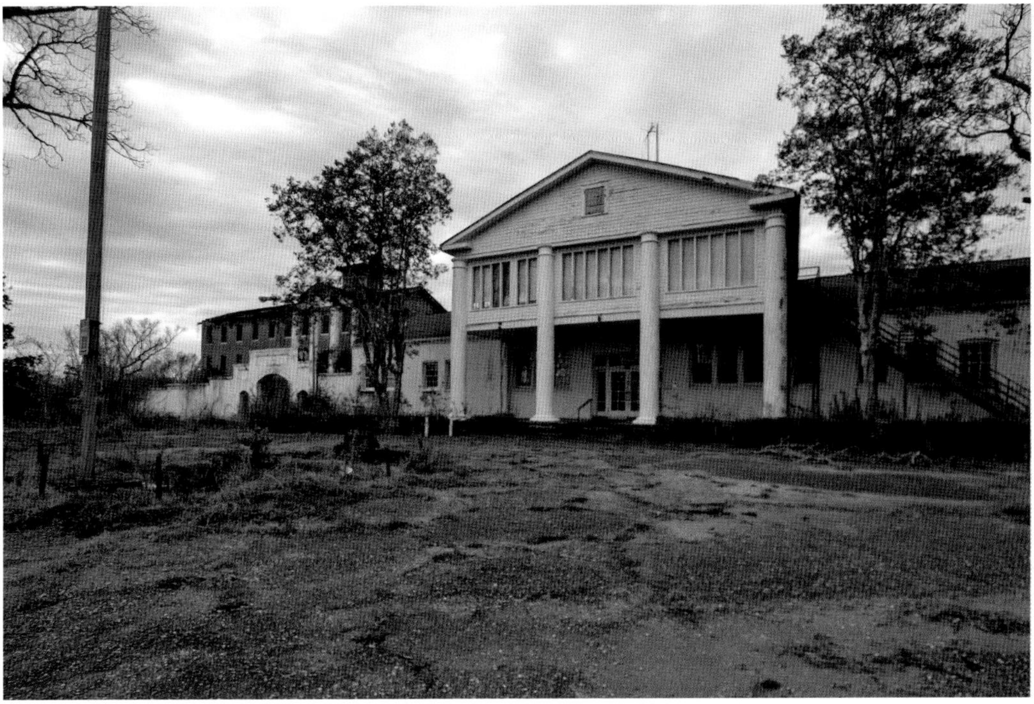

The administration building was created in 1902 when the site became a hospital from the existing guardhouse and dispensary that date to the 1830s.

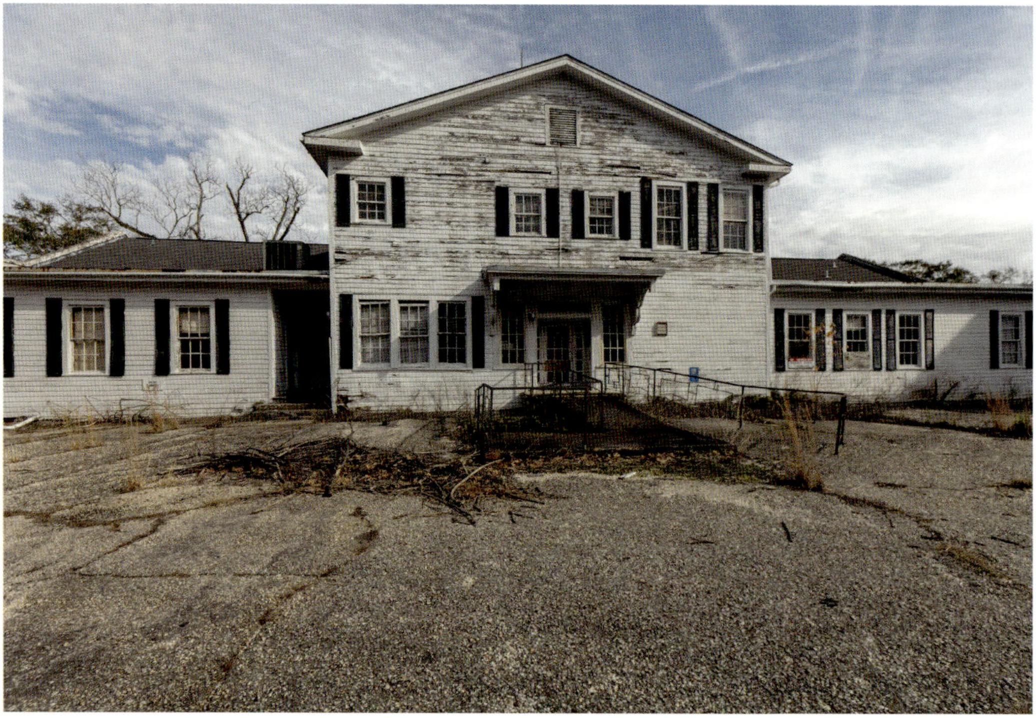

Visitors would come to the administration building before entering the hospital grounds.

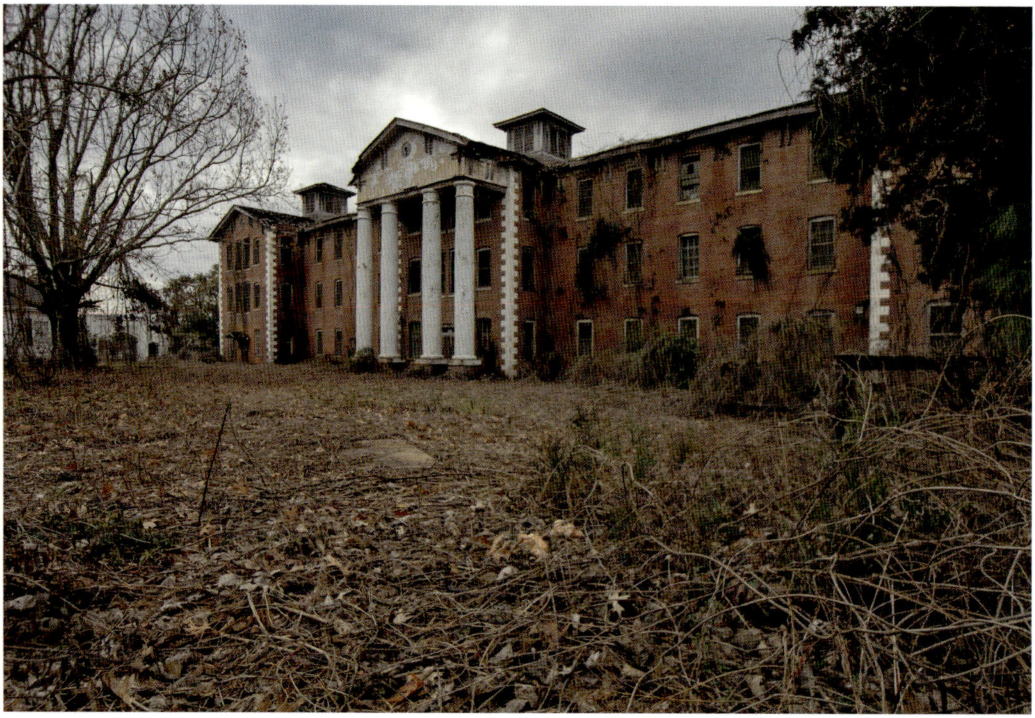

The three-story, H-shaped structure called "Unit 2" was completed in 1932 without state appropriations and on plans and specifications supplied by the superintendent. The building housed male patients.

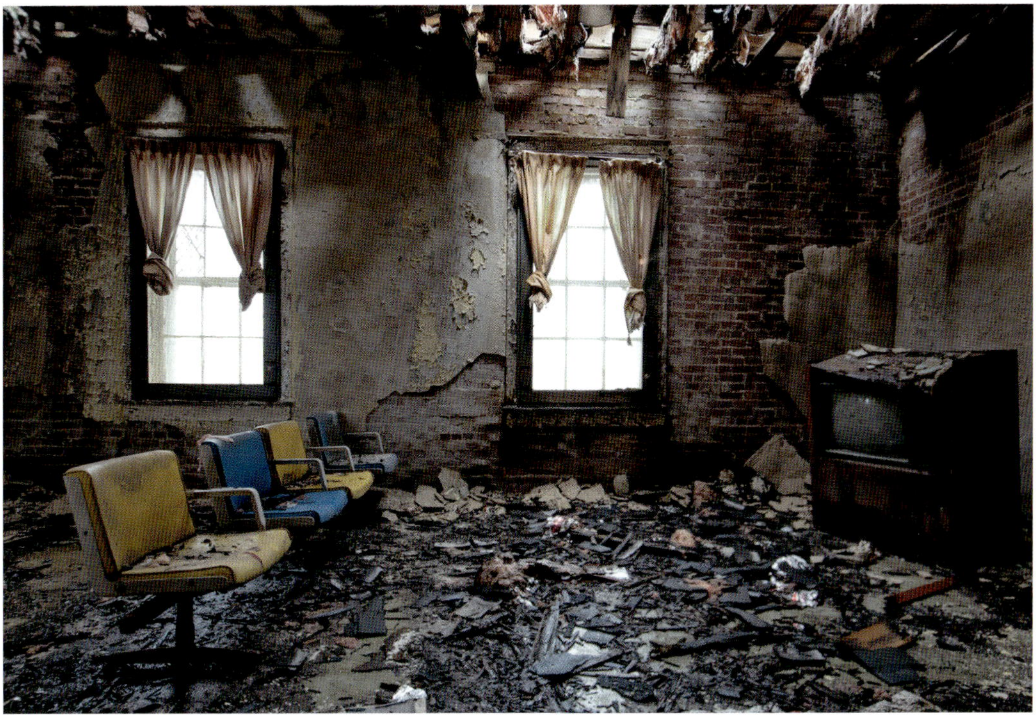

A row of chairs and an old television remain in a Unit 2 day room.

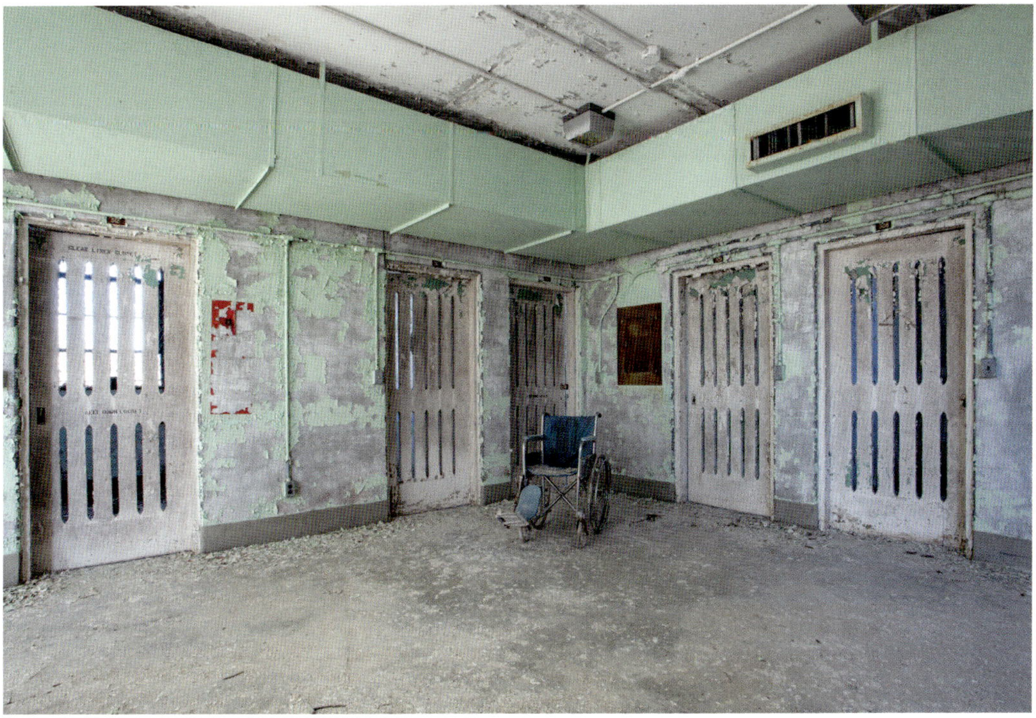

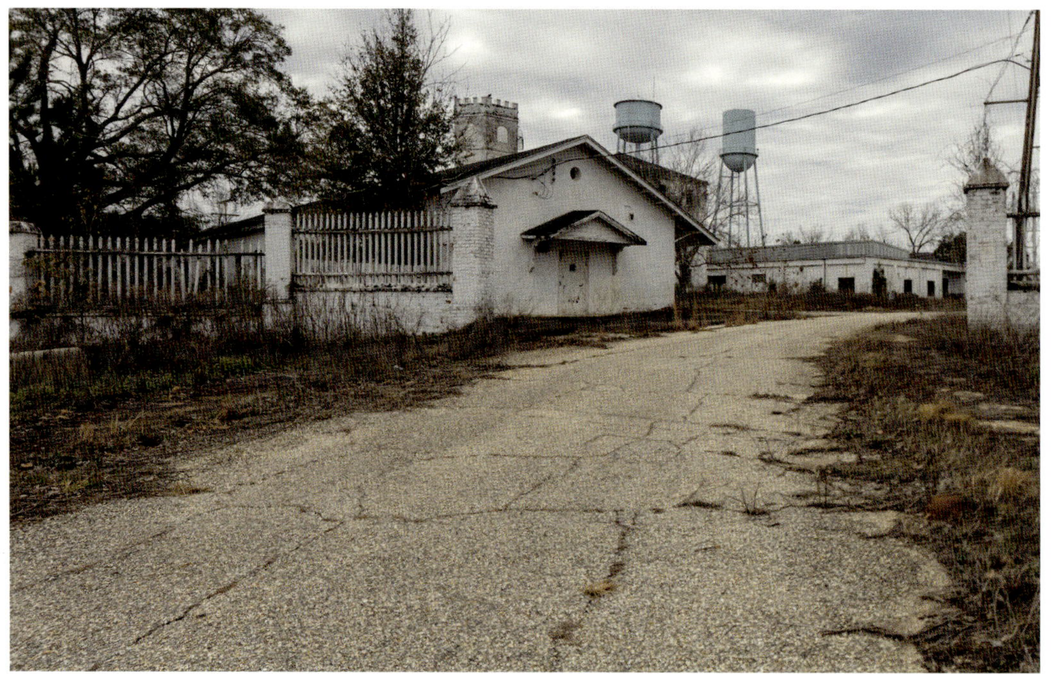

Only portions of the original 1830s picket fence remain. This was a unique type of wooden fence used in nineteenth-century arsenals. According to historians, this is the only known surviving example of its kind.

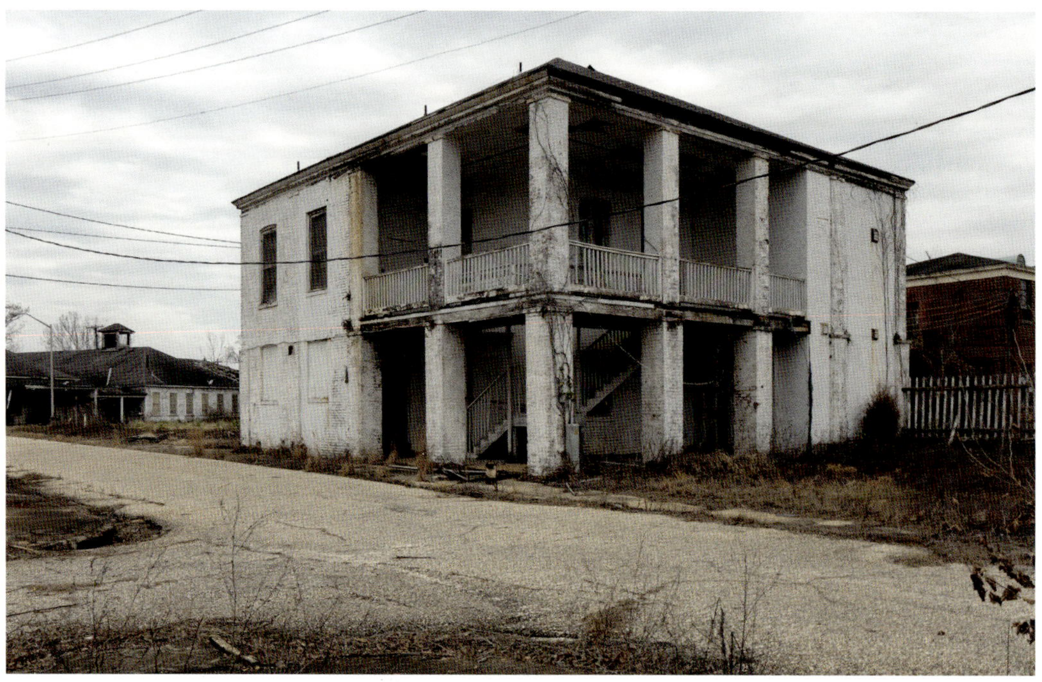

Across from the arsenal is the subaltern's quarters. A "subaltern" is a term common in the British military, which would have been popular in the 1830s. It means "subordinate" and refers to commissioned officers below the rank of captain. The building was used as the doctors' quarters from 1865–1895 when the site was still a military post, as a dining room by the hospital in early years, and as quarters for visiting doctors in later years.

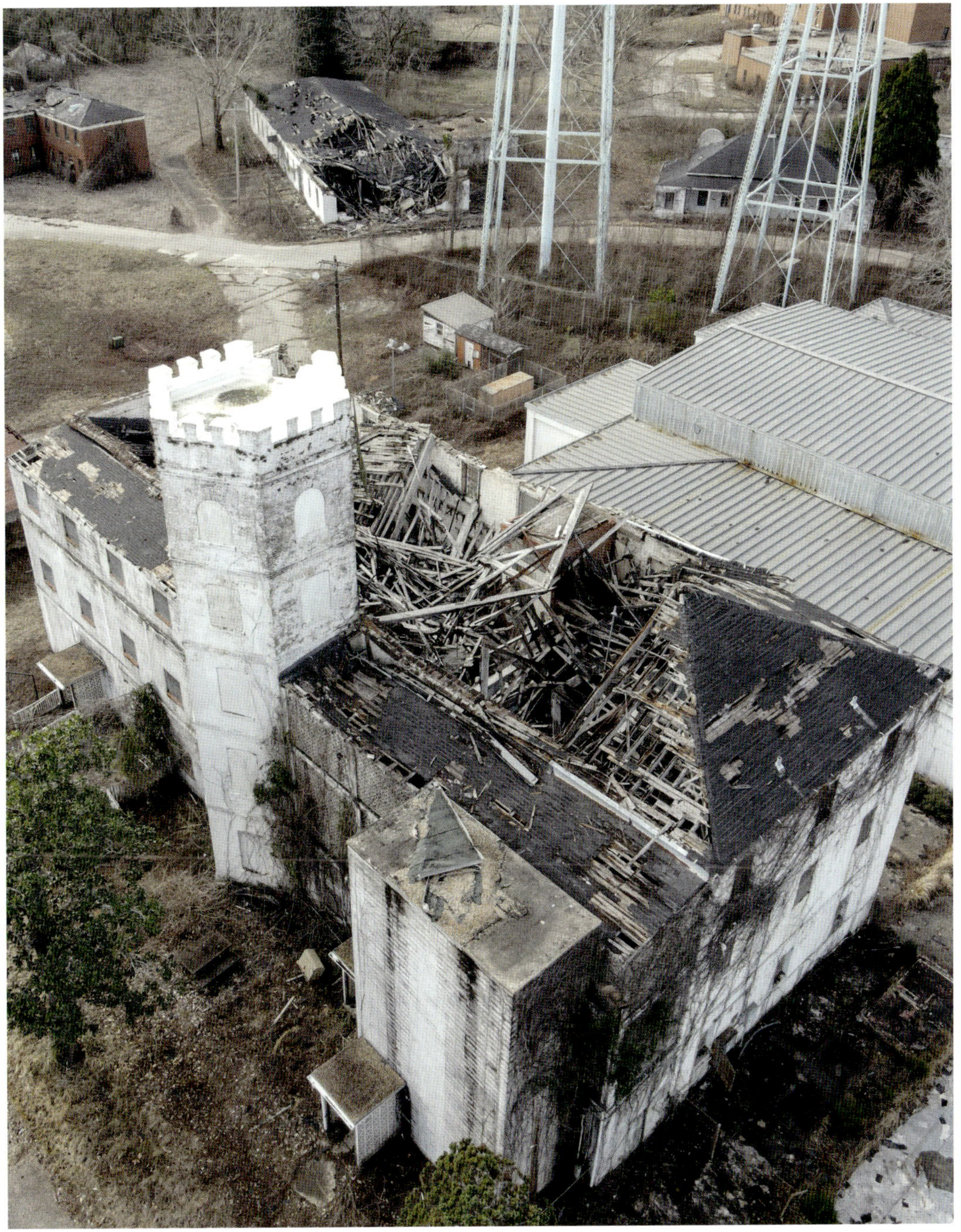

The *c.* 1835 three-story arsenal building with a five-story turret was the largest building constructed during that period. Originally used to house arms, after 1865, it was used as a barracks, then as a patient ward for the hospital.

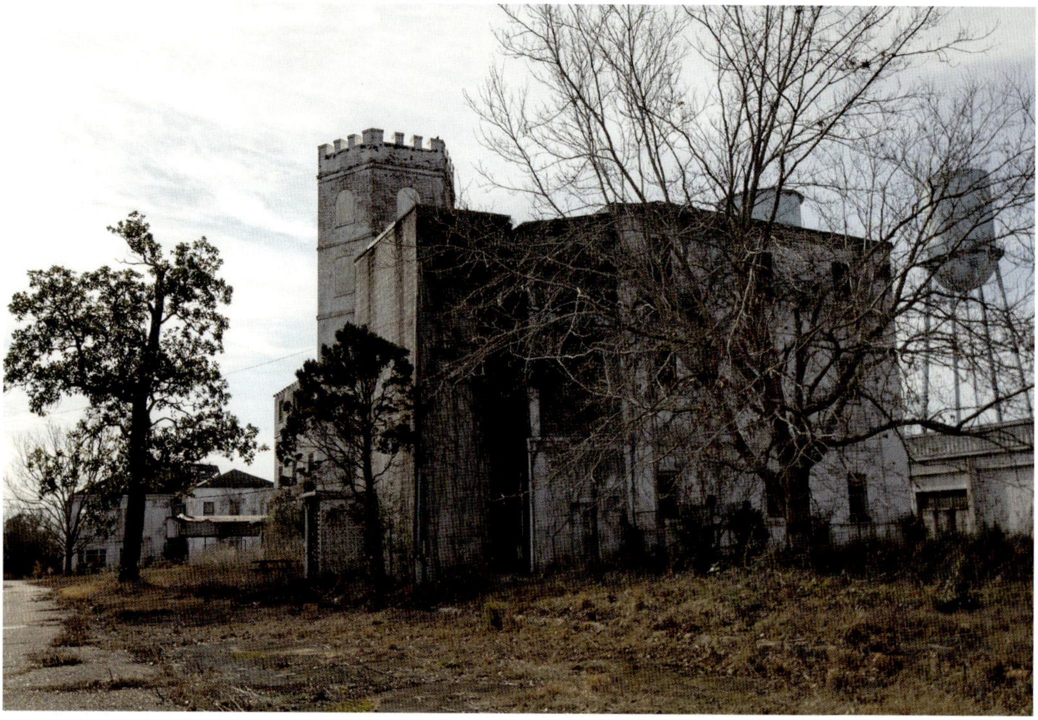

Steeped in more than 200 years of history, the arsenal and many other buildings on the hospital grounds are on the verge of being lost.

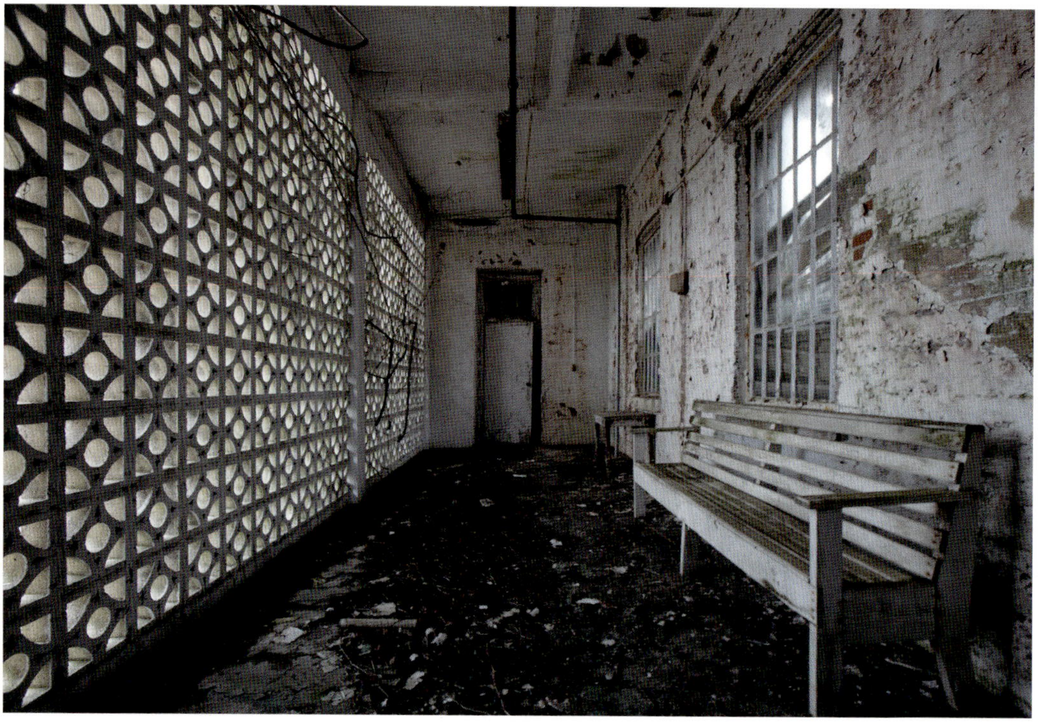

An enclosed porch on an upper floor of the arsenal building.

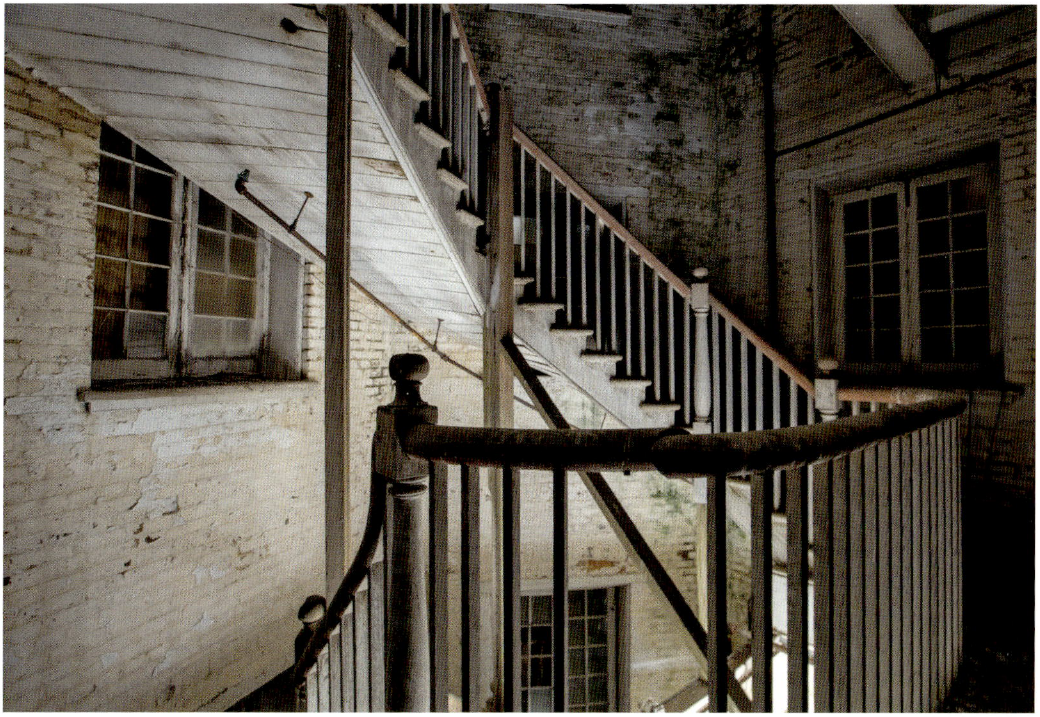

Although the building has partially collapsed, the interior stairwell of the nineteenth-century arsenal remains intact.

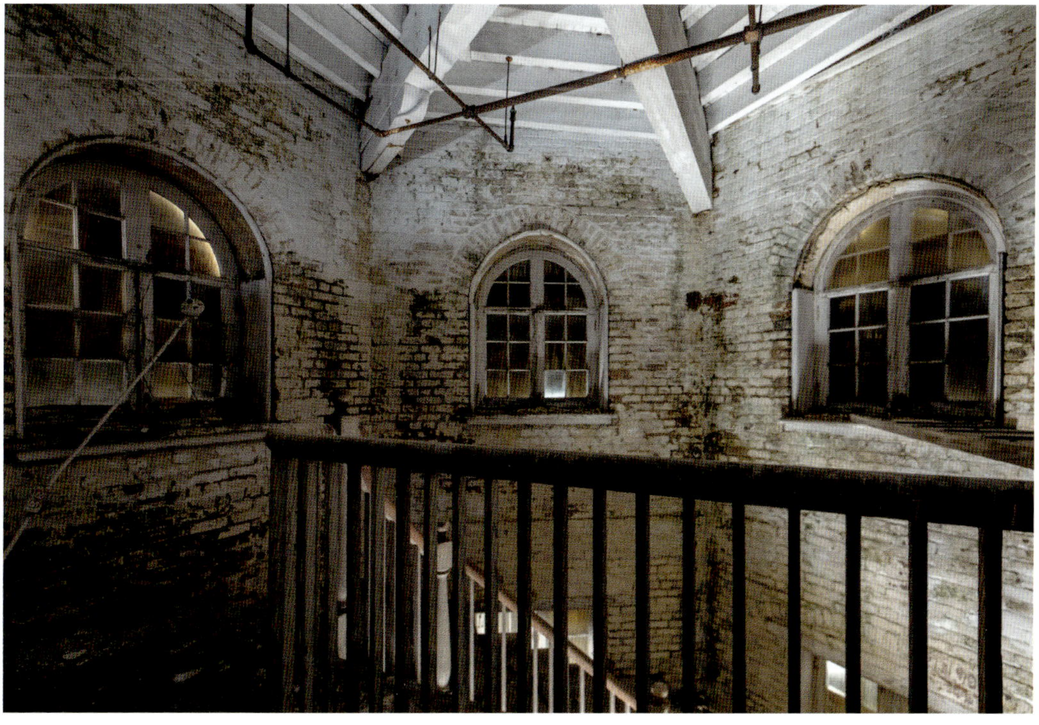

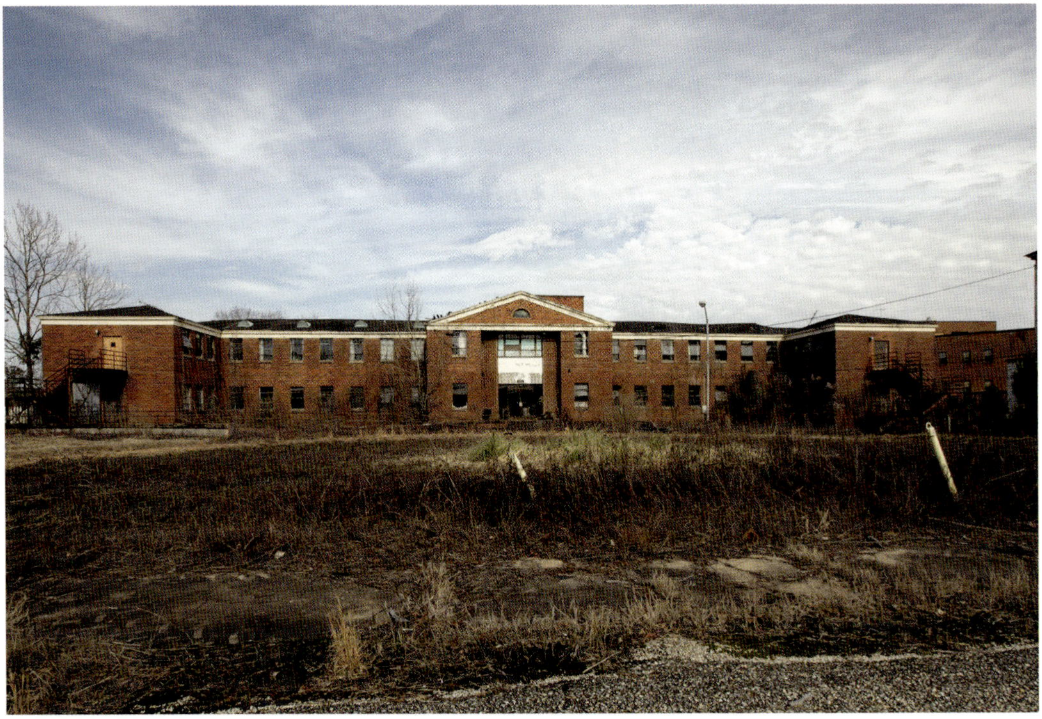

The Hospital for Women was constructed in 1950 along with the Hospital for Men. The two buildings sit across the parade ground from each other and were used as dormitories for patients.

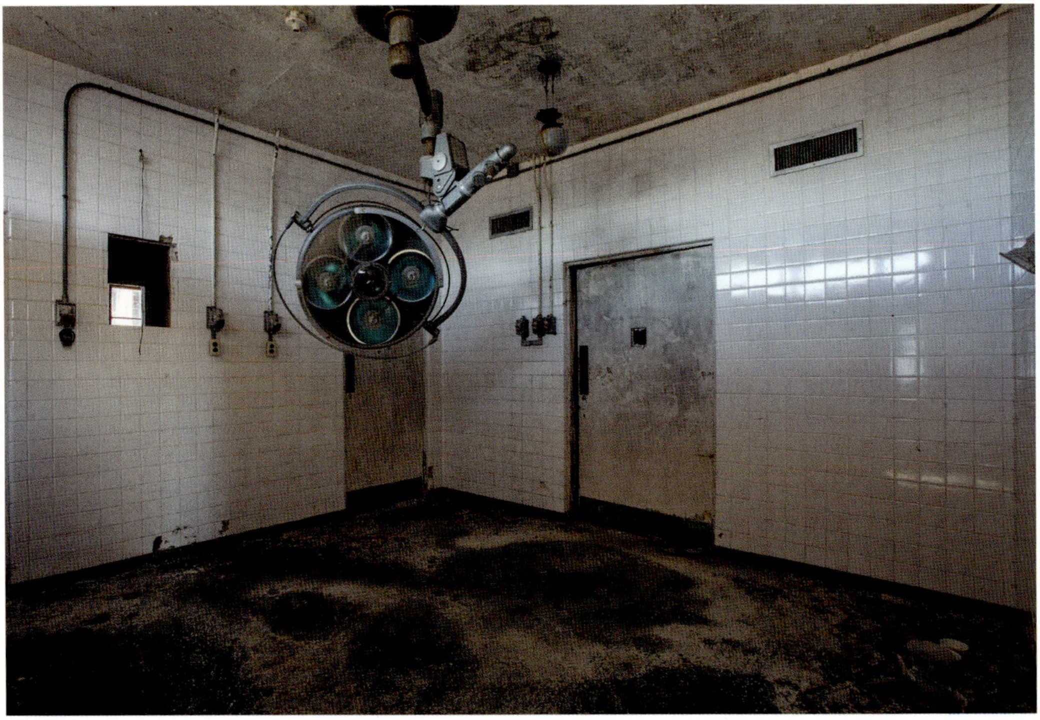

An operating room inside one of the vacant hospital buildings.

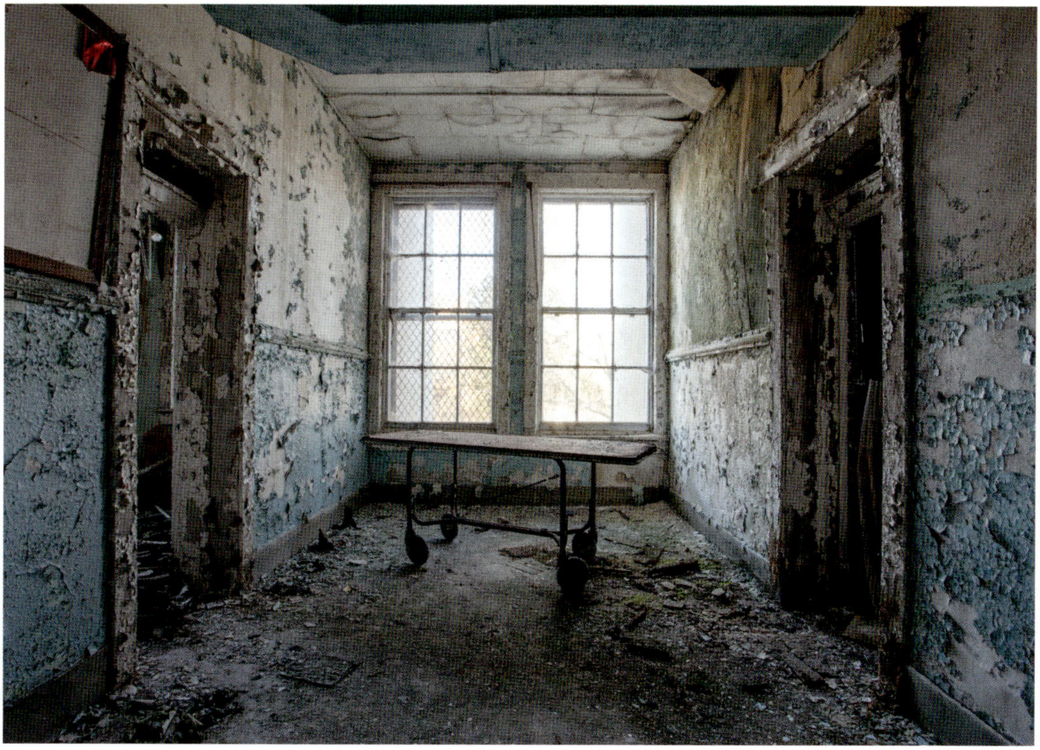

As the buildings closed, old medical equipment (like this gurney) was stored and forgotten.

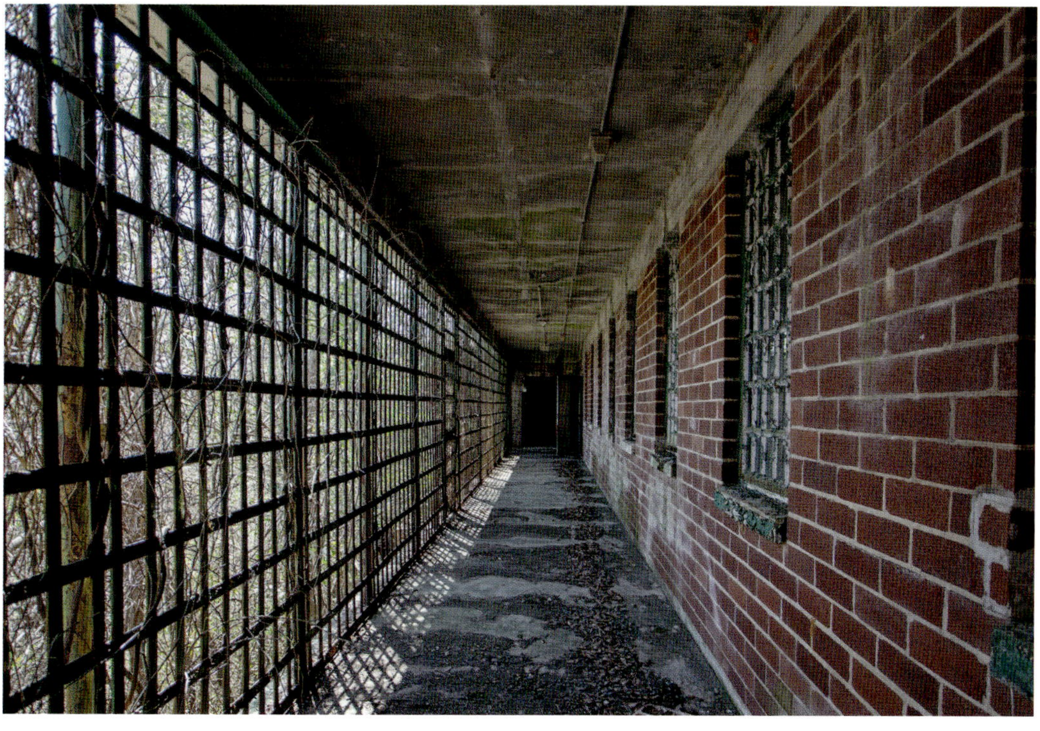

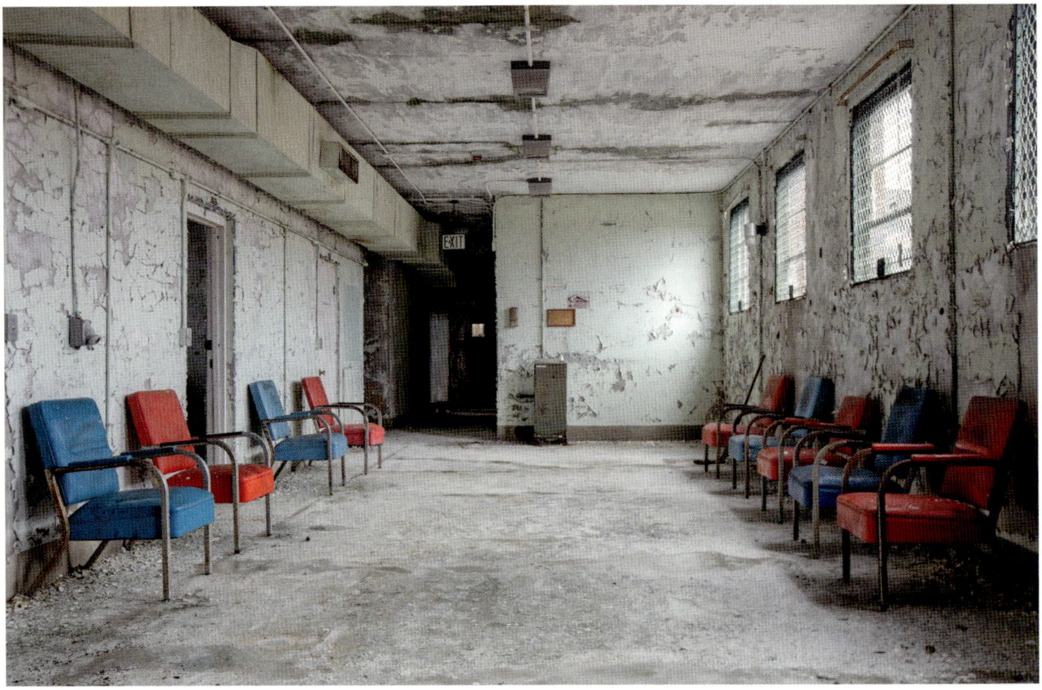

A patients' day room lined with red and blue chairs.

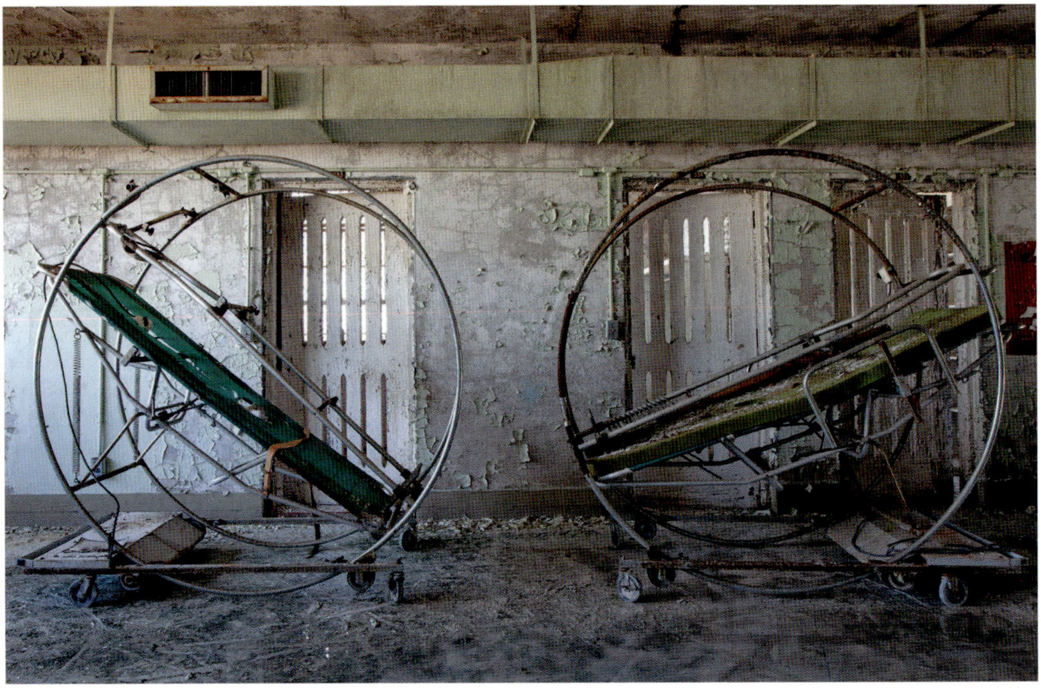

A pair of 1950s Stryker CircOlectric hospital beds. These beds consisted of a bed suspended between two circular frames with an electric motor and was often referred as resembling a small "Ferris wheel." The electric motor enabled the bed to be rotated to different positions, which allowed the patient the mobility needed to maintain normal functioning of their body systems.

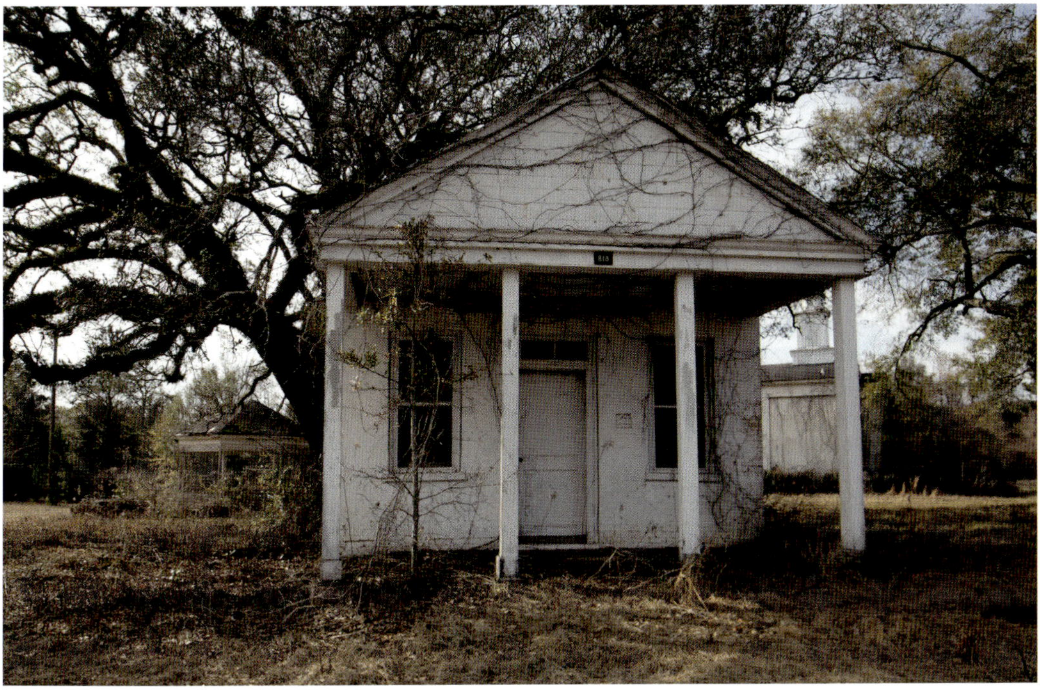

This small building was originally an ordnance lab when the site was used as an arsenal and later as morgue for Searcy Hospital.

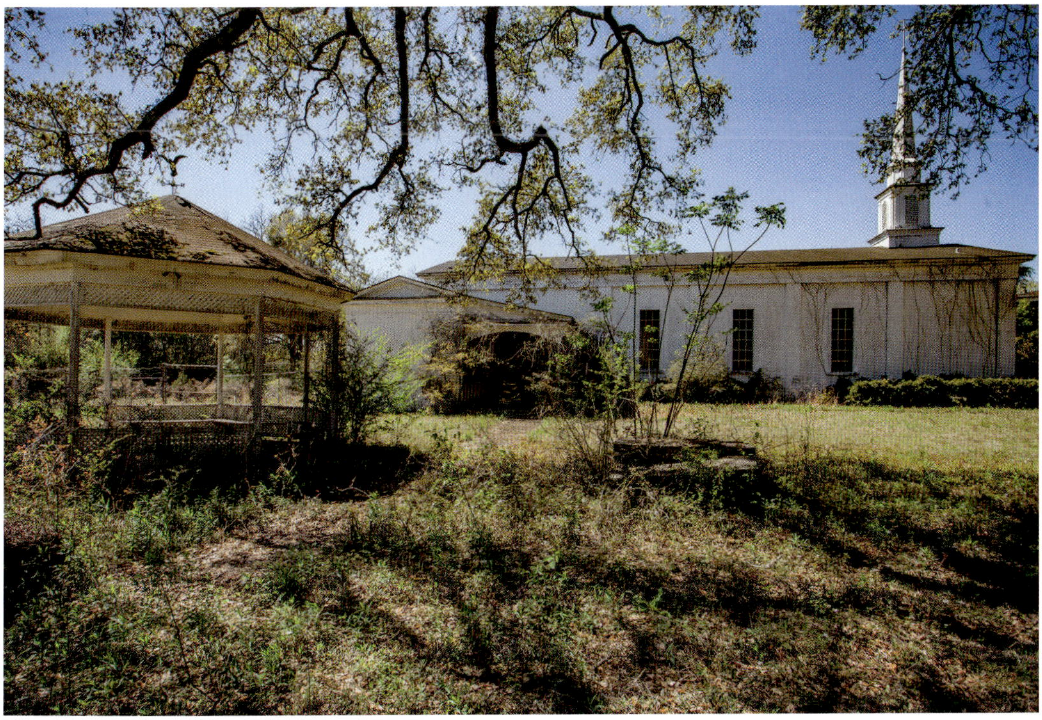

Several buildings survive from the last building period, from 1935–2012, including a picturesque chapel built in 1975 that is now covered in kudzu.

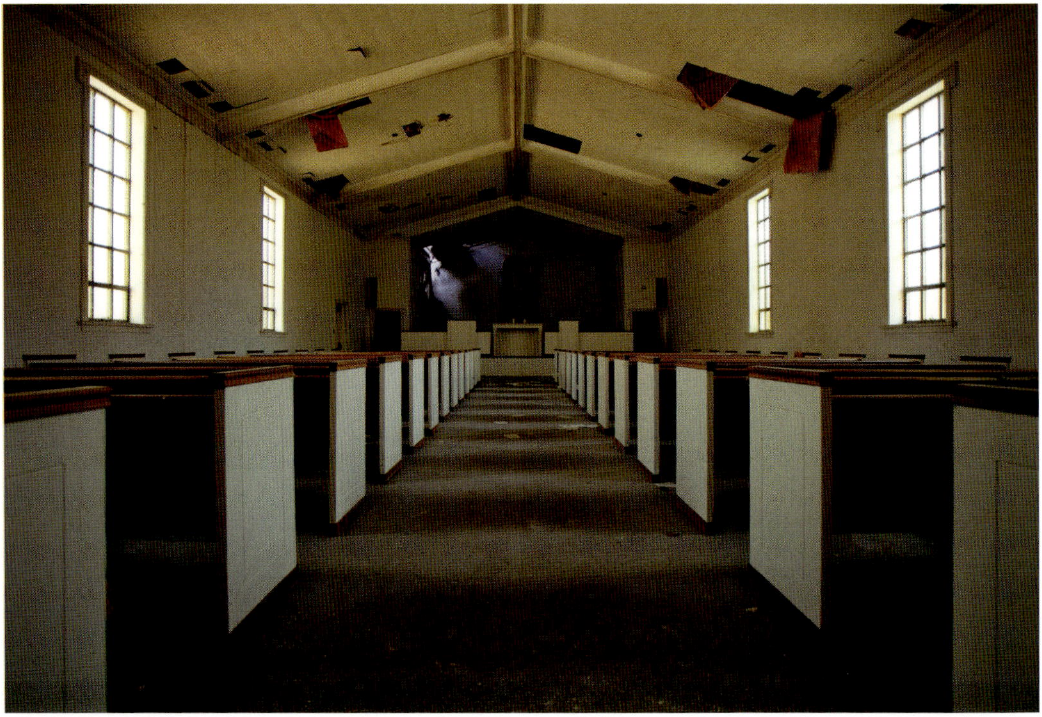

The sanctuary inside the old chapel. This building along with two large, modern hospital wards are not considered to have historical significance.

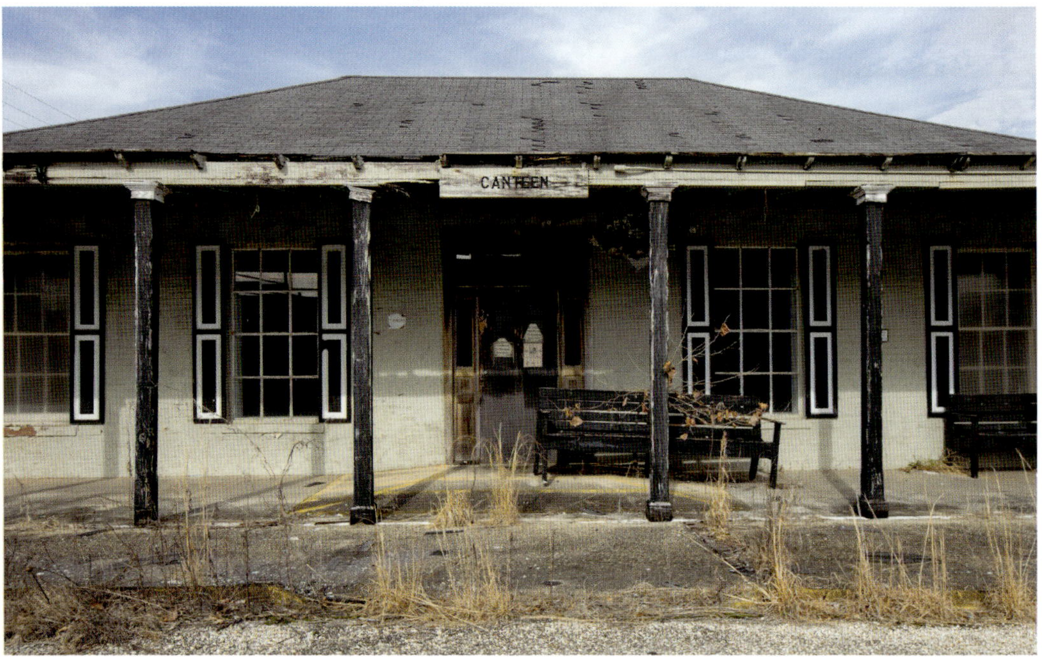

This *c.* 1835 building was originally an armorer's shop, described as a skilled tradesman who kept firearms and munitions in proper working order. From 1865 until 1895, the building was used as the quartermaster's storehouse and later by the hospital as geriatric wards.

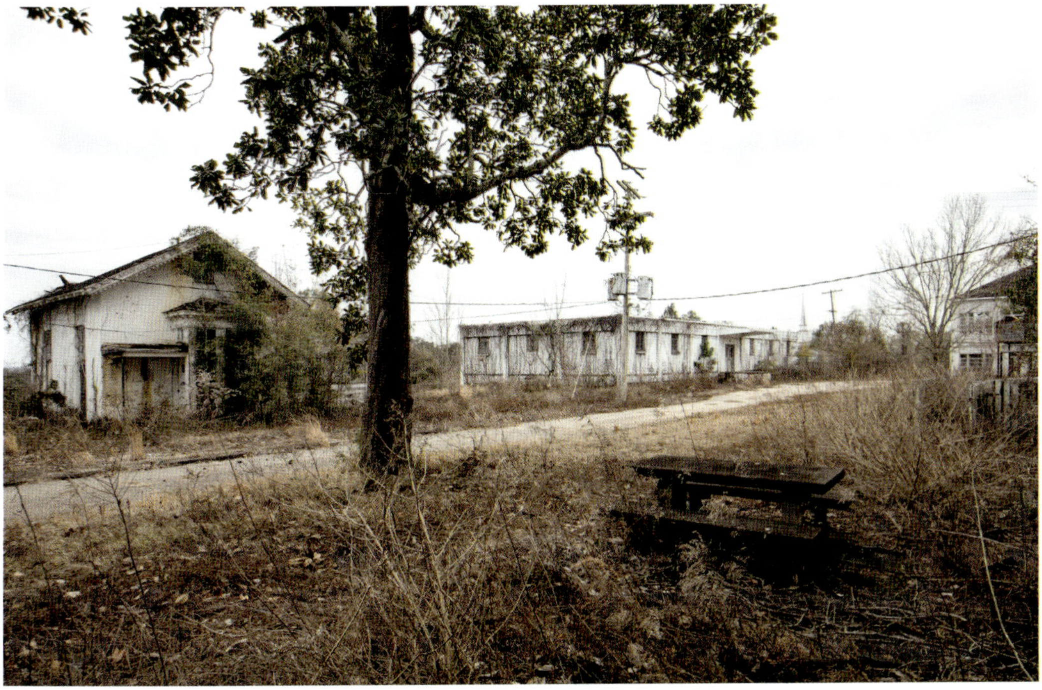

A picnic table sits among the overgrowth under a large oak tree across from a small office for the arsenal. Built in the 1830s, it was used as the paymaster's office until 1895, later as a dining room for the hospital. Its last use was a pharmacy and supply room.

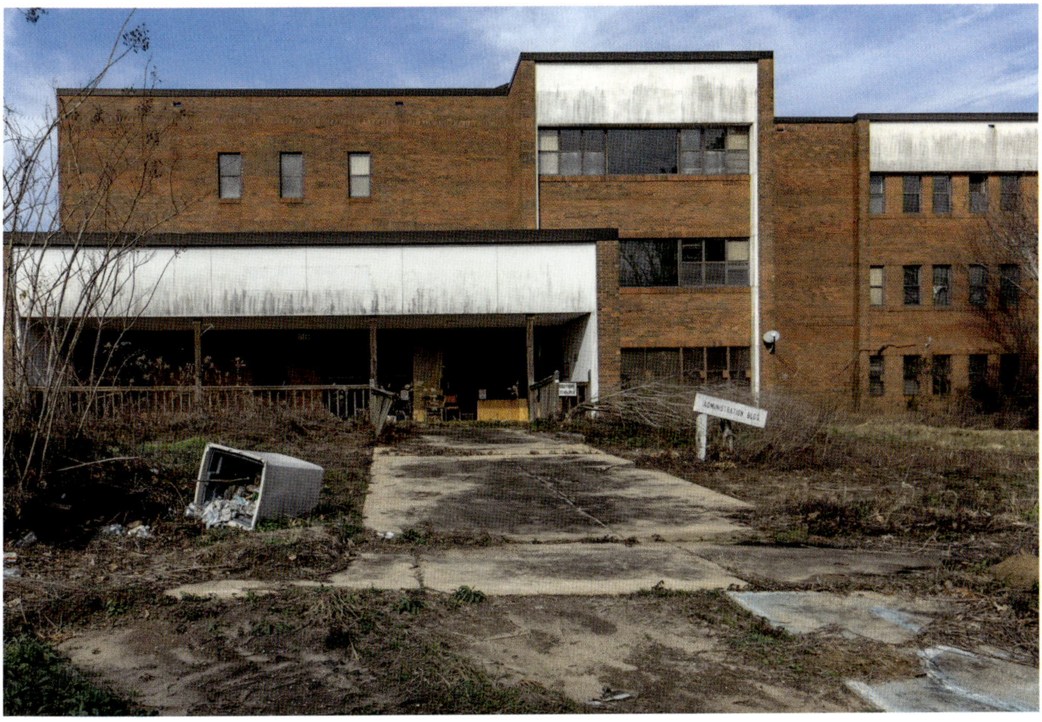

Built in the 1980s, this three-story brick hospital ward was known as "Unit 1."

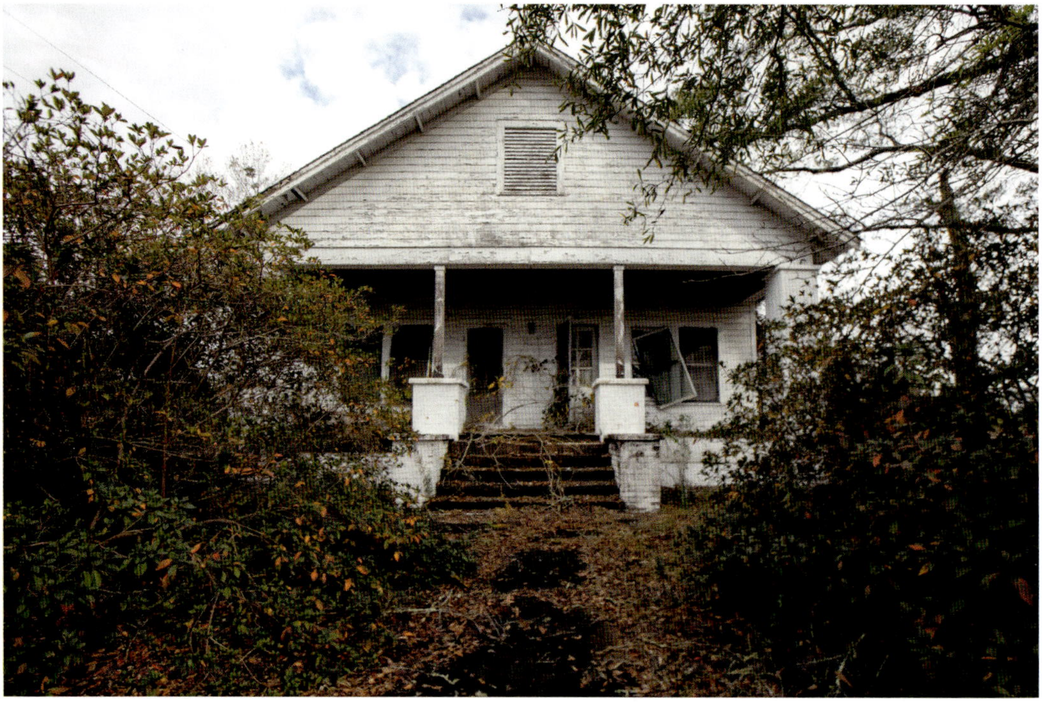

Many of the homes around the perimeter were used for employee housing like this *c.* 1930s cottage.

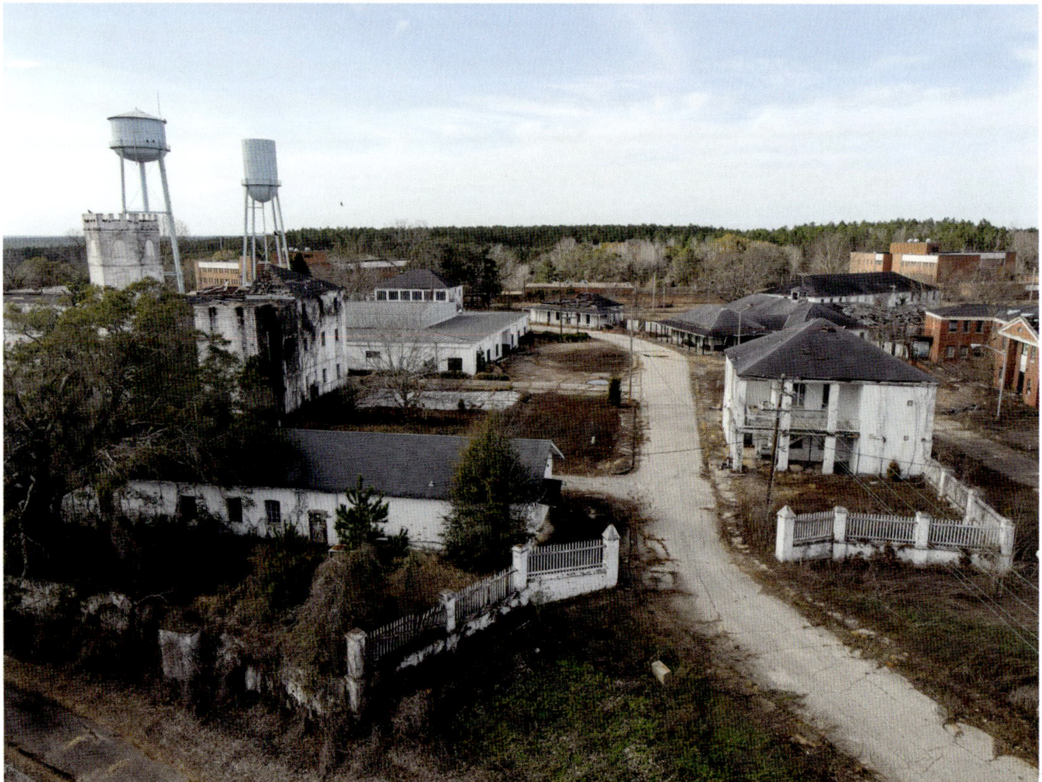